The Society for the Humanities
Cornell University

Studies in the Humanities
Edited by Max Black

THE STUBBORN STRUCTURE

THE STUBBORN STRUCTURE

Essays on Criticism and Society

NORTHROP FRYE

Cornell Paperbacks

CORNELL UNIVERSITY PRESS

ITHACA, NEW YORK

International Standard Book Number 0-8014-9110-x

Library of Congress Catalog Card Number 73-127776

Printed in Great Britain

CONTENTS

Preface   vii
Acknowledgements   xi

PART ONE: CONTEXTS

1   The Instruments of Mental Production   3
2   The Knowledge of Good and Evil   22
3   Speculation and Concern   38
4   Design as a Creative Principle in the Arts   56
5   On Value-Judgements   66
6   Criticism, Visible and Invisible   74
7   Elementary Teaching and Elemental Scholarship   90

PART TWO: APPLICATIONS

8   Varieties of Literary Utopias   109
9   The Revelation to Eve   135
10 The Road of Excess   160
11 The Keys to the Gates   175
12 The Drunken Boat: The Revolutionary Element in Romanticism   200
13 Dickens and the Comedy of Humours   218
14 The Problem of Spiritual Authority in the Nineteenth Century   241
15 The Top of the Tower: A Study of the Imagery of Yeats   257
16 Conclusion to *A Literary History of Canada*   278

Notes   313

PREFACE

This book is a collection of essays and lectures, composed at intervals between 1962 and 1968. I have arranged them not chronologically but thematically, starting with a theoretical group, dealing mainly with the contexts of literary criticism, and following them with more specific studies in English literature, in roughly historical sequence. I hope, and think, that the reader will be able to read them as chapters in a continuous argument, forming a book with a unity of its own. The local allusions are mainly American, because the United States was the milieu of most of the writing. The papers were also written, for the most part, before the rise of what is called student unrest, and while I have also written and spoken a good deal about the latter, I am dealing here with the permanent issues which have been ruffled but not altered by it.

Ever since Cicero it has been assumed that the humanist should also be a professional rhetorician, ready to make speeches on a great variety of occasions and subjects. Of the essays which follow, not one was written purely from my own initiative: every one was suggested to me by someone organizing a conference or programme or book, and the great majority of them were at first delivered orally. Of course, the writing of themes on assigned topics has also been traditionally a part of a humanist's training. But a time when every university has projects and programmes for visiting lecturers, and when the universities themselves are connected by jet planes, puts the humanist under something of a strain. The strain is not in the visit but in producing the manuscript: at that point he is in much the position of the old-style comedians who used to be able to tour the country with one act, until the coming of television exhausted their life's stock of routines in a night or two. What makes publication difficult is precisely what makes oral delivery practicable. In oral delivery there must be a great deal of repetition, because each audience needs its own set of clues: an audience in Chicago has not heard the lecture in Texas which a week previously made some of the same points. When the lectures are published, even separately, such self-cribbing has to be removed: a process at once unrewarding, tedious, and in an irrational way somewhat embarrassing. I have tried to minimize all repetition, and hope that what remains will be more helpful than distracting. Sometimes, of course, repetition can be a sign not so much of lack of ideas as of conviction, even of some consistency about one's convictions.

Each essay, then, was written for a specific occasion: I have not attempted to remove all the marks of those occasions, and I disagree profoundly with the convention which says that I should. Here again I appeal to the humanist tradition: Cicero would have been an idiot to revise his defence of Archias into an essay on the place of the poet in society. Still, a word or two about what the occasions were may be helpful to the reader.

The first three essays were contributed to conferences organized by different universities, usually in connection with anniversary celebrations, on general themes. The universities were, respectively, Chicago, Cornell, and Kentucky, and the questions to be dealt with were, respectively: what knowledge is most worth having? what kind of morality is relevant to scholarship? and, what do the humanities provide that is not provided by the sciences? These questions are referred to in the opening sentences of each paper. All three are concerned to ask the question lucidly rather than to answer it magisterially, and they attempt to be clear enough for the reader to see the gaps in their arguments. The discussion of the informing power of words in 'Speculation and Concern' is particularly tentative, partly because I have not seen the issue raised elsewhere. The essay on design in the arts changes the main context from other verbal structures to other arts: except for this change of context, the argument is not especially new. An earlier version of it was given at a festival on the arts at the University of Rochester: the present version appeared in a *Festschrift* for my friend Philip Wheelwright[1], as a tribute to his versatility of interests.

The next three papers deal with the theory of criticism chiefly in the context of teaching. The attack in the 'Polemical Introduction' of my *Anatomy of Criticism* on the notion that criticism is primarily the evaluation of literature seems to have been a hard pill to swallow. 'On Value-Judgments', a paper given at an MLA conference in Chicago, is one of many efforts I have made to explain my position on this. The most frequent question asked me is: 'But aren't you assuming a value-judgment when you spend more time writing about Shakespeare or Milton than about other poets?' This question was answered in the *Anatomy of Criticism* itself, but I was recently asked it six times in succession by a group of students at a college I was visiting. 'On Value-Judgments' tries to answer it again, and tries also to show that at a certain point the pseudo-question of evaluation passes into the genuine question of the values of literary study itself. 'Criticism, Visible and Invisible' suggests what *those* values are: this was an address given at Trinity College, Hartford, the occasion a conference on my own critical methods, organized by the late Professor Frederick Gwynne. The final paper in this first section was a speech at another M L A meeting, addressed to an audience interested in the sequence and interconnection in the teaching of English from kindergarten to graduate school.

Of the essays in the second group, the one on utopias formed part of a special issue of *Daedalus*, the journal of the American Academy of Arts and Sciences, devoted to that theme. I confined myself to the literary aspect of utopias because the political, philosophical and other aspects were being taken care of more competently by other contributors. I place it first in the second section as a counterpart to the opening essay, with which it has much in common. The Milton essay, given at a tercentenary conference on *Paradise Lost* at the University of Western Ontario, is a kind of distillation of some earlier lectures of mine on Milton also given on that campus, published as *The Return of Eden: Five Essays on Milton's Epics* (I give the sub-title because for some reason this is the only title of the British edition). The two Blake essays differ widely in their interests: the first one, given at the University of Nebraska, tries to outline some of the connections between my own theory of criticism and the study of Blake in which it began; the second is intended simply as an introductory guide to the symbolism of the Prophecies, and hence, perhaps, as an epitome of the long and difficult *Fearful Symmetry*. The Romanticism paper was the opening one of a series of four 'reconsiderations' of Romanticism given to the English Institute in 1962; the view of Romanticism taken in it I have since developed in a later book, *A Study of English Romanticism*, where it is applied to Beddoes, Shelley, and Keats.

Of the two Victorian papers, the one on Dickens was also given at the English Institute, in 1967: it is based on a conception of New Comedy which I had outlined elsewhere, but had never applied to Dickens in detail. The other paper, given at Rice University, was reprinted in a *Festschrift* for my late colleague, Professor A. S. P. Woodhouse: the academic field it covers was one of particular interest to him. The Yeats paper, delivered at the Sligo conference on Yeats in 1968, is my third effort, which by folk-tale convention ought to be the most successful one, to reconcile Yeats's imagery as a whole with the scheme of *A Vision*. It and the Milton paper are preliminary studies for what I am afraid will become a long and intricate book on patterns of imagery in literature.

A Literary History of Canada was a co-operative project, under the general editorship of Professor Carl Klinck of Western Ontario, and embracing about thirty-five contributors. I was asked to write a conclusion trying to sum up what the book as a whole was saying about the poetic imagination as it operated in Canada. I have edited the text, for the comfort of the reader who wants to read it independently of its context, and have eliminated my specific references to my colleagues; but anyone who looks up the original essay can see for himself how much I owe to them, not only in facts and ideas, but in phrasing. I hope that the reader unfamiliar with Canadian literature will read it, not as a quaint and provincial appendix to the present book, but as a glimpse of a new imaginative landscape which is still relevant to his own.

The title is from a passage in Blake's *Jerusalem* (Plate 36 or 40, depending on which copy is used as the basis of the edition), which has always meant a great deal to me, and which looms up with a peculiar power and resonance even in that tremendous setting:

> I call them by their English names: English, the rough basement.
> Los built the stubborn structure of the Language, acting against
> Albion's melancholy, who must else have been a Dumb despair.

And, as some of those who write about me are still asserting that I ignore the social reference of literary criticism, the sub-title calls the attention of those who read me to the fact that I have written about practically nothing else.   N.F.

University of Toronto
November 1969

ACKNOWLEDGEMENTS

'The Instruments of Mental Production' appeared in *The Knowledge Most Worth Having*, edited by Wayne C. Booth, © 1967 by the University of Chicago. Reprinted by permission of the University of Chicago Press.

'The Knowledge of Good and Evil' is reprinted from Max Black, editor: *The Morality of Scholarship*. Copyright © 1967 by Cornell University. Used by permission of Cornell University Press.

'Speculation and Concern' appeared in *The Humanities and the Understanding of Reality*, edited by Thomas B. Stroup, Lexington, Kentucky, 1966, and is reprinted by permission of the University of Kentucky Press.

'Design as a Creative Principle in the Arts' appeared in *The Hidden Harmony: Essays in Honor of Philip Wheelwright*, New York, 1966, and is reprinted by permission of the Odyssey Press.

'On Value-Judgments' appeared in *Contemporary Literature*, Vol. 9, No. 3, Summer 1968, and is reprinted by permission of the University of Wisconsin Press.

'Criticism, Visible and Invisible' appeared in *College English*, Vol. 26, No. 1, October, 1964, and is reprinted by permission of the National Council of Teachers of English.

'Elementary Teaching and Elementary Scholarship' is reprinted by permission of the Modern Language Association of America from *PMLA*, Vol. LXXIX, No. 2, May 1964.

'Varieties of Literary Utopias' is reprinted by permission from *DAEDALUS*, Journal of the American Academy of Arts and Sciences, Boston, Massachusetts, Vol. 99, No. 2.

'The Revelation to Eve' appeared in *Paradise Lost: A Tercentenary Tribute*, edited by Balachandra Rajan, Toronto, 1969, and is reprinted by permission of the University of Toronto Press.

'The Road of Excess' appeared in *Myth and Symbol: Critical Approaches and Applications*, edited by Bernice Slote, Lincoln, Nebraska, 1963, and is reprinted by permission of the University of Nebraska Press. 'The Keys to the Gates' is reprinted from *Some British Romantics: A Collection of Essays* edited by James V. Logan, John E. Jordan, and Northrop Frye, and is copyright © 1966 by the Ohio State University Press. All rights reserved. Reprinted by permission of the Ohio State University Press.

'The Drunken Boat: The Revolutionary Element in Romanticism' appeared in *Romanticism Reconsidered*, New York, 1963, and is reprinted by permission of the Columbia University Press.

'Dickens and the Comedy of Humours' appeared in *Experience in the Novel*, edited by Roy Harvey Pearce, New York, 1968, and is reprinted by permission of the Columbia University Press.

'The Problem of Spiritual Authority in the Nineteenth Century' appeared in *Literary Views: Critical and Historical Essays*, edited by Carroll Camden, published for William Marsh Rice University by the University of Chicago Press, 1964, and is reprinted by permission of the University of Chicago Press.

'The Top of the Tower' appeared in *The Southern Review*, Vol. 5, No. 3, Summer 1969, and is reprinted by permission of *The Southern Review*.

'Conclusion' appeared in *Literary History of Canada: Canadian Literature in English*, General Editor, Carl F. Klinck, Toronto, 1965, and is reprinted by permission of the University of Toronto Press.

I am indebted to Miss Sybil Hutchinson for permission to quote the passage from *A Suit of Nettles*, Toronto, 1958, by James Reaney, who holds the copyright on this material.

I think every other quotation in the book comes under the heading either of fair comment or of public domain.

Part One ∽ CONTEXTS

1 THE INSTRUMENTS OF MENTAL PRODUCTION

The question assigned is: 'What Knowledge Is Most Worth Having?' but I want to quarrel with assumptions in that question. In the first place, the knowledge of most worth, whatever it may be, is not something one has: it is something one is, and the correct response to such a question, if a student were to ask it, would be another question – 'With what body of knowledge do you wish to identify yourself?' In the second place, the phrase 'most worth' is apt to introduce comparative value judgements into areas where they are irrelevant. Whenever students ask me if I would advise them to 'take' sociology or anthropology, ancient history or modern history, a science option or a language option, I realize that there are no objective answers, and no possible means of arriving at any. The answer depends on what criteria they adopt, but not on anything in the structure of knowledge itself that I or anyone else can demonstrate to them. I suppose there is such a thing as practically and inherently useless knowledge, that is, subjects without content or founded on false assumptions, like palmistry or the racial theories cherished by the Nazis; but the danger of a student's being deflected by them is remote. The knowledge of most worth, for a genuine student, is that body of knowledge to which he has already made an unconscious commitment. I speak of an unconscious commitment because for a genuine student, knowledge, like marriage, is too important a matter to be left entirely to conscious choice. Conscious choice is for the uncommitted, and for those the standards employed in the choice can come only from various factors in their own lives, such as a picture of one's future career, a sense of what one is good at, a guess about the market value of one kind of knowledge as compared with another, or simply the kind of instinctive preference that it is not really necessary to rationalize.

I begin by separating general education and scholarship, which are not integrally connected. Intellectually, the world is specialized and pluralistic, and learning, like the amoeba, can reproduce only by subdividing. One may organize colloquia around general topics like communication, and get specialized scholars to 'communicate' with each other in an unsubstantial Eucharist. Scholars may do this kind of thing under pressure, but for the most part they will do it dutifully, like voting, and not with the exhilaration that they would get from discussing their own specialization with some of the very few people in the world who share it. Actual scholarship is esoteric, almost conspiratorial, and the principles of academic freedom require that it should be left that way. The scholar *qua* scholar is responsible only to his subject. Students should not try to 'evaluate' him as a public performer in the classroom; administrators and private foundations should not harass him by telling him that he ought to learn more about different fields; journalists and politicians should not repeat silly clichés like 'ivory tower' to describe his intellectual home. In an age when the word 'dialogue' has acquired so potent a charge of verbal magic, it is worth reminding ourselves that in Plato, who seems to have invented the conception, dialogue exists solely for the purpose of destroying false knowledge. As soon as any genuine knowledge (or what Plato regarded as such) is present, the dialogue turns into a punctuated monologue. What the world of scholarship requires is not two but at least a hundred and two cultures, all more or less unintelligible to one another, and the improvement of scholarship is toward more and not fewer.

What I have just described is the *routine* of scholarship only. Its patron saint is Sherlock Holmes, who never failed to solve any problem put before him because of the purity of his dedication to scholarship. Sherlock Holmes rather resented the fact that Watson had never read his little monograph on the distinguishing of 140 varieties of cigar ash, but when Watson told him that the earth was a globe revolving around the sun, he remarked that that was an irrelevant piece of information that he would do his best to forget. But of course many other things go on as well as the routine of scholarship, notably a process of mutation and metamorphosis. Subjects regroup themselves and other subjects take shape from the shifting relations of existing ones, as geophysics takes shape from a new relation of geology and physics. It is in these moments of regrouping that the great genius, with his colossal simplifying vision, gets his best chance to emerge. I wonder if anyone of Freud's stature could emerge from psychology now: there might be a feeling that he was an armchair theorist who had not served enough time in laboratory routine to be a proper professional psychologist. The Freuds of the future are more likely to emerge, as Freud himself did, from a point of mutation at which psychology begins to turn into something unrecognizable to its scholarly establishment. But these mutations occur from within existing disciplines at a certain stage in their inner development: they cannot be planned or even directly encouraged from the outside.

General education is a social and not primarily an intellectual matter, and has no authority over productive scholarship. All discussion of it must be related to the state of society and the needs, desires, and ideals of that society. There is a body of information and skill that everybody has to know and possess in order to participate in our complex society, and the question is how far up, subjectively in life and objectively in the structure of knowledge, such a body extends, or can profitably be extended. We may assume that we can distinguish two levels in general education: an average or elementary level and a cultivated level; roughly, the difference between being able to read and write and being able to read with some depth and direction and write with some articulateness. At present many believe that raising people to the cultivated level on a huge and unprecedented scale is not merely desirable in itself but a necessity if our civilization is to survive. There has always been a practical distinction between what is important, like cathedrals, and what is necessary, like privies: in our day the important seems, possibly for the first time in history, to be becoming necessary as well.

Ever since Adam was thrown out of Paradise and told to go and till an accursed ground, the most important distinction in human life has been the distinction between labour and leisure. By labour, here, I mean the whole productive aspect of society, the accumulating and distributing of food and the means of shelter and the more specific wants of a settled social order. According to Veblen, Adam soon tires of tilling the ground and compels Eve to do it instead, confining his own activities to hunting and fishing and thereby beginning a 'leisure class', the class that is defined as superior because it contributes nothing to social production. When leisure and labour become personified as an upper and a lower class, the conceptions of waste and alienation come into society: alienation for the worker, who is cheated out of nearly all the fruit of his own labour, and waste for the leisurely consumer, who can put nothing to productive use. American democracy has blurred these social distinctions and has replaced the leisure class with the affluent society, but it has not thereby lessened the feelings of waste and alienation. The sense that society, considered in its producing and distributing aspect, is something cheap and ignoble, that it is not worth loyalty, that many of its products are absurdities and that operating its obsessively busy machinery is spiritually futile, is at least as strong as it ever was. And this time there is nobody to hate, no tyrants or silk-hatted capitalists or swaggering lords, no one essentially different from ourselves for whom can relieve our feelings by abusing.

In a society devoted wholly to labour, leisure would be thought of as merely rest or spare time: if there is continuous leisure, it becomes idleness or distraction. Idleness and distraction are reactions against the unpleasantness or dullness of labour: they make up for the time wasted on work by wasting time in other ways. A life divided only between dull work and distracted play is not life but essentially a mere waiting for death, and war comes to such a society as deliverance, because it relieves the strain of waiting. It is generally realized that idleness and distraction are very close to the kind of boredom that expresses itself in smashing things, and hence there is a widespread feeling, which is at least a century old, that mass education is needed simply to keep people out of mischief. This is not a very inspiring philosophy of education, nor one at all likely to effect its purposes.

Education has nothing to do with this vicious circle of labour and idleness: it begins in that moment of genuine leisure in which Adam is neither tilling the ground nor going fishing and leaving the real work to Eve, but remembering his lost Paradise. Even as late as Milton, articulating the dream of a lost Paradise is still the definition of education. More prosaically, we may say that education is the product of a vision of human society that is more permanent and coherent than actual society. When the students of today were babies, the King of England was Emperor of India, China was a bourgeois friend, Japan a totalitarian enemy, and Nazi Germany was ruling as powerful an empire as the world had ever seen. It is clear that what we think of as real society is not that at all, but only the transient appearance of society. A society in which the presidency of the United States can be changed by one psychotic with a rifle is not sufficiently real for any thoughtful person to want to live wholly within it. What real society is, is indicated by the structure of the arts and sciences in a university. This is the permanent body of what humanity has done and is still doing, and the explanations of why the world around us changes so suddenly and so drastically are to be found only there.

A theory of education, then, implies a theory of society: a theory of society demands the construction of a social model, and all social models, as Max Weber remarks, have something Utopian about them. Conversely, all Utopias are really embodiments of educational theories. We cannot discuss educational theory simply in relation to an existing society, for no educational theory is worth anything unless it can be conceived as transforming that society and, at least to some extent, assimilating it to its own pattern. The moment of leisure, as I have defined it, is that moment which can come only to a fully conscious human being, when he is able to draw back from his activities and compare what he is doing with what he would like to do, or could conceive as better worth doing. This is also the moment at which the sense of a need for education begins, for our words school and scholarship, as Aristotle pointed out, are connected with *schole*, leisure. That is why I spoke of education as something that has for its ultimate goal the vision of an ideal, that is, a theoretically coherent and permanent, social order. In moral terms, we could call this the pattern of the just state.

This leads us to the traditional conception of education that we have inherited from Plato. Plato divides knowledge into two levels: an upper level of theoretical knowledge (theoretical in the sense of *theoria*, vision), which unites itself to permanent ideas or forms, and a lower level of practical knowledge, whose function is to embody these forms or ideas on the level of physical life. What I have referred to in my title as the instruments of mental production consist of the arts, and we may see the major arts in Plato's terms as forming a group of six. Three of these are the arts of *mousike*: music, mathematics, and poetry, and they make up the main body of what Plato means by philosophy, the identifying of the soul of man with the forms or ideas of the world. The other three are the imitative or embodying arts, the arts of *techne*, painting, sculpture, and architecture, which, along with all their satellites and derivatives, unite the body of man with the physical world. In the just state this conception of education is reflected in a hierarchy in which a philosopher-king, supported by guards who have been educated from his point of view, is set in authority over the artisans or producers. Poets who desert their heritage and try to make their art a technical or imitative art have no place in such a state.

The Platonic conception of the relation of education to society is a revolutionary one: the shape of a just society, as education conceives it, is so different from that of society as we know it that the two cannot co-exist: one is bound to regard the other as its enemy. When the conception was revived in the Renaissance, it was modified by a more accommodating outlook. Renaissance education still forms a vision of the permanent form of society, and theoretically, the most important person to impart this vision to is the ruler. Society is best off when its king is a philosopher-king, and the ideal of education is the institute of a Christian prince. In this view, however, the education of the prince does not radically alter the existing structure of society: it merely illuminates it. The model here is Xenophon's *Cyropaedia* rather than Plato's *Republic*. But, as is shown in Machiavelli, the actual prince is much more likely to be a man of force and cunning than of wisdom: an incarnation of will, not of reason. Hence in practice the social role of education is more likely to be found in the courtier, the servant and adviser of the prince. The Renaissance had, besides, inherited a medieval tradition in which the most highly educated people were more likely to be clerics than princes, and hence, in the temporal sphere, confined to a similar supporting and advisory role, a civil service rather than a directing power.

The collision between revolutionary and accommodating views of the just state is clearly set out in More's *Utopia*, in a dialogue between More and his friend Hythlodaye, who has been in Utopia. Hythlodaye has returned from Utopia with a Platonic revolutionary view: only the most drastic recasting of Europe into a Utopian mould will do any good to a society in which the 'commonwealth' is actually a conspiracy of the rich and powerful. More himself, in the first book, displays a different view: Hythlodaye should, he suggests, come to terms with existing society, at least to the extent of using his Utopian vision in an advisory capacity – informing, modifying, improving and rationalizing the structure of that society, and doing what practically can be done toward assimilating sixteenth-century Europe to a more coherent vision of life. The attitude here is closer to Aristotle's conception of justice than to Plato's, yet included in it is a Christian and Augustinian view that is a logical extension of Plato. If the philosopher-king seeks an identity of his immortal soul with a world of immortal forms, he will eventually have to abdicate as king, as full identity would belong to a contemplative rather than an active life. The ultimate form of the just state can only be embodied in a church or monastic community where the real philosopher-king is God. More's Utopia thus has the same elusive relation to the Christian Church that it has to sixteenth-century Europe. There is a real relation to both, along with an underlying antagonism that goes equally deep.

The Renaissance, then, carried on the traditional conception of education as a vision of the just state, but it had ready at hand a powerful practical method of achieving it. This was humanism, the study, not of an ideal civilization, but of an actual one which, having disappeared, could be studied in its ideal form as a structure of arts and sciences. This was an educational instrument of a kind foreshadowed by Plato when he went from his vision of the just state in the *Republic* to its sequel, the story of the civilization of Atlantis learned by the Athenians from the older civilization of Egypt. To a considerable extent Roman culture was humanistic in the sense of re-creating an earlier Greek culture in its own context, and the Renaissance followed the Romans in re-creating a Latinized classical culture in their context. The genuine humanists studied the classics, not as immutable cultural forms in another world, but as informing cultural principles in their world. The classics, in their totality, including Vitruvius on architecture and Columella on agriculture as well as Virgil and Cicero, made up a coherent structure of knowledge that, properly applied, could transform Renaissance society into something like its own pattern of coherence, as the 'embers of dead tongues', in Milton's phrase, kindled a new flame, and the old Roman Empire became renewed into the Holy Roman Empire, the temporal power of Christian Europe. At its best, the study of classical culture promoted a liberalism of outlook that might otherwise have been impossible in ages so heavily burdened with religious and political anxieties. The Greek and Roman cultures could be studied with a genuine detachment, as the student was committed neither to their religions nor to their political views, and hence was able to separate the ideal or permanent structure from the historical one.

The humanist conception of education, as late as Arnold and Newman, still envisaged a roughly Platonic society on two levels. On the lower level were the producers and artisans, the workers and tradesmen, and those who were concerned with the practical and technical arts. On the upper level was an aristocracy or leisure class, freed from the necessity of contributing to social production. The function of education, on this higher social level, was to transform a leisure class into a responsible ruling class, trained in the arts of war and peace, the knowledge of Plato's guards and of his philosopher-king. The arts of peace were primarily the musical arts in Plato's sense: they had expanded into the seven liberal arts in the Middle Ages, but had retained their associations with music, mathematics, and literature. The 'music' part of it, of course, never did have much to do with what we now think of as music, but was rather a branch of speculative cosmology. The supremacy of classics and mathematics, however, was maintained for centuries in university curricula. These arts represented a permanence that the technical arts could not match: buildings crumble, even monuments of perennial brass can disappear, but books, while individually expendable, have a unique power of self-perpetuation. Hence a book culture and the study of words and numbers can be used to build and rebuild the permanent forms of society, to establish the sense of continuity that is the genuine control of the social order, statesmanship as distinct from 'policy, that heretic'[1], as Shakespeare calls it, which merely swims on the stream of time.

By the nineteenth century, humanist education had to meet the challenge of an entirely new conception of society. This new conception was, once again, clearest in its most revolutionary and Utopian form, as, first, the ideals of the American and more particularly of the French Revolution, and, second, the goals of the socialist revolutionary movement as set out by Marx. This view, like that of Hythlodaye in More, regarded the relation of the upper to the lower level of society as essentially predatory and parasitic. The education that made the ruling class feel responsible was thus primarily a rationalization of their power: it constituted what Marx calls an ideology. In its fully developed form society would be identical with productive society: it would consist entirely of workers and producers. According to Carlyle, who expounded a good deal of this attitude while trying to reverse its movement, the real distinction is not between cultivated leisure and work, but between genuine work, as the expression of the energy and intelligence of man, and the two forms of antiwork that corrupt society. One of these is the idleness, or dandyism as Carlyle calls it, of an unworking aristocracy; the other is drudgery, the menial and degrading results of exploitation and the mechanical division of labour. The distinction between genuine work and drudgery, the subject of a recent study by Hannah Arendt[2], is developed in Ruskin and in William Morris: Morris is of particular interest to us here because he thinks of the technical arts as the instruments of social revolution. Architecture and the so-called minor arts, the arts mainly of graphic and pictorial design, are for Morris the forces that transform a society of exploitation into a society of workers and producers.

Faced with this social change, the defenders of humanist education were thrown back, often in spite of themselves, on a conservative view of society, one that emphasizes the permanent values of aristocracy, leisure, cultivation, and of the social conception that Newman calls the 'gentleman'. Even as late as T. S. Eliot this association of humanism and social conservatism persists. In Arnold there is a remarkable attempt to separate the ideal of leisure and cultivation from the members of the dominant class who normally embody it. The fact that he describes the former as 'culture' and the latter as 'barbarians' indicates the strength of the effort. Like the humanists of the Renaissance, Arnold gives the primary place to the study of the classics, though only because he thinks of them much as Morris thinks of the arts of design, as the living powers of imagination that transform a class-ridden society into a classless one. But he shows an uneasy awareness of the dwindling number of people who think of the classics in this way, and the growing number of those who either reject them outright as 'dead tongues' or accept them mechanically as mere symbols of social status.

In those whose bias was toward science and technology, notably

Huxley and Herbert Spencer, we find a liberal view of education half-way between the conservative humanist one and the radical socialist one. Here society is assumed to be primarily a producing society, and the student to be preparing for absorption into a society of producers. Production involves a struggle with nature, and so science, the direct study of nature, comes into the foreground of education. The values of humanistic education, being leisure values, are to be thought of, in a producing society, as spare-time values, not transforming society but refining and ornamenting it. The specific humanist reason for choosing the classics as the basis of literary education thus no longer holds: from this point of view, there are no values in the best Greek and Latin literature that cannot be obtained from the best English literature. Huxley and Spencer were, of course, primarily interested in the new doctrine of evolution, and they thought of evolution as in part a process in which man is constantly being educated by nature. For the most part he is educated reluctantly, involuntarily, and with his mind distracted by his own fantasies, an inattentive and unruly child of Mother Nature. As Huxley says: 'The question of compulsory education is settled so far as nature is concerned. Her bill on that question was framed and passed long ago. But, like all compulsory legislation, that of nature is harsh and wasteful in its operation. . . . Nature's discipline is not even a word and a blow, and the blow first; but the blow without the word. It is left to you to find out why your ears are boxed.' We see that Huxley's Mother Nature is much like any harassed Victorian mother with a large brood of children, except that she is unusually taciturn: she never scolds, she only whacks. But she is not always a mother: she is a white goddess, and if man accepts her discipline and frames his education on her pattern, he may in time become her lover, even, for brief moments, her master.

From this nineteenth-century view has mainly descended the conception of liberal education as a preparatory period, in which the student is allowed four years to get some perspective on the society around him. After that, in the standard phrase of commencement oratory, he is ready to go out into the world, conceived as a world of more or less productive activity, where he will use the small percentage of what he has learned that is relevant to what he is doing, use an even smaller percentage to help ornament and cultivate his spare time, and let the rest gradually erode. A decade or so after graduation one may still have cultivated tastes, but as a rule one can no longer read the Arabian Nights so fluently in the original Arabic, or social science textbooks in the original double Dutch. This conception of education is based on a Rasselas myth of a youthful prison-paradise, a playpen, as Robert Hutchins calls it, followed by a descent to the Egypt of practical life.

It will be seen that this view of liberal education has a basis that is really antiliberal: a grimly utilitarian standard is the logical response to it. This standard is modified in various ways: some things are good in themselves, their own ends as Newman says, and we have to think of the values of education as including them too. Or, more obviously, a knowledge of the more permanent principles of the arts and sciences turns out to be more practically useful than the kind of technical training that becomes obsolete as soon as one has learned it. But as long as we accept, even unconsciously, a vision of society in which the machinery of production assumes an overwhelming and inescapable urgency, our defences of the liberal arts and sciences will continue to have a panic-stricken tone. There is residual panic even in the question of what knowledge is most worth while, for in the time-word 'while' lurks the thought 'so little time', with its suggestion that a pathetically small part of one's life is spent in acquiring knowledge. The conception of society as consisting functionally only of workers and producers was one of the great nineteenth-century contributions to thought. But considering that it has become a stock response to say that the main problem of the twentieth century is the problem of leisure, surely we need to develop a view of education that incorporates this problem. The natural drive of the producing society is not democratic but oligarchic or managerial: it increases inequalities of privilege instead of reducing them, and in itself is no longer capable of leading us to the vision of the just state.

Today, the machinery of production appears to be steadily declining in the proportion of time and attention that it requires. I am not speaking of automation, which is not a cause but an effect of this process: I mean simply that the proportion of work to leisure which according to the Book of Genesis was established by God himself on a ratio of six to one is rapidly changing in the direction of a ratio of one to one. This makes for a social situation in which dull, meaningless, and exploited labour is less inevitable, and hence idleness and distraction are less inevitable as reactions against it. We are accustomed to thinking that everyone needs to be functionally related to this society through the work he does. But if leisure comes to occupy so much of so many people's lives, the question of finding a social function in leisure becomes increasingly important. This is already a problem of some urgency with women, as middle-class housewives are the obvious victims of a machinery of production so overefficient that it can only continue to operate by turning as many people as possible into full-time consumers. We appear, then, to be entering a period in which work and leisure are not embodied in different classes, but should be thought of as two aspects, nearly equal in importance, of the same life. Every citizen may be not only a Martha, troubled about many things, but a Mary who has chosen the better part, and the question 'What does he know?' becomes as relevant to defining one's social function as the question 'What does he do?'

The vast network of educational and cultural activities which includes schools, universities, churches, theatres, concerts, art galleries and museums, adult education programmes, and many other things, such as recreational and physical education, which I cannot deal with here, is thus gradually taking shape as the *other half* of society. Some countries, including Canada, have a nationalized programme of television, radio, and films, which is, or is supposed to be, more educational in its aims than the so-called private media that are conscripts in the army of production. One would hope to see an increasingly large proportion of such media desert advertising for education, or, at least, become more concerned to guide than merely to reflect public taste. One would hope to see the present notion disappear that mass media must be controlled either by propaganda or by advertising, that the former means totalitarianism and slavery and the latter democracy and freedom. The confusion of the liberal and the *laissez-faire* is still very much with us. One would hope to see the machinery of production operated with less hysteria through the gradual elimination of superfluous goods, including the waste products of war. These are Utopian hopes, but without Utopian hopes there can be no clear vision of social reality. In such a society it would be appropriate that universities should no longer be almost wholly concerned, as teaching institutions, with young people in the few lucid intervals that occur during four years of the mating season, but would make a place also for adults who could keep dropping into the university at various periods of their lives as an intellectual retreat.

In this social context, the question of what knowledge is worth while would not have the implication that knowledge is obtained mainly during a period of preparing for life. Life will not stay around to be prepared for, nor, in a world where the coding, housing, and retrieving of information is itself one of the biggest activities there is, can life be conceived as anything apart from a continuous learning process. The essential aim of all early education should be the inculcating of a lifetime habit. This takes me back to my original remark that for a genuine student the knowledge of most worth is the subject to which he has already committed himself. One would normally expect that the subject which forms a student's 'major' would be the basis of a permanent interest in that subject. It is one function of general education, I should think, to establish a context for special cultural interests. Every field of knowledge is the centre of all knowledge, and general education should help the student to see how this is true for his chosen field.

It is obvious, as was also said at the beginning, that a cultivated and well-informed interest in a subject is something different from scholarship, with its dependence on research libraries and laboratories. As the somewhat sinister phrase 'productive scholar' indicates, scholarship is part of the army of production: the scholar is not necessarily, *qua* scholar, an educated man at all, and he works in an area where the division of labour is at its most thoroughgoing. The editor of Shakespeare and the chemist live in different scholarly worlds, and proposals to make the humanist memorize the second law of thermodynamics and the scientist a speech from *Macbeth* will not bring them together. What brings them together is social, not intellectual, the fact that they are both citizens of their society with a common stake in that society. The only knowledge that is worth while is the knowledge that leads to wisdom, for knowledge without wisdom is a body without life. But no form of knowledge necessarily does or cannot do that: the completing of the structure has something to do with one's sense of the place of knowledge in the total human situation, ideal as well as actual.

Because we have tended to think of leisure as occasional or preparatory, and leisure-time activities as merely filling up the cracks of a

busy life, the creative arts, which are particularly the symbols of cultivation, have never reached their true educational proportions. I think
that what is true of scholarship is also true of the creative arts: those
who paint and write and compose are, again, producers. The process of
liberal education seems to me to be concerned more with understanding
and responding to the arts than with producing them, though, of course,
this is a matter of emphasis, not of definition. As Castiglione showed for
the Renaissance courtier, the artist needs to be complemented by the
cultivated amateur, who represents the social vision of an educated
public that has some idea what to do with the artist's work. Hence
education in the arts is primarily critical: it struggles to attain a conscious knowledge and understanding of a kind that is normally detached
from the creative process itself, though it should be as useful to the
creative artist as to anyone else. The chief deficiency in today's literature, for example, is not the lack of good writers, but the lack of a
reading public sufficiently large, informed, and articulate to establish
the real social importance of the good writer.

The importance of the creative arts becomes obvious in proportion
as social leisure increases: they are the primary elements of the cultivated life and of all social ideals. But their importance does not stop
here: they are also, in the phrase of my title, the primary instruments of
mental production. We have seen that two arts, literature and mathematics, held a leading place in Platonic, medieval, and humanistic
conceptions of education, and their place today is as central as ever,
although the classical literatures are now reinforced by the modern
ones. The contemporary reason for their importance is that the arts of
words and numbers are not only arts in themselves but informing languages for other disciplines. Words inform the bodies of knowledge
that we call the humanities, as well as most of the social sciences;
mathematics informs the sciences, more particularly the physical
sciences. I suppose the scientific part of general education would be
general science, and it is always something of a *tour de force* to make
science accessible and profitable to the unspecializing student. But, of
course, the more the student understands of the language of mathematics, the less difficult the *tour de force* has to be. I think that literature,
the art of words, has a similar relation to the other verbal disciplines,
and that the shape of the arguments of the controversial subjects,

religion, philosophy, political theory, is ultimately a poetic shape. Education is concerned with two worlds: the world that man lives in and the world he wants to live in. It would, of course, be nonsense to say that the former was the business of the sciences and the latter the business of the humanities and the arts. But it is true that science is primarily the study of the order of nature, the world that is there: it is true also that the form of the world man wants to live in is revealed by the form of the world he keeps trying to build, the world of cities and gardens and libraries and highways that is a world of art. We come closer to their relation if we say that the two great divisions of liberal knowledge embody two moral attitudes which are also intellectual virtues. The distinctive intellectual virtue of science is detachment, the objective consideration of evidence, the drawing of rational conclusions from evidence, the rejection of all devices for cooking or manipulating the evidence. Such a virtue is most obvious in the sciences that are founded on the repeatable experiment. But even in fields that are non-experimental and non-predictive, such as history, the scholar needs the same kind of detachment and is bound by the same code of honour to the extent that the nature of his subject permits. Only in the creative arts, perhaps, is one free of the scientific code, and only there because detachment is replaced by a kind of craftsmanship that is psychologically very similar.

But in the arts, particularly the literary arts, we become aware of many human factors relevant to them but not to science as such: emotion, value, aesthetic standards, the portrayal of objects of desire and hope and dream as realities, the explicit preference of life to death, of growth to petrifaction, of freedom to enslavement. Literature is not detached but concerned: it deals with what is there in terms of what man wants and does not want. The same sense of the relevance of concern enters into many other verbal areas, into religion (where the concern is 'ultimate', in Tillich's phrase), and a great deal of philosophy and history and political theory and psychology. It extends into most areas of applied science, and if it does not enter pure science as such, that is only because the detachment of science is the aspect of concern that is appropriate to science. And just as the language of science seems to be largely mathematical, so the language of concern is verbal, but verbal in a certain way. Briefly, the language of concern is the language of myth. Myth is the structural principle of literature that enters into and gives form to the verbal disciplines where concern is relevant. Man's views of the world he wants to live in, of the world he does not want to live in, of his situation and destiny and heritage, of the world he is trying to make and of the world that resists his efforts, forms in every age a huge mythological structure, and the subjects I have just listed form the main elements of it. I call it a structure, and sometimes, as in the Middle Ages, it really does seem to be one, the extent to which the Middle Ages unified its mythology being a source of great admiration to later times. In our own day we are more aware of variety and disagreement in our mythology, but the connecting links are there, and it is a part of the task of general education to try to expose them.

Many of those who are engaged in building up this mythopoeic structure – poets, theologians, philosophers, cultural historians – keep eagerly scanning the physical sciences for formulae that they can annex, thereby showing that scientific evidence confirms their world-picture. In the eighteenth century there was great religious, philosophical, and poetic excitement over the world-view that Newton had developed, though on analysis it was not so much his actual science that caused the excitement as the fact that Newton, who himself had speculative interests, had thrown out such suggestions as that space was the sensorium of deity, in addition to framing his laws of motion and gravitation. Evolution, similarly, set off a great wave of mythopoeic speculation ranging from Bernard Shaw's creative will to theories about society that had much more to do with Malthus than with Darwin. Various conceptions borrowed from Einstein, Planck, and Heisenberg have been used to decorate more recent world-pictures, and the law of entropy, taken out of its thermodynamic context and applied to the entire universe, gives us a cosmology sufficiently pointless and lugubrious to sound very modern in this existential age.

These examples are somewhat discouraging: they all seem to me to be phony, and I doubt if any of them would be regarded, in the sciences that suggested them, as founded on a genuine and well-proportioned knowledge of those sciences. I would even risk the suggestion that the physical sciences have never contributed anything to the mythopoeic world-picture except through misunderstanding and misapplication. If that is true, then the moral is clearly that science is its own world-view, and should be distinguished from the mythical one, even though it may be another mythology. Any cultivated person can become acquainted with both without trying to reconcile them, and without suffering from schizophrenia through failing to do so. Doubtless the world we see and the world we create meet somewhere at some point of identity, but keeping the two eyes of knowledge focused on that point seems better than a Cyclopean single vision. It is particularly in the religious area of the mythical vision that this is true. There is a natural impetus of religion towards idolatry: the instinct that created gods out of nature in primitive life still keeps trying to project God from human concerns into the order of nature. The God of nature is dead, because he was never alive, but the fact that there is no time and no place for God in the scientific world-view does not refute the religious aspect of the mythical one.

I am not, of course, speaking of philosophical efforts to co-ordinate scientific world-views in themselves, which form a different kind of activity. And what I am attacking, in any case, is not the integrating of myth and science, if it can be done, but the forcible conversion of science to myth. I spoke of detachment and concern as the virtues of the two attitudes, but for each virtue there is a corresponding vice. The vice of detachment is indifference: the feeling that one's immediate concern is separable from the total human concern – that a man can be an island entire of himself. The indifferent man, in science or business or whatever, does what seems useful to himself at the moment, and disregards the suggestion that it might be harmful to society, or even to his own better self. The trouble with indifference is that it cannot remain indifference. The only forms of human reality are life and death, and if the hopes and dreams and desires and values of humanity which are essential to life are rejected, life itself is rejected. Sooner or later indifference must be conscripted by aggression, and find its fulfilment in war, in the promotion of death on a total scale.

The vice of concern, on the other hand, is anxiety. We have anxiety when a society seizes on one myth and attempts to pound the whole of knowledge and truth into a structure conforming to it. The simplest statement of this kind of anxiety is the remark attributed to the Caliph Omar, when about to burn the Alexandrian Library, that all the books in it either agreed or disagreed with the Koran, and were therefore either superfluous or blasphemous. Similar anxieties dominated Christian Europe for centuries, and provided more than enough evidence that the desire to persecute was an essential part of them. Marxism forms the same kind of anxiety-myth today, and it too has its Omars demonstrating that all forms of knowledge are either consistent with it or wrong. Hysterical anxiety-groups on the extreme right in American life also work in the direction of setting up a myth of 'Americanism' as the criterion for all statements of fact or opinion. It is generally felt that such groups exert a subversive influence on American culture that is out of all proportion to their numbers, to say nothing of their intelligence. If so, then something is lacking in the educational resources of the saner part of the country.

To sum up: the instruments of mental production are the creative arts and the bodies of knowledge they inform. These bodies make up two larger bodies, mythology and science, man's view of his own destiny and his view of the world around him. These larger bodies are distinguishable, but not separate, and the moral attitudes that make them possible, concern and detachment, interpenetrate in all knowledge. Mythology in particular, on the level of general education, forms an initiatory pattern of education: understanding the traditional lore of one's society. The basis of it is social mythology, the clichés and stock responses that pour into the mind from conversation and the mass media, including school textbooks. The purpose of social mythology is to create the adjusted, that is, the docile and obedient citizen, and it occupies an overwhelming proportion of American elementary education. I think this is the source of the deficiency I have just noted: the myth of the American way of life does not distinguish the reality from the rationalized façade of that life. Above social mythology is the mythical structure formed by the humanities and the vision of nature afforded by general science, the purpose of which is to create the informed and participating citizen. Above this is the world of art and scholarship, which is to be left to shape itself, and acknowledged to have the authority to reshape the structure of general education below it at any time. Where an initiatory mythology controls the whole structure of education, as it did in medieval Europe and does now in Communist China, tolerance is a negative virtue, a matter of deciding how much deviation is consistent with the safety of the myth. Where art and scholarship are autonomous, tolerance is a positive and creative force, the unity of detachment and concern.

When I say that education is the study of society in its stable and permanent form, I do not, naturally, mean an unchanging form. I mean that genuine society preserves the continuity of the dead, the living and the unborn, the memory of the past, the reality of the present, and the anticipation of the future which is the one unbreakable social contract. Continuity and consistency are the only sources of human dignity, and they cannot be attained in the dissolving phantasmagoria of the newspaper world, where we have constantly to focus on an immediate crisis, where a long-term memory is almost a handicap. The term 'liberal' applied to education, again, reminds us that there is not necessarily any principle of freedom in political democracy, in economic *laissez-faire*, or in the separation of state and church. All these may be signs of a measure of freedom in society, but they are not sources of it. There can be no freedom except in the power to realize the possibilities of human life, both in oneself and for others, and the basis of that power is the continuing vision of a continuing city.

2 THE KNOWLEDGE OF GOOD
AND EVIL

In the eighteenth century there was some confidence that, in Samuel Johnson's words, no new discoveries were to be made in the field of morality. But new discoveries continued to be made elsewhere, most remarkably in science, and these have had their effect on our conceptions of morality as well. The development of science emphasized the value of the 'scientific method', but most expositions of that method turn out to be not so much methodologies as statements of a moral attitude. To achieve anything in the sciences, one needs the virtue of detachment or objectivity. One starts out with a tentative goal in mind, but on the way to it one must consider evidence impartially and draw only the strictly rational conclusions from that evidence. Cooking or manipulating the evidence to make it fit a preconceived idea works against detachment. And though we may say that detachment is an intellectual rather than a moral virtue, it becomes increasingly clear as we go on that such a distinction is without meaning. The persistence in keeping the mind in a state of disciplined sanity, the courage in facing results that may deny or contradict everything that one had hoped to achieve – these are obviously moral qualities, if the phrase means anything at all.

The triumphs of these virtues in modern civilization have naturally, and rightly, given them a high place in our scale of values. They are most clearly displayed in the physical sciences, which are so largely informed by mathematics, but as the social sciences developed, they too felt the powerful pull of detachment, and so they became increasingly behaviouristic, phenomenological, and restricted to what can be observed and described. At present it may be said that the principle, which is also a moral principle, that every discipline must be as scientific as its subject-matter will allow it to be, or abandon all claim to be taken seriously, is now established everywhere in scholarship.

Thus in the general area of the 'humanities', history is a subject which can doubtless never be a science, in the sense of being founded on repeatable experiments, informed by mathematics, or leading to prediction. But there is a scientific element involved in the choice of historical evidence which distinguishes history from legend, and prevents, say, a British historian from including Atlantis, Merlin, and King Lear in his purview. Again, if the historian is attempting to set up a system of causation in his history, he will avoid indefinable causes and restrict himself to what he can observe and describe. And while one historian may believe in something incredible to another, such as the resurrection of Jesus or the miracles of a medieval saint, the sense of a predictable order of nature is so strong that the incredulous historian will set the pattern for his colleague. That is, whatever any reasonable and well-disposed historian finds incredible is likely also to be historically unfunctional in the work of another historian who believes it.

Similarly, literary critics are slowly and reluctantly beginning to realize that the evaluative comparison of literary works and traditions gives us no knowledge of literature, but merely rearranges what we already know, or think we know. Whatever gives us knowledge of literature has, like genuine history and genuine philosophy, a detached and objective element in it that distinguishes it from elegant rumination. The hope of developing an axiological science in criticism, as elsewhere, remains so far only a hope. As for religion, its resistance to the same pressure has been long and stubborn, but is visibly collapsing. For long it was felt that the religious mind, like the White Queen in Alice, specialized in believing the impossible. The present tendency to 'demythologizing' in religion means, first, that beliefs which are contradicted by the plainest evidence of history or science, such as the quasi-historical fantasies of the Anglo-Israelites or the 'fundamentalism' that translates the hymn of creation in Genesis into a textbook of geology, are intellectually wrong. Consequently, because of the way that such beliefs shut doors in the mind and prevent the whole mind from coming into focus on anything, they are in the long run morally wrong as well. In all areas of knowledge we distinguish the observed fact, which depends on sense experience, from the context of the fact, which depends not so much on reason as on a sense of convention about what is, at the time, felt to be reasonable. Truth in religion is increasingly felt to be something that conforms to scientific and scholarly conceptions of truth, instead of being thought to reside primarily in the miraculous, or in the transcendence of other conventions of truth.

Demythologizing is a very inappropriate, not to say foolish, term for what is actually mythologizing, as any withdrawal of religious structures from ontological assertion is bound to transform them into myths. This process has now reached a crucial stage. As the principle of objectivity as the guide to truth continues to make its way, certain types of conceptions, which do not lend themselves to observation, tend to become unusable. What reality can now be attached to the word 'God', if it no longer means anything objective? Is it a word that can still be used, like 'mind' in psychology or 'life' in biology, as a kind of metaphorical signpost, pointing to things that manifest themselves as complexes of observable behaviour? If so, what complexes? Or is it a word that depends solely on projection or hypostasis, like such terms as devil, angel, god with a small *g*, daemon, or (in most contexts) soul, which can only be asserted to exist? It is so fatally easy to name things that are not there: the lion and the unicorn have exactly the same *grammatical* status. Or, finally, is the conception of 'God', which has never been anything but a nuisance as a scientific hypothesis, simply a dead word, like 'ether' in physics, which does not even need a Michelson-Morley experiment to knock it on the head? The case of religion is of particular importance in discussing morality in scholarship, because our traditional morality has been bound up with religion, and religion with belief in the existence of a personal God. In Tourneur's *Atheist's Tragedy* (1611), the word 'atheist' also means what we should now mean by a psychopath. Anyone at that time who renounced a personal God would be assumed to have renounced every moral principle as well. Today, most responsible theologians would agree that the statement 'There is a God' is of very little religious and no moral significance. It is clear that the conviction we began with, that no new discoveries are to be made in morality, was premature, even if we are still only at the stage of unmaking some of our old discoveries.

In the creative arts the virtues of detachment and objectivity do not, at first sight, seem to apply. The artist is not bound to evidence and rational deduction: he makes a functional use of emotional and even repressed factors in his mental attitude which the scientist as such must sublimate. Yet the cult of objectivity has been very strong in the arts, too, for over a century, especially in literature. Zola thought of his novels as applied sociology; Flaubert and Joyce recommended an Olympian detachment as the only position worthy of the artist; even the poets insisted that writing poetry was an escape from personality. If any serious contemporary writer were attacked on moral grounds, his defence would almost certainly be based on the moral virtue of detachment. He is trying, he would say, to tell the truth as he sees it, like the scientist. Such a defence would relate to content, but, in form, perhaps the *craftsmanship* of the artist, his effort by re-working and revising to let his creation take its own shape, is what corresponds in the arts to the scientist's objectivity. Art being also a mode of communication, the artist's personal emotions have only a typical or representative status in his art.

The permeation of ordinary scholarly life by the same virtue is marked in the deference paid to impersonality. A scholar is supposed not to write or to read an unfavourable review with any personal application; his friendships are not supposed to be affected by theoretical disagreements; students are instructed that 'failure' means only not meeting an objective standard, and does not refer to them as human beings. It is significant that the *personal appropriation* of knowledge is not considered the scholar's social goal. The scholar whose social behaviour reflects his knowledge too obtrusively is a pedant, and the pedant, whatever the degree of his scholarship, is regarded as imperfectly educated.

Yet there is a widespread popular feeling, expressed in many clichés, that the pedant, the scholar who does not accurately sense the relation between scholarship and ordinary life, is in fact typical of the university and its social attitude. The forward impetus of the scientific spirit backfires in the public relations department: the disinterested pursuit of knowledge acquires, for its very virtues, the reputation of being unrelated to social realities. The intellectual, it is thought, lives in an oversimplified Euclidean world; his attitude to society is at best aloof, at worst irresponsible; his loyalties and enmities, when they exist, have the naïve ferocity of abstraction, a systematic preference of logical extremes to practical means. A fair proportion of incoming freshmen, in my experience especially women, though mildly curious about the scholarly life, are convinced that it is an 'ivory tower', and that only a misfit would get permanently trapped in it. I call this popular view a cliché, which it clearly is, but the clichés of social mythology are social facts. And what this particular cliché points to, rightly or wrongly, is the insufficiency of detachment and objectivity as exclusive moral goals.

The scholarly virtue of detachment, we said, is a moral virtue and not merely an intellectual one: what is intellectual about it is its context. It turns into the vice of indifference as soon as its context becomes social instead of intellectual. Indifference to what? Indifference, let us say, to what we may call, with the existentialists, concern. By concern I mean something which includes the sense of the importance of preserving the integrity of the total human community. Detachment becomes indifference when the scholar ceases to think of himself as participating in the life of society, and of his scholarship as possessing a social context. We see this clearly when we turn from the subject itself to the social use made of it. Psychology is a science, and must be studied with detachment, but it is not a matter of indifference whether it is used for a healing art, or for 'motivational research' designed to force people to buy what they neither want nor need, or for propaganda in a police state.

The challenge of concern may come in many forms, and from either a revolutionary or a conservative attitude. Marxism has done much to popularize the view that all social detachment is illusion. On the other hand, Burke laid down a programme of pragmatic and short-range concern in opposition to revolutionary tendencies of his time which he described as 'metaphysical', a deductive effort to force human destinies into conclusions from large and loose premises about the rights of man. Such conceptualizing of social activity tends to sacrifice the immediate for the distant good: it achieves a detachment from the present situation which is really only indifference to it. The kind of progressivism that says: 'If we shoot a hundred thousand farmers now, we may have a more efficient system of collectivized agriculture in the next generation', or: 'We need something like a nuclear war if we are to stabilize the population explosion', are examples of the kind of indifference that Burke had in mind.

It is clear that concern and morality are closely connected: morality, in fact, in the sense of the kind of obligation that enables man to preserve his relation to society, is the central expression of concern. What we have to determine is to what extent concern is a scholarly virtue, and whether or not it is, like detachment, a precondition of knowledge. Traditionally, morality has been primarily the safeguarding of the community against all attacks on it. Its ultimate sanction is the giving up of the individual life to preserve the social one, whether in war or in capital punishment. But the safeguarding of the community is not the whole of concern. Concern includes a dialectical value-judgement: the assumption that life is better than death, happiness better than misery, freedom better than slavery, for all men without exception, or significant exception. Human life is socially organized and cannot achieve its goals without such organization, yet any given society may bring death, misery, or slavery on many or even the majority of its members. A man who feels such concern can thus never wholly repudiate nor wholly support his particular society: there must always be a tension between one's loyalties and one's projected desires.

Traditionally, however, what I have called the dialectic of concern has been strictly subordinated to accepting one's own society. In proportion as this is true, society incorporates the dialectic of concern in a class-structure wherein one class derives a greater share of leisure, privilege, and personal liberty from the labour of the rest of society. The same pattern appears in religion, where the division takes the form of heaven and hell, salvation and damnation. As long as the dialectic concern was assumed to be completed in another world, the class-structure of this one could be accepted as a necessary transition to it. To that extent the instinct of western Europe was sound in regarding Christianity as the palladium of its social structure. A more radical tension has begun to develop since, say, around Rousseau's time. It was probably Rousseau who brought out most vividly the contrast between what civilization demands and what man most profoundly wants. Since then, the reconciling of the dialectic of concern with the social structure has tended to take one of two forms, depending on whether the general-will side or the noble-savage side of Rousseau's thought is stressed. One form, clearest in Marxism, calls for a revolutionary movement from the depressed part of society to put an end to the perversion of concern in the social structure, along with its religious projection. The other, which has taken hold in America, calls for the maintaining of an open society to resist any such revolution, on the ground that it would merely set up a new establishment, and one much harder to dislodge.

The traditional assumption that man can do nothing without a specific organization takes different forms in our day. One of these is the sense of the futility of individual effort, which in turn leads to a rationalizing of 'commitment' or 'engagement', that is, attaching oneself to something that looks big and strong enough to get somewhere on its own. The attraction of Communism for many European intellectuals is usually rationalized on this basis. You obviously can't lick them, the argument runs, so you'll have to join them, or their most powerful enemy. Yet the expression of concern seems morally much more clear-cut when it takes the form of a minority resistance movement, like the resistance of the French to the Nazis, of the Hungarians to the Communists, of Negroes to white supremacy, of the Vietcong to the Americans. It is still more so in proportion as the cause appears quixotic, hopeless, futile, or abandoned by others. Those who die for their country in war help to preserve the life of their community in time, but the hopeless cause is invisible, though believed by its martyrs to be present. In religion, an invisible but present heaven may be the guarantee, so to speak, of the reality of the community to which martyrdom bears 'witness' (the original sense of martyr). The apocalyptic visions of the Phaedo and the New Testament make the deaths of Socrates and of Christ more intelligible. But even without religion the non-participating expression of concern, when carried to the point of death, has an intense moral challenge about it. The self-cremating of Buddhist and American conscientious objectors to the Vietnam war is an example. The Nuremberg and other Nazi trials even raised the question whether a (necessarily hopeless) resistance to the demands of a perverted social order was not only morally but legally binding, and whether one who did not make such a resistance could be considered a criminal. It was feared at the time, no doubt correctly, that the nations who prosecuted these trials would not show enough moral courage to respect this principle where their own interests were involved. In contrast, the more powerful the social structure, the more apt one's loyalty to it is to modulate from concern to concerned indifference. The enemy become, not people to be defeated, but embodiments of an idea to be exterminated. The real growing-point of concern, we have indicated, is not the mere wish that all men should attain liberty, happiness, and more abundant life, nor is it the mere attachment to one's own community: it is rather the sense of the difference between these two things, the perception of the ways in which the human ideal is thwarted and deflected by the human actuality. If there is no moral concern for all humanity, and only concern for one's own society, then concern is reversed into anxiety, which is the vice of concern, as indifference is the vice of detachment. Anxiety in this sense is a negative concern, a clinging to the accustomed features of one's society, usually connected with a fear of something that has been made into a symbol of the weakening of that society. Every social change, even the most obvious improvements, like abolishing slavery or giving votes to women, or the most trifling novelties in fashion, stirs up anxieties of this sort. Religion is a particularly fruitful source of such anxieties, which it inherits from the primitive anxiety known as superstition. Those who are not capable of faith have to settle for anxieties instead.

The wider concern based on the preference for life, freedom, and happiness to their opposites is, as we have just called it, a projection of desire. The source of all dangers to social routine, real or fancied, is man's feeling that his desires are not fulfilled by his community. And when we think of the individual man in this way, as a potential disturber of society, we tend increasingly to think of him, not as reasoning man or feeling man, but as sexual man. Eros is the main spokesman for the more abundant life that the social structure fears and resists. When we begin to think along these lines, we soon become aware of the extent to which social anxieties are preoccupied with channelling and sublimating the sexual energies. We begin to understand why certain overt expressions of sexual activity, such as public nakedness or 'four-letter words', provide an automatic shock to such anxieties. This familiar Freudian view of anxiety has developed an unexpected social importance in the last decade, when American life has begun to show some contrasting parallels with Communism. The programme of Marxism calls for a separation of social loyalty from the ruling class's defence of its privileges, and attaches loyalty to a 'proletariat' or group of dispossessed. The contrasting social movements in America have recently

taken on a strongly Freudian cast, in which 'beat', 'hip', and other dis-
affected groups attempt to define a proletariat in a Freudian sense, as
those who withdraw from 'square' or bourgeois anxiety-values and
form a society of the creative and spontaneous. Associated with them
are novelists and poets who emphasize the sexual side of human activity,
sometimes with a maundering and tedious iteration. Considered as
moralists, such writers are attempting to destroy or at least weaken the
anxiety-structure founded on sexual repression.

It is becoming apparent that concern is a normal dimension of everybody, including scholars, and that for scholars in particular it is the
corrective to detachment, and prevents detachment from degenerating
into indifference. It remains to be seen what its relationship to the
learning process is. It seems obvious that concern has nothing directly
to do with the content of knowledge, but that it establishes the human
context into which the knowledge fits, and to that extent informs it. The
language of concern is the language of myth, the total vision of the
human situation, human destiny, human inspirations and fears. The
mythology of concern reaches us on different levels. On the lowest
level is the social mythology acquired from elementary education and
from one's surroundings, the steady rain of assumptions and values and
popular proverbs and clichés and suggested stock responses that soaks
into our early life and is constantly reinforced, in our day, by the mass
media. In this country most elementary teaching is, or is closely connected with, the teaching of 'the American way of life'. A body of
social acceptances is thus formed, a myth with a pantheon of gods,
some named (Washington, Franklin, Lincoln), others anonymous (the
pioneer, the explorer, the merchant adventurer). This body of acceptances gradually evolves into a complete mythology stretching from
past golden age to future apocalypse. Pastoral myths (the cottage away
from it all, the idyllic simplicity of the world of one's childhood) form
at one end of it; stereotypes of progress, the bracing atmosphere of
competition, the threat of global disaster, and the hope of preserving
this life for one's children form at the other. Such a popular mythology
is neither true nor false, neither right or wrong: the facts of history and
social science that it contains are important chiefly for the way in which
they illustrate certain beliefs and views. The beliefs and views are primarily about America, but are extended by analogy to the rest of the

human race. Such social mythology expresses a concern for society, both immediate and total, which may not be very profound or articulate, but which is a mighty social force for all that. Similar social mythologies have been developed in all nations in all ages: contemporary Americans, in fact, have an unusually benevolent and well-intentioned one.

Above this is a body of general knowledge, mainly in the area of the humanities, which is also assimilated to a body of beliefs and assumptions. This forms the structure of what might be called initiatory education, the learning of what the cultivated and well-informed people in one's society know, within the common acceptances which give that society its coherence. Initiatory education enters into the university's liberal arts curriculum and is reinforced by the upper strata of the mass media, ranging from churches to the more literary magazines. In our society, the structure of initiatory education is a loose mixture of ideas, beliefs and assumptions, different in composition for each person, but not so different as to preclude communication on its own primarily social level. It forms a body of opinion which I call the mythology of concern. By a myth, in this context, I mean a body of knowledge assimilated to or informed by a general view of the human situation. Some myths in this sense are pure expressions of belief, like the myth of progress. Some are beliefs which are not so much true as going to be made true by a certain programme of social action: this is the sense in which Sorel generally uses the word, and it also characterizes the myth of Marxism, according to the *Theses on Feuerbach*.

The traditional picture of scholarship as an intensely specialized activity, motivated by detachment and the pursuit of truth for its own sake, is correct as far as it goes. The arts, and the detailed research which is scholarship in this more restricted sense, emerge out of initiatory education like icebergs, with an upper part which is specialized and a lower part which is submerged in the scholar's general activity as a human being. The mythology of initiatory education is not itself scholarship in the restricted sense, but its upper levels modulate into a scholarly area of great and essential importance. The scholar is involved with this area in three ways: as a teacher, as a popularizer of his own subject, and as an encyclopedist. That is, if he happens to be interested in conspectus or broad synthesizing views, he will spend much or all of his time in articulating and making more coherent his version of his society's myth of concern. A great deal of philosophy (in fact, this is often supposed to be philosophy's role), of history, and of social science takes this form. Relatively few such myths are so firmly embedded in the facts as to be actual hypotheses, capable of being definitely proved or disproved; their importance is rather in their effectiveness in extending the reader's perspective. The mythology of concern, taken as a whole, is not a unified body of knowledge, nor is the knowledge it contains always logically deduced from its beliefs and assumptions, nor does one necessarily believe in everything that one accepts from it. But it does possess a unity none the less, and those who have most effectively changed the modern world – Rousseau, Marx, and Freud have come up at different times during this discussion – are those who have changed the general pattern of our mythology.

The world of scholarship, in the restricted sense, is too specialized and pluralistic to form any kind of over-all society. Each scholar, left purely to his own scholarship, would see the human situation only from his own point of view, and the resulting sectarianism would probably destroy society, as the confusion of tongues led to the abandoning of Babel. Hence the importance of having an area of scholarship inter-mediate between general information and the pursuit of detailed research. It is essentially an activity of exploring the social roots of knowledge, of maintaining communication among scholars, of formulating the larger views and perspectives that mark the cultivated man, and of relating knowledge to the kind of beliefs and assumptions that unite knowledge with the good life.

But it is equally important to recognize where this kind of scholarship is. There is a persistent belief that the unifying of the different fields of scholarship is the final aim of scholarship. But in an open society the unifying of the myth of concern should never be carried to the point of losing the sense of the autonomy of scholarship. A completely unified myth of concern tends to assume that it already has all the important answers, that whatever scholarship has yet to disclose will be either consistent with what is now believed or else wrong, and that it has the right to prescribe the direction in which scholarship is to go. In this situation the myth of concern becomes an anxiety-myth. The mythology of the Middle Ages was much more completely unified than ours, so much so as to inspire envy in every age since, down to the revival of

Thomism in the last generation. Yet it fought hard for its fictions: the resistance of authority to scholarship did not stop with Galileo, and it is hard to believe that it has stopped now. Marxism is also a myth of concern which has become an anxiety-myth when it has been politically established. It interferes less with the autonomy of science than with the arts and humanities, which are more likely to develop rival myths of concern. Its interference with the sciences, for one thing, has usually been disastrous. An extreme example, now officially repudiated, was Lysenko's genetics, whose proponent revived a curious neoscholastic method of arguing, first proving the correct attitude to genetics out of Marx and Lenin, and then asserting that this attitude would be found to fit the facts when the facts were examined. Extreme right-wing groups in America, working, of course, mainly on the level of stock response, also attempt to set up a myth of 'Americanism' as a criterion for all cultural activity that they get to hear about. When art and scholarship are left autonomous, it is assumed that all unification of knowledge is provisional, and that new discoveries, new ideas, and new shapings of the creative imagination may alter it at any time. The open society thus has an open mythology; the closed society has a controlling myth from which all scholarship is assumed to be logically derived.

One reason why our myth of concern is not as well unified as that of the Middle Ages is that all myths of concern are anthropocentric in perspective, and physical science, at least, refuses to have anything to do with such a perspective. The physical scientist finds his subject less rooted in the myth of concern than the philosopher, the historian, or the theologian. The latter find it more difficult to separate their subjects from their social commitments: they may even find it something of a struggle to preserve intellectual honesty in their arguments, to let facts speak for themselves and avoid twisting them into the directions called for by their commitments. But the physical scientist's enemy is more likely to be indifference than anxiety, and even a genuine interest in the social context of his scholarship has some unexpected barriers to surmount. Naturally the main outlines of the scientific picture of the world are a part of our general cultural picture, and naturally, too, any broad and important scientific hypothesis, such as evolution or relativity, soon filters down into the myth of concern. But scientific hypotheses enter the myth of concern, not as themselves, but as parallel or translated forms of themselves. An immense number of conceptions in modern thought owe their existence to the biological theory of evolution. But social Darwinism, the conception of progress, the philosophies of Bergson and Shaw, and the like, are not applications of the *same* hypothesis in other fields: they are mythical analogies to that hypothesis. By the time they have worked their way down to stock response, as when slums are built over park land because 'you can't stop progress', even the sense of analogy gets a bit hazy. If a closed myth like official Marxism does not interfere with physical science, we have still to remember that physical science is not an integral part of the myth of concern.

We have spoken not merely of scholarship but of the arts also as needing autonomy if society is to preserve its freedom. The reasons why the arts are not included belong to another paper, but the role of literature in the myth of concern is relevant here. It is an ancient belief that the original framers of the myth of concern were the poets, acting as 'unacknowledged legislators', in Shelley's phrase. In literature the dialectic of concern, the separation of life, freedom, and happiness from their opposites, expresses itself in two tonalities, so to speak: the romantic and the ironic visions. The romantic vision is of the heroic, the pleasurable, the ideal, of that with which one feels impelled to identify oneself. The ironic vision is the vision of the anguished, the nauseated, and the absurd. Besides these, there are the two great narrative movements, the tragic and the comic, which move towards the ironic and romantic cadences respectively.

The ironic vision is the one which is predominant in our day, and its features of anguish, nausea, and absurdity have been deeply entrenched in the contemporary myth of concern. We have noted the importance of detachment in scholarship and its close connection with the scientific method. Science is based on a withdrawal of consciousness from existence, a capacity to turn around and look at one's environment, which is perhaps the most distinctively human of all acts. It is the act that turns the experiencing being into a subject, confronting an objective world from which it has separated itself. The ironic vision is, so to speak, a detachment from detachment: it recognizes the emotional factors of alienation, loneliness, and meaninglessness lurking in the subject-object relationship which the activity of science ignores. The heart of the ironic vision, however, is the vision of the kind of society that such a solitude creates, a society unable to communicate and united only by hatred or mutual contempt. Perhaps the most concentrated form of the ironic vision is what has been called the dystopia, the description of the social hell that man creates for himself on earth, the society of Orwell's *1984*, Koestler's *Darkness at Noon*, Huxley's *Ape and Essence*, Kafka's *In the Penal Colony*, where the individual finds his identity in seeing his own self-hatred reflected in the torment and humiliation of others.

The goal of the romantic vision is less easy to characterize. Although we should expect it to be the opposite of the ironic vision, some form of social heaven or city of God on earth, it is certainly not, at least not in literature, that anxiety-ridden form known as the utopia. It is rather the happy and festive society formed in the final moments of a comedy around the marriage of the hero and heroine, where the 'hero' is not, as a rule, an exceptionally brave or strong person, but only a modest and pleasant young man. It is rather the idyllic simplified world of the pastoral, where the hero is a shepherd with no special pretensions, except that he is also a poet and a lover. We notice that what we feel like identifying ourselves with in literature tends to be social rather than purely individual, a festive group rather than an isolated figure. Even the tragic hero who is necessarily isolated by the action – Achilles or Beowulf or Hamlet – seems to regard his heroism not as something that marks him off from others but as something that he has contributed to his society. It is not the characters but the brave deeds of great men that the Homeric heroes wish to emulate. If they die, they look for nothing more for themselves than the batlike existence of a shadow in Hades: their reputation will be their real immortality. It seems a cold and thin immortality, and yet perhaps there is something in this final trust in fame that is more than a 'last infirmity', more than the mere wistful pathos it appears to be.

It is becoming clearer that the impulse which creates the mythology of concern and makes it socially effective is a central part of the religious impulse. Religion in this sense may be without a God; certainly it may be without a first cause or controller of the order of nature, but it can never be without the primitive function of *religio*, of binding together a society with the acts and beliefs of a common concern. Such an impulse starts with one's own society, but if it stops there it sets up a cult of state-worship and becomes perverted. We know in our own experience how our mythology of concern works against exclusiveness: all genuine concern recognizes the claims of Negroes to full citizenship, for example. Yet the kind of problem represented by the disabilities of Negroes is much broader in scope, as many suffer from similar disabilities who are not Negroes, and if we make the symbol of coloured skin an end in itself, like some of the proponents of 'black power', we merely set up a new kind of anxiety. The force that creates the myth of concern drives it onward from the specific society one is in to larger and larger groups, and finally toward assimilating the whole of humanity to the ideal of its dialectic, its concerned feeling that freedom and happiness are better for everyone without exception than their opposites. All national or class loyalties, however instinctive or necessary, are thus in the long run interim or temporary loyalties: the only abiding loyalty is one to mankind as a whole.

If this were the whole story, the myth of concern would end simply in a vague and fuzzy humanitarianism. But in proportion as one's loyalty stretches beyond one's nation to the whole human race, one's concrete and specific human relationships become more obvious. A new kind of society appears in the centre of the world, a society which is different for each man, but consists of those whom he can see and touch, those whom he influences and by whom he is influenced: a society, in short, of neighbours. Who is our neighbour? We remember that this question was asked of Jesus, who regarded it as a serious question, and told the story of the Good Samaritan to answer it. And, as the alien figure of the Samaritan, in a parable told to Jews, makes obvious, one's neighbour is not, or not necessarily, a member of the same social or racial or class group as oneself. One's neighbour is the person with whom one has been linked by some kind of creative human act, whether of mercy or charity, as in the parable itself; or by the intellect or the imagination, as with the teacher, scholar, or artist; or by love, whether spiritual or sexual. The society of neighbours, in this sense, is our real society; the society of all men, for whom we feel tolerance and goodwill rather than love, is in its background.

We have spoken of the religious impulse as one that creates social ties, and that is as far as we can take it here. The universal goodwill to men which is one logical form of its development is one that could be expressed by statistical formulas, like the greatest happiness of the greatest number. But the sense of a society of neighbours takes us beyond ethics and values into the question of identity. It would perhaps be a reasonable characterization of religion to say that a man's religion is revealed by that with which he is trying to identify himself.

Throughout civilization there runs a tendency known in the Orient as 'making oneself small', of being modest and deprecating about one's own abilities, and being much more ready to concede the abilities of others. Some of this is self-protective hypocrisy, but not all of it is. When we think about our own identity, we tend at first to think of it as something buried beneath what everyone else sees, something that only we can reach in our most solitary moments. But perhaps, for ordinary purposes at least, we may be looking for our identity in the wrong direction. To identify something is first of all to put it in the category of things to which it belongs: the first step in identity is the realization *humanus sum*. We belong to something before we are anything, nor does growing in being diminish the link of belonging. Granted a reasonably well-disposed and unenvious community, perhaps our reputation and influence, what others are willing to think that we are, comes nearer to being our real selves than anything stowed away inside us. In the imagery of Blake's lyric, one may be more genuinely a 'clod', something attached to the rest of the earth, than a separated 'pebble'. In an ideal community there would be no alienation, in the sense used in Marx's early writings: that is, one's contribution to one's community would not be embezzled, used by others at one's expense. In such a community perhaps we could understand more clearly why even the tragic heroes of literature attempt to identify themselves with what they are remembered for having done. In the society that the mythology of concern ultimately visualizes, a man's real self would consist primarily of what he creates and of what he offers. The scholar as man has all the moral dilemmas and confusions of other men, perhaps intensified by the particular kind of awareness that his calling gives him. But *qua* scholar what he is is what he offers to his society, which is his scholarship. If he understands both the worth of the gift and the worth of what it is given for, he needs, so far as he is a scholar, no other moral guide.

3 SPECULATION AND CONCERN

As I understand it, I am being asked to discuss the question: What do the humanities provide for human culture that the sciences do not provide? My own field is literature, and literature seems to belong to two groups: the creative arts, including music and painting, and the verbal disciplines, including history and philosophy. Both may be regarded as humanities, but we have to distinguish them even when we associate them. The question itself is, I suppose, legitimate enough: it is, I take it, simply a matter of trying to indicate the different functions of different things. It is difficult, and perhaps impossible, to contrast the arts and the sciences without a good deal of oversimplifying and making some false or half-true antitheses. There may be some value in over-simplifying the contrast, if one has to do that to make it at all: a more serious difficulty is that nobody is likely to approach such a problem with his mind fully made up, his convictions firmly held, and his tentative and exploratory notions outgrown. In what follows I am thinking aloud, expecting the kind of indulgence that is accorded to such improvisation.

It will not have escaped your notice that I have so far said nothing except 'harrumph'. But there is something to be said for the convention of beginning with an apology, or topos of modesty. This kind of question is often called, as I have just called it, a 'problem', and one expects a problem to be solved. A genuine problem is a specific formulation of experience that can be adequately stated in other terms: to use a common analogy, it is like a knot in a rope that can be untied or retied without affecting the identity of the rope. A question like this is only metaphorically a problem: it is actually a subject of study, and the word solution is not appropriate. All I can do with a subject of study is to individualize it, to make a suggestion or two about how it looks from the standpoint of a literary critic who is living in the mid-twentieth century.

As a subject of study, the question can hardly be called new: a whole line of philosophers from Hegel onward have beaten their brains out over the difference between the knowledge of science and the knowledge of what the Germans call *Geist*, and over the methods and techniques appropriate to the study of history or sociology as distinct from biology or chemistry. It is an appropriate question for a centennial celebration, because it was one of the liveliest issues being debated a hundred years ago. The level of debate has not improved notably in tone since then. No contemporary treatment of the subject known to me matches the lucidity of Walter Bagehot's *Physics and Politics*, published in 1867, or the amiable and urbane discussion of Arnold and Huxley about the proportioning of humanities and sciences in the curriculum of a liberal education. A few years ago we had the Leavis-Snow dispute, where neither contribution was in the least amiable or urbane, and where it is hard to say which of the two documents was the more stupefyingly wrongheaded. Other essays purporting to defend the humanities have all too often a querulous and self-righteous air, like that of a striptease performer who informs a newspaper reporter that while all the other girls just take off their clothes, she is an authentic artist. And so, after more than a century of giving answers to the question of what is distinctive about the humanities, it is still quite possible that the real answer is 'nothing at all'. Freud concludes his *Future of an Illusion* by saying: 'Science is not an illusion, but it would be an illusion to suppose that we could get anywhere else what it cannot give us.' He was talking about religion, but he may be unconditionally right, beyond the limits of his context, and everything non-scientific, except possibly the creative arts, may be only pre-scientific or pseudo-scientific. And the arts may be an exception only because their function may be a purely ornamental or decorative one. This conference, after all, deals with 'The Humanities and the Quest for Truth', and the arts not only never seem to find truth, but do not even appear to be looking for it very seriously.

The best way to approach our question, I think, is to begin by reversing it, as Freud's phrasing suggests. What does science provide for human culture that the arts and the humanities do not provide? The traditional answer, and doubtless the right one, is 'nature'. What I am saying here is that science gives us nature, not the understanding or conception of nature. This may only be bad grammar, but I mean something more than understanding. The human mind can operate in different ways, but one very obvious way for it to operate is as a subject. That is, it can start by saying: Here am I, and I am here. Everything else is there. As soon as the mind does this, nature springs into being, like Athene from Jove's forehead, and reality appears to the mind as objective, as a field. It seems to me that it is peculiarly the function of science to objectify reality, to present the world in its aspect of being there. The world of science is the world of space: as has often been noted, science deals with time as a dimension of space. The subject itself becomes an object in this process, for there is nothing inside the scientist, from the structure of his spine to his infantile complexes, which is not also available for scientific study. Everything is there: nothing is really here except the consciousness with which he studies nature. And this consciousness, or scientific intelligence, is ideally disembodied. The theory of physics, for example, has been complicated, in its more rarefied aspects, by the fact that the scientist possesses a body, and cannot comprehend nature without physical contact. To see the world as an objective field of operation is also to quantify reality, to make it something measured rather than simply seen or heard. Isaiah praises a God 'Who hath measured the waters in the hollow of his hand, and meted out heaven with the span, and comprehended the dust of the earth in a measure, and weighed the mountains in scales, and the hills in a balance.' In science man takes over this traditional function of God, replacing the divine balance by the mathematician's equations.

Because science deals with reality as objective, there is no such thing as subjective science. What this means in practice is that science stabilizes the subject. It assumes a mind in the situation that we think of as sane or normal, ready to accept evidence and follow arguments. Thus science assumes a mind to some extent emancipated from existence, in the state of freedom or detachment that we call clarity. The sense of truth as an ideal, and of the pursuit of truth for its own sake as a virtue, go with the process of objectifying reality on which science is founded. The word truth itself carries with it the sense of a recognition of what is there. So does the sense of facts as given, as irreducible data to be studied in their inherent arrangements instead of being arranged. There may actually be no facts of this kind, but it is important to pretend that there are, that facts lie around immovably where they have been thrown, like rocks carried down by a glacier. As Wallace Stevens says:

> The arrangement contains the desire of
> The artist. But one confides in what has no
> Concealed creator.[1]

What science stands for in human life, then, is the revolt of consciousness against existence, the sense of his own uniqueness in nature that man gets by drawing his mind back from existence and contemplating it as a separated thing. The animal is immersed in existence without consciousness; the human being has consciousness, and consciousness means being capable, up to a point, of seeing existence as external to oneself. Of course, to withdraw from existence means to stop existing, and some philosophers, notably Sartre, even go so far as to associate consciousness with nothingness or non-being. However, it seems clear that conscious human beings can externalize their world and still go on living. Human existence, then, is a complex, of which consciousness is one of many functions, and the concentrated consciousness that produces science is a stylizing or conventionalizing of human behaviour.

I do not wish to suggest that science is founded on a narrowly empirical view of the world: that its end is only to describe and understand what it sees. The physical sciences at least are not simply descriptive, but are based on prediction as well: they see their phenomena in time – or their version of time – as well as space, and their end is rather a vision of nature under law. It is not the experiment but the repeatable experiment that is the key to the understanding of nature in the physical sciences, and the repeatable experiment is what makes prediction possible and gives to science a prophetic quality. Telepathic communication, poltergeists, mediums, have been approached experimentally and certain typical phenomena recur, but the experiments are not repeatable (except where they are fraudulent)[2], no laws can be established, and so science applied to such things never gets off the ground. Where the phenomena are unconscious or where the units involved are small and numerous, like atoms, molecules or cells, so that there is no practical difference between the highly probable and the certain, the language of science is primarily mathematical. From the natural sciences we move toward the social sciences, where the phenomena are relatively large, few, and complicated, like human beings. Here prediction on a statistical basis is as important as ever, but, except for some specialized aspects, the repeatable experiment is no longer at the centre of the study. In proportion as this is true, the subject tends to be organized verbally rather than mathematically. We then move into what are generally regarded as the humanities. History and philosophy are almost purely verbal, non-experimental, and non-predictive. But accuracy of statement, objectivity of description and dispassionate weighing of evidence, including the accepting of negative evidence, are still required. Hence a scientific element is still present in them that distinguishes history from legend, philosophy from rumination, and, as I think, literary criticism from a good many of the activities that go under that name. From there we move into the creative arts proper, where the requirements even of accurate descriptive statement and the basing of conclusions on fair evidence are no longer made, or at least not in the same way, and where therefore we may feel that we have finally escaped from science. But except for the arts, which pose separate problems, all scholars, whatever their fields, are bound by the same code of honour. All of them have to be as scientific as the nature of their subjects will allow them to be, or abandon all claim to be taken seriously.

The philosophers who moved from Kant and Hegel towards the establishing of modern historical and sociological methods were largely preoccupied with the question of boundary lines. At what point does *Natur* turn into *Geist*? Precisely where do the methods that work in the physical sciences cease to become effective or appropriate? But it is surely possible that there are no boundary lines at all, and that this whole way of looking at knowledge as divided into two complementary bodies is wrong. The crudest form of this view is the one that I call the heart-of-darkness theory. It is a type of argument that used to be fashionable in natural theology (perhaps still is), and has been transferred to the humanities from there. There have been theories among religious apologists that religion, like the ghost of Hamlet's father, or the dancing fairies of Milton's Nativity Ode, belongs to a dark preserve of mystery on which the sun of science has not yet risen. Religion, according to this approach, deals with whatever seems at the moment to be beyond the capacities of science: creation at first, then the origin of life or the human soul, then moral values, and so on – it has to keep moving fairly fast, like the lunatic in Blake's 'Mad Song', to make sure of staying in the dark while science pursues it. Even yet there is a strong popular belief that if we once get hold of something that 'science cannot explain', whether it is extrasensory perception or the principle of indeterminacy or finding underground water with a hazel twig, we have a guarantee of free will and immortality and the existence of God.

The basis of such notions, when applied to the arts, is the assumption that if science deals rationally, factually, impersonally with an external world, the arts can only deal with an inner world of emotion, personality, and value. This really reduces itself to the assumption that if science is objective, the arts must be subjective. But subjective art is as impossible a conception as subjective science. The arts are techniques of communication: they are fostered by schools and groups and depend on convention quite as much as science does. In fact, there seems to be nothing that is really subjective except a rebellion against the stability of the attitude toward the world on which science is based. It is very tiring to keep on being open to involuntary sense impressions, to be detached and clear-headed, to weigh evidence and fit judgements to it, and very easy to relapse into an emotional colouring of experience, such as we get from day-dreaming or bad temper or private memories and associations. But however important and normally human in itself, the individual's emotional colouring of his own experience is not what the arts or the humanities are primarily concerned with. So whenever I read critical theories that begin by saying, in effect, 'Poetry is whatever mere science isn't', I flake out very quickly, because I know that some version of the subjective fallacy is about to follow.

The genuine basis of this complementary view of the arts and sciences is the distinction, already glanced at and most elaborately set out in Bergson, between time as externalized by science, where it is really a dimension of space, and time in its other form of the continuous awareness of one's own existence. This latter does elude science, so here is something that science cannot explain. But nothing else can explain it either, so that is not much help. All explanation contains some traces of scientific method, unless the explanation is really a clouding up of the question, like the doctor's explanation in Molière that opium puts people to sleep because it has a dormative faculty. But while the direct awareness of being cannot be explained, it can, up to a point, be expressed, and this expression is the basis of the arts. The role of art, then, is primarily to express the complex of human existence, humanity's awareness of being itself rather than its perception of what is not itself and is outside it. This self-awareness is neither subjective nor objective, for man in himself is both an individual and, no less essentially, a member of the society which is partly inside him; and it is neither rational nor irrational. It does not quantify existence like science: it qualifies it: it tries to express not what is there but what is here, what is involved in consciousness and being themselves. The arts, then, belong to the phase of experience that we have learned to call existential, to an awareness that cannot be external to itself nor have anything external to it.

The production of art is, of course, a stylizing of behaviour like the production of science. As far as the actual man doing the work is concerned, I doubt whether there is any essential psychological difference between the artist and the scientist, any 'creative' factors present in one that are not present in the other. Both have to use the entire mind; both have much the same difficulties in getting that very complicated machine to work. But when we consider the finished product only, it is clear that the arts do not stabilize the subject in the same way that science does. Emotions, repressed or mythopoeic elements in the subconscious, the manipulating of data, the summoning up of controlled hallucinations (as expressed in the traditional phrase about poetry, *ut pictura poesis*), all have a function in the creation of art. The stabilized subject of science is usually identified with the reason; the unstabilized subject is normally called the imagination. The individual artist is a representative of human imagination, just as the individual scientist is a representative of human reason. But at no point, *qua* artist, is he outside the human world we call culture or civilization, just as the physical scientist, *qua* physical scientist studying 'nature', is never inside it.

I speak, of course, of the arts in the plural because there is a group of them: music, literature, painting, sculpture, architecture, perhaps others. The dance, for instance, is in practice a separate art, though in theory it is difficult to see it as anything but a form of musical expression. It seems inherently unlikely, at the time of writing, that we have yet to develop a new art, despite all the strenuous experiment that there has been, some of it in that direction. Marshall McLuhan says of the new media of communication that 'the medium is the message', and that the content of each medium is the form of another one. This surely means, if I understand it correctly, that each medium is a distinctive art. Thus the 'message' of sculpture is the medium of sculpture, distinct from the message which is the medium or painting. But, as McLuhan also emphasizes, the new media are extensions of the human body, of what we already do with our eyes and ears and throats and hands. Hence they have given us new forms or variations of the arts we now have, and the novelty of these forms constitutes a major imaginative revolution in our time. But though distinctive arts they are not actually new arts: they are new techniques for receiving the impression of words and pictures.

Of these arts, literature is the art of words, and words are also the medium for the humanities and much of the sciences. This suggests that the arts, besides being arts, may also be informing languages for other disciplines. A painting or a poem is a construct: you look first of all at the associative factors in it, the things that make it hold together. But besides having paintings we have pictures of things: that is, there are things outside painting that we understand pictorially. For centuries philosophers expressed themselves in words, taking words for granted, forgetting that there is an art of words, not realizing that the verbal basis of philosophy constitutes a philosophical problem in itself. It seems to have been only in our own time that philosophers and logicians have really tried to become aware of the limitations of form (as distinct from the mere pitfalls or fallacies) inherent in the use of words. Even now their interest seems to be mainly linguistic rather than properly literary, and some philosophers are so ignorant of the source of their own subject that they regularly use 'literary' in a pejorative sense. It is obvious that words lend themselves very readily to being an informing language for a descriptive discipline. Literature was not, up until the Romantic movement at least, regarded as the most impressive thing man does with words, the more objectified structures of theology and philosophy being regarded as higher in status and coming closer to what is called the quest for truth. As compared with music, or even painting, there is always some reference to the outer world implicit in every use of words. Even if in the future we leave painting to the chimpanzees and music to chance, I do not see how literature can ever lose its kernel of externalizable meaning. And yet the capacity of words for informing other disciplines is not unlimited. Compared with mathematics at least, words are incurably associative: multiple meanings lurk in them and the structures of grammar twist them into non-representational forms. It seems more likely that words have a certain radius of descriptive power, and that it is important to determine the approximate limits of that radius.

The other arts seem to differ widely in their powers of being able to inform other studies. Painting and sculpture, like literature, can be employed to represent the external world, and, again like literature, their descriptive or representational aspect has had more prestige in the past than their associative or constructive aspect. We can understand what their informing capacity is if we think not only of painting but of the pictorial arts, including illustrations, sketches, blueprints, diagrams, and models, and not only of sculpture but of the sculptural arts, including three-dimensional models. Some modern painters and sculptors, such as Miró or Giacometti, indicate the inherent relation of their arts with diagram and model very clearly. In some areas, such as geometry, the pictorial and the mathematical overlap, and of course the role of diagram in the sciences, as in the structural formulas of chemistry, is of immense importance. The question of whether light consists of waves or particles is surely, to some extent, a picturing problem. In my *Anatomy of Criticism* I have raised the question of the role of diagram in verbal thought as well. But to what extent and in what ways the pictorial and sculptural arts inform the humanities and sciences I do not know, nor have I read anybody who did know.

Music, on the other hand, has often been said to be the existential art par excellence, the hieratic, self-enclosed expression of 'pure being' with no relation to an externalized order of any kind. Perhaps this is because it is, as Mrs Langer[3] suggests, the art of 'virtual time', the closest expression of the continuous awareness of being which is the core of non-scientific experience. Or perhaps it is only because, up to the rise of electronic music, the music we know has been founded on a set of conventions as arbitrary as chess. On my piano as I write this is a sonata of Clementi called 'Didone Abbandonata': we are supposed to think of the story of Dido while we listen. The finale is a rondo beginning with what for Clementi is a sharp discord, a minor ninth, and the movement is hopefully marked 'con disperazione'. But it soon collapses into the ordinary rondo structure, and by the time we reach the second subject it is clear that poor Dido has been abandoned once more. A greater composer would have been more tactful or created a more compelling musical mood, but that is why the mediocre example illustrates more clearly my point, which is that music is not an informing art: it sets up a powerful centripetal force that resists being drawn into the structure of anything outside itself. We do use metaphors from music a good deal ('harmony', 'overtones', and the like), and the old fables about the music of the spheres suggest that music may have an unsuspected informing power about it. Perhaps the myth of heaven as a place where harp playing is a compulsory cultural accomplishment will come true, and the theology and metaphysics of the future will be understood musically rather than verbally. When I read or try to read Heidegger I get the same feeling that I get when trying to read *Finnegans Wake*, of language dissolving into a mass of associative puns, and language of this kind is surely heading in the direction indicated by the squeals and groans of electronic music.

If words can be used both to construct an art and to inform some of the descriptive disciplines, there seems no reason why we should not think of mathematics, which informs so much of the physical sciences, as an art too. It is a self-contained construct like the arts, and I do not see how it is possible to frame a definition, or even a description, of the arts that would include the five I have listed and exclude mathematics. But mathematics is the art of numerical or quantitative relationships, and so it has a unique capacity for giving order and coherence to the sciences, of providing their descriptions and experiments with the repeatable element of law. In contrast to the other arts, it stabilizes the subject on the 'rational' level, as science does, and is so constantly informing the physical sciences that it is often regarded as simply a part of them. Hence some of the more speculatively minded scientists and philosophers are occasionally surprised to discover that nature has a mathematical form. Of course it has: they put it there. And because it informs science so readily, mathematics practised as an art in its own right is a rare and esoteric achievement, though its tradition can be traced from the semi-occult use of it associated with the name of Pythagoras down to the later work of Einstein.

The rise of modern science involved a new way of looking at the external world which is most lucidly set out in Locke, though it had been there at least since Galileo. According to this the world has secondary qualities which are experienced by sensation, and primary qualities independent of such experience, which can only be weighed and measured. This distinction has a rough but significant analogy to the role of words in rendering the external world as compared with the role of mathematics. Mathematics is the language that can render the world of primary qualities: words never lose their connection with human action and human sensation on which the two primary categories of words, verbs and nouns, are based. To the extent that an electron, for instance, is given a name and made a noun, it becomes a potential object of perception, unlikely as it is that it will ever be an actual one. The radius of verbal information, then, apparently runs between the human body and its environment as perceived and experienced by that body. The non-literary function of words is thus, in the broad Kantian sense, critical: words can be used to explain the human situation, instead of merely expressing it as literature does, but they always remain connected with that situation.

The conception of science, as a systematic understanding of nature under law for which the appropriate language is mathematics, is, of course, a relatively recent one. For thousands of years before the great scientific explosion of the last few centuries, thinkers had been making constructs of the outer world, mainly verbal and pictorial. In these constructs the associative characteristics of the arts from which they were derived are very obvious. Poets find it much easier to live in the Ptolemaic universe than in ours, because it is more associative; modern poets turn from science to occultism because the latter still features associative patterns. Very early the two great containing conceptions of the scientific attitude made their appearance: 'substance', or the objectified world visible and invisible, and 'soul', the ideally disembodied intelligence which contemplates it. These parents then peopled the world with various offspring, ideas, essences, universals, atoms, and the like. The great difficulty with using words, when attempting to deal with primary qualities, is the readiness with which words adapt themselves to what we may call, altering Whitehead's phrase, pseudo-concreteness. Adam named the animals because he could see them, but, as Theseus says in Shakespeare, it is just as easy to name airy nothings, to bestow nouns on and make verbal objects out of things that are not there, or cannot be proved to be there. Again, the prestige of the subject-object relationship meant that attempts to express what is genuinely existential, the human situation itself, could take the form of the *metaphorically* objective. The conception of a spiritual world is a metaphorical verbal object of this kind. With the rise of modern science, words have become more limited in their range. Metaphysics seemed for a time to be taking the form of a verbalized general science, expressing for its age some sense of what scientific activity as a whole is doing. It is more at home, however, with the assumptions on which scientific work is based, because those assumptions are part of the human context of science, and so they can be dealt with critically, which means verbally.

The principle of metaphorical object is of central importance when we try to see what the place of content is in the arts. The activity of consciousness, of externalizing reality, is always part of the whole existential complex. The aspect of painting that reproduces or 'imitates' an outer world exists in painting, as, so to speak, a metaphor of externality. Even music has, in the witty and paradoxical form of 'programme' music, a metaphorical external world of this kind, and literature has it in everything that we call realism. We are constantly using quantitative expressions (e.g. 'I love you very much') as metaphors for things that are not quantities. Aristotle, who approached the arts from a scientific point of view (one of his most illuminating comments on art is in the *Physics*), spoke of the arts as imitative of nature. But as soon as we examine this conception of imitation, the notion of a continuous relation to the external world begins to dissolve, and we can see that 'nature' exists in the art only as the content of art, as something that art surrounds and contains. So while science deals with the consolidating of what is there, the arts deal with the expanding of what is here; the circumference of science is the universe, the circumference of the arts is human culture. In our time the sense of cleavage between the expression of what is here and the study of what is there is very sharp. We tend to feel that whatever is objective or external belongs only to the spatial world of science: every other 'there' is a metaphor derived from that spatial world, and such metaphors no longer carry much conviction. Theology, for example, or at least the Protestant versions of it that I am more familiar with, is now trying to come to terms with the fact that nothing it is talking about is actually 'there'. God is certainly not 'there': he has been deprived of all scientific function and he has no status in the spatial world of science, including the temporal world that can be divided and measured. So whatever the present or future of theology may be, it cannot be the queen of sciences as we now think of science: science deals only with It, and can take no part in an I-Thou dialogue.

For a long time, of course, it was assumed that the study of nature was also the study of a revelation of God, the order and coherence of nature being assumed to be the result of divine design. This view was contemporary with the view that the models of human civilization themselves, the city and the garden, were also of divine origin. But just as man came finally to believe that he had created and was responsible for his own civilization, so he came also to believe that the real basis of science was the correspondence of nature and human reason. Whatever is there in nature, the mind can find something in verbal or mathematical reasoning that will explain, assimilate or inform it. 'The external world is fitted to the mind', as Wordsworth says. So although nature is an externalized reality, it is not, for science, an alien one. In fact, science, as a form of knowledge, could even be thought of as a gigantic human narcissism, the reason falling in love with its own reflection in nature. Whenever there have been anti-scientific trends in human culture, they have usually seized on some aspect of this principle, though their target has been less science itself than the kind of essential philosophy that preceded it. Existentialism, for example, insists that if we think of the external world as a human world, certain elements become primary that are carefully kept out of science: the imminence of death, the feeling of alienation, the pervading sense of accident and of emptiness, and the direct confrontation with something arbitrary and absurd. Once we take away from externality the rational structure that we have put into it, it becomes what Milton calls a universal blank. All science is founded on the equation A equals B, where A is the human reason and B the rationally comprehensible element in nature. The existentialists may be described as the people who have discovered that if A equals B, then A minus B equals nothing. We notice that existentialists have some difficulty in making their philosophy self-sufficient. Most of the best of them have incorporated it into a religious attitude, and of the atheistic ones, Heidegger went along with the Nazis and Sartre has recently collapsed on the bosom of the Church Marxist. It looks as though the attitude, along with whatever anti-scientific bias it may have, belongs in a larger context which is normally either religious or revolutionary, or both. That larger context is a view, found in very different forms in Blake, Kierkegaard, Nietzsche and D. H. Lawrence, which might be paraphrased somewhat as follows:

Reality is primarily what we create, not what we contemplate. It is more important to know how to construct a human world than to know how to study a non-human one. Science and philosophy are significant as two of the creative things that man does, not as keys to the reality of the world out there. There is a world out there, but science sees it as a world under law, and no vision under law can ever give us the whole truth about anything. Science moves with greatest confidence, and makes its most startling discoveries, in a mechanical and unconscious world. If we remove science from its context and make it not a mental construct but an oracle of reality, the logical conclusion is that man ought to adjust himself to that reality on its terms. Thus moral law imitates natural law, and human life takes on the predictable characteristics of nature as science reveals it. What begins as reason ends in the conditioned reflexes of an insect state, where human beings have become cerebral automata. The real world, that is, the human world, has constantly to be created, and the one model on which we must not create it is that of the world out there. The world out there has no human values, hence we should think of it primarily not as real but as absurd. The existential paradoxes help us to do this, and they thereby reduce the world to the *tohu-wa-bohu*, the waste and void chaos of a world which man has once again to create.

In science applied to the human world, that is, in applied science and technology, we see the mathematical shape of science itself, from the pyramids of Egypt and the highways and aqueducts of Rome to the chessboard cities and cloverleaf intersections of our day. For Blake, and in some degree for Lawrence, these mathematical shapes in human life are symbols of aggression: human life is at its most mathematical and automatic in military operations, and in Blake the pyramid, and more particularly the 'Druid' trilithon, the ancestor of the Roman arch, are symbols of imperialistic hysteria and malevolence. Every advance in technology is likely to cause an immense legal complication in life, as the automobile has done, and the sheeplike panic-stricken stampeding of modern life, of which the totalitarian state is a by-product, is part of a technological way of life. Popular fiction has been exploiting the figure of the mad scientist for over a century, and there really does seem to be such a thing as mad science: psychology used to enslave people, nuclear physics used to exterminate the human race, microbiology suggesting even more lethal methods of trying to improve it. However, even in their most anti-scientific pronouncements such writers as Blake and Lawrence seldom if ever say that science is the direct cause of the sinister will to slavery in modern times. They say rather that man has lost his nerve about taking charge of his own world, through a false theory of knowledge in which he is 'idolatrous to his own shadow', as Blake says, and that this loss of nerve expresses itself as a perversion and parody of science. The world out there is real, but if we *deify* its reality, if we make it an object of imitation, it takes on the outlines of Satan the accuser, belittling us with its vast size in time and space, contemptuous of our efforts to be free of its colossal machinery.

The contrast I am paraphrasing is more conventionally phrased in other writers, and is often put into the form of an antithesis between values and facts. But the word value still has something prefabricated about it, a suggestion of something immutable laid up in a Platonic heaven. It is man's right to create his world that must be safeguarded, and every creation is likely to require a transvaluation of the past. Besides, values are really for the most part still forms of law, and do not get us out of our dilemma. The same is true of the moral categories of Kierkegaard, the 'ethical freedom' of the man who has passed beyond speculation. It would be better to use the existential terms engagement or concern to express the contrast between a reality which is there to begin with and the greater reality which, like religious faith or artistic creation, does not exist at all to begin with, but is brought into being through a certain kind of human act.

Science is increasingly a communal and corporate activity. The humanities are more individualized, and the arts are intensely so: schools and isms in the arts are a sign of youth and immaturity, of an authority not yet established in the single artist. When we think of the scientist as voyaging through strange seas of thought alone, as Wordsworth did Newton, we are probably thinking of him primarily as a mathematician. We are, in contrast to Communist countries, extremely permissive about a writer's loneliness: we allow our writers to retire into what sometimes seem very neurotic fairylands, because they may also be areas of the unstabilized imaginative vision. The result is that communication in and from the arts is a slow and cumbersome business, and that is why we need the dimension of criticism, the vision of artists as a society engaged in a communal enterprise.

As soon as we take this critical perspective on literature, we see that literature is organized by huge containing conceptions which establish the literary societies and the family resemblances among large groups of writers. We call these containing forms myths, and it is in these myths that the nature of man's concern for his world is most clearly expressed. Our own age expresses itself chiefly in the ironic myth, and irony marks the ascendance of a technological society and the tendency of man to imitate the natural law outside him. It is in the ironic mode that the writer deals with the human situation as though it were external to him and as though he were detached from it, and in this mode that he sees human behaviour as mechanized, frustrated, and absurd. If one were to say to almost any serious contemporary writer: 'But I don't like the characters and situations you present to me', he would almost certainly answer: 'That's because I'm trying to tell the truth as I see it.' In our day the writer defends himself in language parallel to the language of science and other objective disciplines. These myths also inform the structures built out of words that exist outside literature, that is, in general, the humanities. Existentialism, with its conceptions of anguish, nausea, and the like, is an ironic philosophy, a fact which accounts for the lack of self-sufficiency I spoke of before. Irony, in literature, is a sophisticated myth, best understood as a frustration or parody of the more primitive comic and romantic myths in which a quest is successfully accomplished. These romantic and comic myths are those that inform Christianity and the revolutionary myth of

Marxism. Earlier in this paper I quoted from Freud's *Future of an Illusion*. Religion was a subject Freud had a Freudian block about, mainly because he wanted to be a lawgiving Moses in his own right, contemplating the back parts of his own God. As a literary critic, I am interested in the fact that Freud and Marx are the two most influential thinkers in the world today, that both of them developed an encyclopedic programme that they called scientific, and that nine-tenths of the science of both turns out to be applied mythology.

These mythical expressions of concern, in which man expresses his own attitude to the culture he has built, are subject to a disease of thinking which is best called anxiety, in the Freudian and not the existential sense. We often find that those who are committed to a religious or revolutionary faith have a peculiar difficulty in being intellectually honest in their arguments: their commitment wants to twist and manipulate facts, to maintain tendentious lines of reasoning, to rationalize or simply assert things for which there is no evidence. The record of Christianity is full of persecutions in the name of absurdities, and Marxism is also an anxiety structure, with a sensitive nose for heresies and deviations. The reason for this kind of anxiety is, again, a failure of nerve, a refusal to accept the fact that man continually creates his world anew, a desire to have it fit something outside itself. What is outside, in this sense, cannot be in space: it can only be in time, a pattern established in the past, or to be established in the future, to which all facts and discoveries somehow must be adjusted.

In the sciences it is possible to carry on one's studies with an undeveloped sense of concern. There are scientists who irritably brush off the suggestion that what they are doing may have momentous consequences for good or evil, and that they should be concerned for those consequences. A sense of concern would make such a scientist more presentable as a human being: it would also unite him to the community he lives in, and work against the dehumanizing tendency inherent in all specialization. There is no way of overcoming the barriers of specialization, no way of making a Romance philologist and a solid-state physicist intellectually intelligible to each other. But they are united by being both citizens of their society, and their realization of this makes both Romance philology and solid-state physics liberal arts, studies that liberate mankind. In science this social concern affects the scientist as man, but not so much *qua* scientist. But in the humanities the great poetic myths are also shaping forms: in history, in philosophy, in criticism, a scientific detachment and a humane engagement are fighting each other like Jacob and his angel. That is why the humanities are difficult to characterize, not only in methodology, but even as a distinctive group of studies in themselves.

To sum up, then: it does not seem to me that the really important difference between the humanities and the sciences is in the difference in their subject-matter. It is rather that science exhibits a method and a mental attitude, most clearly in the physical sciences, of a stabilized subject and an impartial and detached treatment of evidence which is essential to all serious work in all fields. The humanities, on the other hand, express in their containing forms, or myths, the nature of the human involvement with the human world, which is essential to any serious man's attitude to life. As long as man lives in the world, he will need the perspective and attitude of the scientist; but to the extent that he has created the world he lives in, feels responsible for it and has a concern for its destiny, which is also his own destiny, he will need the perspective and attitude of the humanist.

4 DESIGN AS A CREATIVE PRINCIPLE IN THE ARTS

There is a time-honoured distinction which divides the arts into a major and a minor group, the fine and the useful, but this distinction is rapidly losing all its fineness and most of its usefulness, and is now practically vestigial. It was never in any case a distinction among artists, only among the arts themselves. In reading Cellini's autobiography we can see how the well-trained artist of that day was ready to switch from a commission in the 'major' arts to one in the 'minor' ones and back again, with no loss of status or feeling of incongruity. We think of Michelangelo as dwelling on the loftiest summits of the major arts, but Michelangelo too had his handyman assignments, such as designing the uniform of the Papal Guards, in which he acquitted himself indifferently but not incompetently. Similar conditions still prevail. In the early years of our marriage, when finances were a bit difficult, my wife assisted the family fortunes by getting a job painting magnolias on coffee trays. She met a sculptress at a party, and approached her with some trepidation, feeling that anyone who practised so majestic an art might take a dim view of her magnolia project. The sculptress, however, had been living on a private income cut off at the source as a result of the war, and she was making her living painting roses on babies' chamber pots.

One of the primitive functions of art is the production of luxury goods for a ruling class: armour for the warrior, vestments for the priest, jewellery and regalia for the king. Eventually the same kind of social demand produces temples, cathedrals, castles and palaces, with all their contained treasures. Such art is often characterized by great complexity and ingenious skill, a skill sometimes regarded with superstitious awe by contemporaries who do not possess it. One thinks of the legends of the mysterious smiths and forgers of weapons like Weyland and Hephaestus, of the long series of enchanted spears, magic swords and helmets of invisibility in romance, of the deities begotten by the Greek veneration for such work, the Cabeiroi and Dactyls and Cyclops and Telchines, of the many elaborate descriptions of works of 'minor' art from Homer's shield of Achilles onward. The *Beowulf* poet's favourite aesthetic judgement is 'curiously wrought', a phrase he usually applies to armour.

In our own day we notice how often an unsophisticated eye falls with particular delight on elaborate embroideries or Chinese ivory carvings, the delight being expressed in some such formula as 'look at all the work in that'. As a ruling class becomes less primitive, the work done for it begins to look more and more like unusually expensive and elaborate toys, as we can see in Fabergé, for example. It is understandable that Yeats should associate his nostalgia for aristocracy with 'many ingenious lovely things' of this sort, including the toy bird in *Sailing to Byzantium*. At the same time, as an ascendant class gets more and more of a monopoly of the art produced in its society, it extends its ownership over the 'major' arts, too, especially of painting and sculpture, which, unlike works of literature, may become the exclusive possession of their purchaser. And although patronage normally restricts such works of art to a small minority, other patrons, such as the church, may in the stained glass and frescoes of its cathedrals make them to some degree a genuinely public art. I say to some degree, as the old cliché about the art of cathedrals being a 'Bible of the poor'[1] could apply only to those of the poor who had exceedingly long-range vision.

Sheer elaboration, as an aesthetic form of conspicuous consumption, still exists, or did until recently. My own city of Toronto possesses an extraordinary example: a palace of an exuberant millionaire known as 'Casa Loma', one wing of which is bastard French Renaissance and the other wing bastard Spanish Renaissance, like Siamese twins born out of wedlock. But the rise of democracy (in contrast to the oligarchy of which Casa Loma is an expression) gives a functional cast to public art, and thereby to public taste generally, and the industrial revolution has transferred the 'curiously wrought' arts from craftsmanship to mechanism. Elaboration is now mainly in the area represented by the housewife with a new garbage-disposal unit or the teenager with his attention absorbed by the viscera of a motor cycle. Such things, of course, belong to the useful rather than the fine arts, but so did their ancestors: even the most useless of aristocratic toys still had the social role of dramatizing a certain standard of living.

As a result the 'creative' arts have tended increasingly to form a united front, with the 'major' and 'minor' distinction becoming of less account. We can see this tendency starting in William Morris. For Morris there were two forms of production, the creative and the mechanical. The former is genuine work, and in Morris's thought work is identified with the creative act. Genuine work is true 'manufacture', in the original sense of something made by a brain-directed hand, and it tends towards social freedom as surely as mechanical production leads toward exploitation and mass slavery. Morris thus assigns a revolutionary social role to the creative arts, but what he sees as essentially creative in the creative arts is design, and design is something that fine and useful arts have in common. Because of his interest in the social role of art, Morris found his centre of gravity in the 'minor' arts, and when he practised painting and poetry he treated them as 'minor' arts. In doing so he threw down a challenge to the theory of criticism. Is not what we consider 'major' about the major arts simply their association with the luxury goods of a ruling class? Even literature has always regarded the most major forms of its art as being connected, as in epic and tragedy, with the portrayal of ruling-class figures.

Any exhibition of abstract or non-objective art today will illustrate how far we have gone in the direction of emphasizing design in painting and sculpture. And if we compare such an exhibition with one of handcrafts or industrial design, we can see that the real relation between them now is not that of major to minor art, but of theory to practice, the disinterested to the applied forms of the same constructive principles. The kind of modern building which seems the result of an armaments race between the makers of glass and the makers of curtains shows similar tendencies. It seems almost as though in the visual arts there is now only one art, the art of design, and what used to be different arts are variations of it in different media. This is naturally a considerable overstatement, though it may have some value as that.

Painting and sculpture differ from the applied arts most markedly in the extent of their capacity for representation. Hence representationalism tends to separate the major from the minor visual arts, and formalism tends to unify them. We notice that the more successful nations show a matter-of-fact realism in their arts, but that many aspects of such realism seem to have little creative staying power. Roman art is a good example of the way in which a realistic approach to art tends to become, first derivative, then pedestrian, and finally insipid, while the real creative energy of the culture goes into engineering. Something similar has happened in the totalitarian societies of our time, and there are strong tendencies toward it in the democracies. The reason is that what representational public art represents is mainly a society's idealized picture of itself. A Roman goddess, say the Barberini Juno, suggests, not awe or veneration or majesty, but the impressiveness of a well-to-do Roman matron. 'Beauty' in the human form tends to mean, in such an art, the representing of youth, good looks and physical health. One feels of the wax mannequins in a modern shop window that any girl who succeeded in being as haughty and aloof as they look would be in an advanced stage of narcissism, and ought to see a psychiatrist before going out of business entirely. But the abstracted gaze of these models is directly descended from the placid idols of earlier cultures who mirror their own society's dream of realizable pleasure.

Realism in a healthy condition is another form of socially revolutionary art: it explores society, shows compassion with misery, brings strange gleams of beauty out of suffering, and ridicules absurdity and pomposity, especially in those with authority. In an unhealthy condition it expresses the will of the ascendant social group to preserve its *status quo*, and when it does this it seeks the facile idealizing which is what the word 'beauty' so often means. Marxist criticism in Russia is now struggling to work out the paradox of a 'social realism' which works properly in a genuinely revolutionary context, but can only turn sickly and parasitic when designed to support the party which achieved its revolution and has now the role of a ruling class. Realism is often associated with, and often rationalized as, a scientific view of the world, but the impetus behind realistic art, good or bad, is of social and not scientific origin. There is a curious law of art, seen in Van Gogh and in some of the surrealists, that even the attempt to reproduce the act of seeing, when carried out with sufficient energy, tends to lose its realism and take on the unnatural glittering intensity of hallucination.

There are two aspects of contemporary art in the democracies which are of particular importance as indicating that democracy is a genuinely revolutionary society, neither about to be revolutionized nor trying to retain its present structure, but mature enough to provide for both change and stability. One of these is realism doing its proper job of social criticism; the other is experimentalism in pure or abstract form. It is, quite consistently, an essential part of Marxist theory to attack 'formalism' as the essence of the bourgeois in art. Both of the democratic tendencies are signs of a society that regards its social order as expendable and created for its convenience, the order being made for the sake of man and not man for the sake of the order.

We said that with the growth of democracy and industry the production of luxury goods for a small minority gradually extends itself over a greater part of society. In proportion as it does this, it tends to extinguish another form of art: the popular creation of the minor arts. The immediate production of domestic arts, from pottery to household fetishes, and from peasants' blouses to the weather-vanes and bowsprits of American folk museums, can lead only the most furtive existence in our society, for what we call handcraft follows a different tradition, as we have just seen. Folk art is both popular and primitive, two words which mean much the same thing in the arts. These terms ordinarily mean that representation is subordinated to more geometrical and abstract forms of expression, sometimes merely through incompetence in drawing, sometimes through a naïve but genuinely simple wisdom. But despite the pleasure with which we seize on any sign of such creativity, especially when it reaches into the major arts, as it does with painting by Grandma Moses and others, this current of creative energy in our society is now largely diverted into more expert and sophisticated channels (or canals, which mixes the metaphor less). It is still active and influential as a tradition, but hardly as a source of production in its own right.

In contrast to the luxury goods spoken of earlier, which are produced for the centralizing forces in society, the aristocracy and the church, the popular arts are decentralized. William Morris's conception of the social role of art takes off from here. Morris's association of the minor arts with social freedom and stability is anarchist rather than communist, and assumes as its goal a decentralizing of society. For Morris the state, and *a fortiori* the huge industrial empire, is a crude form of human community, the genuine form of which he restores and depicts in his *News from Nowhere*. If we realize that we associate the minor arts today mainly with the smaller countries, and think most readily of Swedish furniture, Swiss watches, Irish linen, or (until recently) Czecho-Slovakian glass, we can see some force in his idea. *News from Nowhere* is, however, an application of a more general principle that all culture, including the major arts, demands the decentralizing of society. Shelley's preface to *Prometheus Unbound* proposes to break England down into a group of small communities, in which anonymous masses would become identifiable people, so that each community could follow in its own way the tradition of the small-town cultures of Periclean Athens, Renaissance Florence, or Elizabethan London. T. S. Eliot's *Notes Towards a Definition of Culture* is preoccupied with Welsh nationalism, Scottish nationalism, the encouraging of local peculiarities of all kinds, and with the advisability, for most people, of never leaving the place where they were born. But whatever the merits of the art produced in our time, it will certainly be an international art,[2] and decentralizing theories seem at present to be a hopeless anachronism. I am a Canadian intellectual, and therefore (in Canada it is a therefore) I am a cultural regionalist, but the extent to which Canadian culture can grow out of the Canadian soil I realize in advance to be an exceedingly limited one.

The present organization of educational media in the universities, the museums, the art galleries, seems almost deliberately designed to bring about a change from decentralized to international culture. For the contemporary artist, all the arts of all traditions and epochs are available for comparative study, the primitive and the historical, the barbaric and the sophisticated. The basis for comparison, when any is made, is obviously design. The contemporary artist is as free to follow the influences of Benin bronzes as of Rodin, of Etruscan cave paintings as of Cézanne. The enormous expansion of technical resources has united the artist more closely with the educational media, so closely, in fact, that an 'arts' course can be a preparation for the understanding of contemporary art in a way that it could hardly have been a century ago.

At the same time most of the expansion, as compared with the cultural traditions of a century ago, has been in the area of the popular and primitive arts.

If these somewhat random remarks about the visual arts have any cogency, is it possible to see analogies between the visual arts and literature which will throw any light on the situation of literature and its criticism today? Analogies are tricky things, and even striking analogies may be specious. Some of the phenomena noted above have no genuine literary analogues at all. If the visual arts have many practitioners who, like Cellini, can tackle either a statue or a salt cellar, one might expect the same situation in literature. The poet or novelist could well be a verbal handyman, able to turn out a piece of advertising copy or a newspaper report or ghost-write a politician's speech as part of his professional competence with words. This is by no means the rule, because the applied verbal arts, especially journalism and advertising, are imprisoned in conventions so rigid that no one who has learned them is fit for anything else unless he starts all over again. Those who followed in *The New Yorker* the record of Miss Marianne Moore's struggles to make her poetic talents useful to the Ford Motor Company in its search for a name for its new car (it was finally called 'Edsel') will understand that the gap between the poet and society is one that the poet cannot do much to bridge.

In the production of luxury goods, again, the role of literature is not always easy to trace. One can see that in literature, as elsewhere, what is designed as a toy or plaything is mechanically complex: detective stories are more ingenious than serious novels, and light verse is more deliberately contrived than heavy verse. There has, of course, been a constant demand for the services of the poet in congratulatory odes, masques, and the kind of work associated with the office of poet laureate. The masque, however, as Ben Jonson, the first official poet laureate, discovered, follows the general rule of drama that the more spectacular the conception of the drama is, the less important the poet's role. The remarks above on the importance of experimentalism in a democratic society and of keeping realism to its proper critical role would apply to literature equally with the other arts. But there are two features of literature which make all analogies with visual arts difficult. One is the way in which literature is decentralized by the barriers of language. The other is the fact that no art of words can ever be wholly abstract, in the way that painting and sculpture and music can be. There must always be an identifiable content, which corresponds to representation in painting and sculpture. Content, unlike design, demands some knowledge of the cultural background of the work. Hence the presence of a representational core, along with a specific language to learn, helps to slow down the internationalizing of literature. Perhaps it is a good thing that it is slowed down, but it is reasonable to expect that literature will to some degree follow the tendencies of the other arts, and, if so, its criticism needs to be prepared for such tendencies. The real problem for our analogy is this: what are the principles of design in literature which enable us to take something of the same perspective towards it that we can take toward the visual arts and music?

We notice that one form of literature seems to make its way easily across all barriers of language and culture, and this is the folk-tale. The reason for its ability to travel is clearly that it is pure verbal design. It is made up of a number of stock themes that can be counted and indexed; its plot belongs to an identifiable type; there is hardly any content beyond the plot, and therefore the plot can be readily abstracted from the language in which it is expressed. There is little of the feeling, which every translator of a fully developed work of literature has, that some elements are so bound up with the conventions of a specific culture that they are hard to convey, and that other elements are so bound up with the features of a specific language that they cannot be conveyed at all. It is, then, the *mythos*, Aristotle's word for plot or narrative, which is the element of design in literature. It has been an established principle in literary criticism ever since Aristotle that the poetic, as distinct from the historical, narrative presents the typical or universal event rather than the specific and particular one.

If we keep the plot in mind as the principle of design in any work of literature which contains a fiction, we can see a host of family likenesses which ought to make 'comparative literature' as comprehensible and systematic a study as the comparative study of folk-tales. What begins to emerge from the chaos of literature are certain recurring principles of verbal design, embodied in such conventions and genres as comedy, romance and tragedy, which link Shakespeare with

Kalidasa, Melville with the Old Testament, Proust with Lady Murasaki. This is a less myopic approach to the study of comparative literature than the one employed at present, but one which promises more fruitful results. Such typical plots (*mythoi*) shows also a clear line of descent from the myths of early mythologies, and illustrate the place of literary fiction and drama as a cultural descendant of mythology.

Plot is a clear and simple example of over-all verbal design; but, apart from the fact that not all works of literature have plots, we need to isolate also an example of a *unit* of design. Poetic language is associative rather than descriptive language, and the primitive function of poetry, a function it never loses and frequently returns to, seems to have something to do with identifying the human and the non-human worlds. We see this function clearly in the kind of mythology out of which a great deal of literature grows: stories of gods who are human in conception and character and yet are identified with aspects of nature, and are sun-gods or tree-gods or sky-gods. The unit of identity, where two things are said to be the same thing and yet preserve a twofold aspect, appears in poetry as metaphor, and this I take to be the fundamental unit of verbal design in literature. Here again the actual process of identification is one that does not depend either on language (though of course there may be linguistic identifications, as in puns), or on the peculiarities of a specific culture. When an Italian and a Chinese poet both employ metaphor, it makes for very little difficulty if one chooses a rose and the other a lotus.

The tendency of contemporary poets, and many novelists and dramatists as well, to be attracted toward myth and metaphor, rather than toward a realistic emphasis on content, is thus a cultural tendency parallel to the emphasis on abstract design in the visual arts. It exhibits also the same paradox, or seeming paradox: it is usually a highly sophisticated, even erudite and academic, approach to the art, yet the features of the art which are most interesting to it are primitive and popular features. Dylan Thomas seems more complex and baffling than Theodore Dreiser, yet it is easier for me to imagine Dylan Thomas genuinely popular than to imagine Dreiser, for all his obvious and considerable merits, genuinely popular. This is not to suggest a preference between two utterly incomparable things, but to suggest that writers who concentrate on literary design rather than content, despite their superficial difficulties, are the writers most likely to reach the widest public most quickly. The principles of literary design are also the readiest means by which literature can be effectively taught, at any level from kindergarten to graduate school. And as myth and metaphor are habits of mind and not merely artificial devices, such teaching should lead us, not simply to admire works of literature more, but to transfer something of their imaginative energy to our own lives. It is that transfer of imaginative energy which is the aim of all education in the arts, and to the possibility of which the arts themselves bear witness.

5 ON VALUE-JUDGEMENTS

I have nothing new to say on this question, and I must bring it down to the context of professional routine. I might rationalize this context as being existential, committed, and the like, but even here all I can offer is an analogy that seems to me pedagogically instructive. The pursuit of values in criticism is like the pursuit of happiness in the American Constitution: one may have some sympathy with the stated aim, but one deplores the grammar. One cannot pursue happiness, because happiness is not a possible goal of activity: it is rather an emotional reaction to activity, a feeling we get from pursuing something else. The more genuine that something else is, the greater the chance of happiness: the more energetically we pursue happiness, the sooner we arrive at frustration. The more one says he is happy, the more quickly we get out of his way to prevent him from making us miserable.

So with the sense of value in the study of literature. One cannot pursue that study with the object of arriving at value-judgements, because the only possible goal of study is knowledge. The sense of value is an individual, unpredictable, variable, incommunicable, indemonstrable, and mainly intuitive reaction to knowledge. In knowledge the context of the work of literature is literature; in value-judgement, the context of the work of literature is the reader's experience. When knowledge is limited, the sense of value is naïve; when knowledge improves, the sense of value improves too, but it must wait upon knowledge for its improvement. When two value-judgements conflict, nothing can resolve the conflict except greater knowledge.

The sense of value develops out of the struggle with one's cultural environment, and consists largely of getting an instinct for the different conventions of verbal expression. All verbal expression is conventionalized, but we quickly realize that some conventions are more acceptable to the social group we are associated with than others. In some societies, including our own until quite recent times, the different conventions were linked to different social classes, and high and low speech were at least symbolic of the conventions of lord and peasant respectively. Today we still have, despite the linguists, distinctions between standard and substandard speech, and a corresponding distinction, though one quite different in its application, between standard and substandard writing. The critic who fights his way through to some kind of intuitive feeling for what literary conventions are accepted in his society bevomes a representative of the good taste of his age.

Thus value-judgements carry with them, as part of their penumbra, so to speak, a sense of social acceptance. One of the first papers I heard at an MLA conference was a paper on Yeats by W. H. Auden, given at Detroit in 1947. He referred to Yeats's spiritualism in terms of its social overtones of lower-middle-class credulity and drawn blinds in dingy suburban streets, and remarked that A. E. Housman's Stoicism, while it may have been no less nonsense, was at any rate nonsense that a gentleman could believe. There was, of course, an intentional touch of parody here, but actually Auden was putting an evaluating criticism into its proper, and its only proper, context. Every attempt to exalt taste over knowledge has behind it the feeling that the possessor of taste is certainly a gentleman, while the possessor of knowledge may be only a pedant.

The task of the evaluating critics, who review contemporary books and plays, is partly to prevent us from trying to read all the books or see all the plays. Their work is quite distinct from that of the literary scholar who is trying to organize our knowledge of our past culture, even though it is called by the same name and engaged in by many of the same people. The literary scholar has nothing to do with sifting out what it will be less rewarding to experience. He has value-judgements of selectivity, just as any scholar in any field would have, but his canons of greater and less importance are related to the conditions of his specific research, not directly to the literary qualities of his material.

There is a vague notion that historical criticism is a scholarly establishment, and all critical methods which are not simply branches of historical study, whether explicatory or archetypal, are anti-historical, and ought to be applauded or denounced as such. But of course, every great writer who lived in a different time or cultural orbit from ourselves is a challenge to the assumptions on which our evaluative statements are made, and knowledge of his assumptions makes our own more flexible. The fundamental critical act, I have said elsewhere, is the act of recognition, seeing what is there, as distinct from merely seeing a Narcissus mirror of our own experience and social and moral prejudice. Recognition includes a good many things, including commentary and interpretation. It may be said that it is not really possible to draw a line between interpretation and evaluation, and that the latter will always remain in criticism as a part of the general messiness of the human situation. This may often be true as regards the individual critic. Nevertheless there is a boundary line which in the course of time inexorably separates interpreting from evaluating. When a critic interprets, he is talking about his poet; when he evaluates, he is talking about himself, or, at most, about himself as a representative of his age.

Every age, left to itself, is incredibly narrow in its cultural range, and the critic, unless he is a greater genius that the world has yet seen, shares that narrowness in proportion to his confidence in his taste. Suppose we were to read something like this in an essay published, say, in the eighteen-twenties: 'In reading Shakespeare we often feel how lofty and genuine are the touches of nature by which he refines our perceptions of the heroic and virtuous, and yet how ignobly he condescends to the grovelling passions of the lowest among his audience. We are particularly struck with this in reading the excellent edition by Doctor Bowdler, which for the first time has enabled us to distinguish what is immortal in our great poet from what the taste of his time compelled him to acquiesce in.' End of false quote. We should see at once that that was not a statement about Shakespeare, but a statement about the anxieties of the eighteen-twenties.

Now let us suppose that an evaluating critic of our own age goes to work on Dickens. He will discover that melodrama, sentimentality, and humour bulk very large in Dickens. He feels that a critic of our time can accept the humour, but that the melodrama and sentimentality are an embarrassment. He has to pretend that melodrama and sentimentality are not as important as they seem, or that Dickens has a vitality which carries him along in spite of them. He will also realize that his own age sets a high value on irony, and disapproves of coincidence or manipulated happy endings in plots and of exaggerated purity in characters. So he will bring out everything in Dickens, real or fancied, that is darkly and ambiguously ironic, or hostile to Victorian social standards, and the coincidences and the pure heroines and the rest of it will be passed over – in short, bowdlerized. To interpret Dickens is first of all to accept Dickens's own terms as the conditions of the study: to evaluate Dickens is to set up our own terms, producing a hideous caricature of Dickens which soon becomes a most revealing and accurate caricature of ourselves, and of the anxieties of the nineteen-sixties.

As long as criticize means evaluate, the answer to the question: 'Whom does the critic criticize?' seems at first a very easy one. The person the critic criticizes is, of course, the poet, whom the critic, in the traditional metaphor, judges. The drama critic attends a play and then writes a review judging it; if he is a literary scholar, then he reads the great poets in order to judge them too. Who would bother to be a critic unless one could be in the position of judging the greatest poets of the past? Alas, this carryover from studying to judging does not work, and the literary scholar, many bitter and frustrating years later, discovers that he is not judging the great poets at all. They judge him: every aspect of past culture shows up his ignorance, his blind spots, his provinciality, and his *naïveté*. When criticize means evaluate, the answer to the question 'Whom does the critic criticize?' turns out to be, in scholarship, the critic himself. The only value-judgement which is consistently and invariably useful to the scholarly critic is the judgement that his own writings, like the morals of a whore, are no better than they should be.

Of course literature, as an object of study, is a limitless reservoir of potential values. Think of how largely American nineteenth-century writers bulk in our cultural imaginations today, and of how impoverished those imaginations would be if they did not include such figures as Ethan Brand or Billy Budd or Huckleberry Finn. Yet it is not so long ago that the question was frequently and seriously asked: 'What on earth could you find to say about *American* literature?' There is, in fact, nothing in past literature that cannot become a source of imaginative illumination. One would say that few subjects could be duller or less rewarding than the handbooks studied by Miss Frances Yates in *The*

Art of Memory, yet her study has all the mental exhilaration of the discovery of a fine new poet. But when value is totally generalized in this way, it becomes a superfluous conception. Or rather, it is changed into the principle that there is value in the study of literature, which is an unobjectionable way of stating the relationship.

The experience of literature is not criticism, just as religious experience is not theology, and mental experience not psychology. In the experience of literature a great many things are felt, and can be said, which have no functional role to play in criticism. A student of literature may be aware of many things that he need not say as a critic, such as the fact that the poem he is discussing is a good poem. If he does say so, the statement forms part of his own personal rhetoric, and may be legitimate enough in that context. Naturally a reader of a work of criticism likes to feel that his author is a man of taste too, that he enjoys literature and is capable of the same kind of sensitivity and expertise that we demand from a good reviewer. But a writer's value-sense can never be logically a part of a critical discussion: it can only be psychologically and rhetorically related to that discussion. The value-sense is, as the phenomenological people say, pre-predicative.

The study of literature, then, produces a sense of the values of that study incidentally. The attempt to make criticism either begin or end in value-judgements turns the subject wrong side out, and the frequency of these attempts accounts for the fact that more nonsense is written in literary criticism, especially on matters of theory, than in any other scholarly discipline, not excluding education. Fortunately, its practice is considerably better than its theory, even when its practice includes MLA papers and doctoral theses on the birthday odes of Colley Cibber. No one deplores more than I do the purblind perspectives of scholarly critics, or the fact that so much criticism is produced with so little intellectual energy that it has all to be done over again. Still, it is better not to adopt a critical approach which makes the writing of sense impossible, however lugubrious the result of better premises may often be. With the enormous increase of personnel required in the humanities, I foresee a time when demands that every scholar be productive may be reversed into efforts at scholarly contraception. This may lead to a growing awareness of the difference between the criticism which expands our understanding of literature and the criticism which merely reflects and repeats it.

In the meantime, the effort to reverse the critical machinery continues to be made, usually in some such terms as these: Is not a value-judgement implied in, say, choosing Chaucer rather than Lydgate for an undergraduate course? Surely if we were to elaborate a theory explaining *why* some writer is of the first magnitude, and another only of the tenth, we should be doing something far more significant than just carefully studying them both, because we should also be proving that it was less important to study the smaller man. I do not know of anybody who claims that a valid theory of this sort exists, but I have often been reproached for not devoting my energies to trying to work one out. The argument reminds one a little of that of Sir Thomas Browne that a theory of final causes, working through universal principles of design like the quincunx, would give us a master key to all the sciences.

It is also part of the great Northwest-Passage fallacy of criticism which always gets stuck in the ice of tautology. The greatest writers are – let me see – imaginative rather than fanciful, or possessed of high seriousness, or illustrative of the sharpest possible tension between id and superego. The critic invariably discovers these qualities in the writers he considers best, overlooking the fact that they are merely synonyms for his preferences. The circumambulation of this prickly pear can go on for centuries, as long as the terms are brought up to date in each generation. Or one may draw up a list of categories that appeal to the sensibilities of the critic because they are fashionable in his age, and call them characteristic of all great literature of all periods. The effect of this is to canonize the taste of that age, and make it into a dogma binding on future generations. I. A. Richards made a parenthetical suggestion about such universal categories in *Practical Criticism*, but obviously soon realized, not only that the procedure involved was a circular one, but that, once again, such phrases as the 'inexplicable oddity' of birth and death merely echoed the anxieties of the nineteen-twenties. For those who wish to persist with this or similar methods, a certain degree of paranoia will be found most helpful, if not essential.

It is because I believe in the value of literary scholarship that I doubt that value-judgements have a genuine function in acquiring it. Those who try to subordinate knowledge to value-judgements are similarly led, with similar consistency, to doubt that genuine knowledge of literature is possible, or, if possible, desirable, There are many ways of expressing this doubt, or disapproval. One is the chorus that has for its refrain: 'But literature is alive, and you're anatomizing a corpse.' Such metaphors take us back to the vitalism that has long since disappeared from biology, and the scholarly critic is constantly being told that he is leaving out whatever the objector regards as the seat of the author's soul, whether his heart, his blood, his guts, or his testicles. The basis of this response is a fixation derived from adolescence, when the sense of social approval is so highly developed, and when it seems so utterly obvious that the end of reading is to assimilate everything into the two great dialectical categories of value-judgement, which in my own adolescence were 'swell' and 'lousy'. But it seems to me (if we must use these metaphors) that there is only one thing that can 'kill' literature, and that is the stock response. The attempt of genuine criticism is to bring literature to 'life' by annihilating stock responses, which, of course, are always value-judgements, and regularly confuse literature with life.

On the next stage there is the notion that university deans and chair-men demand a certain amount of historical research from new recruits as part of a kind of hazing process, before one is allowed to start on one's proper evaluating work. This research is assumed to exist all on one level, and to be nearly exhausted, so that one is now forced to look for something like the Latin exercise-books of Thomas Flatman or the washing bills of Shackerley Marmion. The appearance of every genuine work of literary scholarship knocks the bottom out of this notion, but it revives in each generation of graduate students. More sophisticated versions of the rejection of knowledge are, first, the helpless historical relativism which says that as Samuel Johnson or Coleridge made some of the mistakes likely to be made in their day, so we can only go on making a fresh set of mistakes, and can learn nothing from our pre-decessors. Second is the assumption that most interpretation, if at all subtle or difficult, is something that the author could not have under-stood, and hence has simply been imposed on him by the critic, a pre-text for an activity begun in self-hypnosis and sustained by group hysteria. If anyone doubts that such a reaction exists, he has probably never written a book on Blake's Prophecies.

In short, the more consistently one conceives of criticism as the pursuit of values, the more firmly one becomes attached to that great sect of anti-intellectualism. At present it seems to be fashionable to take an aggressive stand in the undergraduate classroom, and demand to know what, after all, we are really trying to teach. It appears that we are concerned, as teachers, with the uniqueness of human beings, or with the fullness of humanity, or with the freedom to be aware, or with life itself, or with the committed ironies of consciousness, or with learning to be at home in the world, or in fact with anything at all, so long as it sounds vaguely impressive and is not reducible to treating literature as something to be taught and studied like anything else. Seek ye first the shadow, we are urged, and the mere substance will be added unto you, if for some reason you should want it. It seems to be in literature that the teacher is most strongly tempted to co-operate with the student's innate resistance to the learning process, make himself into an opaque substitute for his subject instead of a transparent medium of it, and thereby develop his charisma, which is Greek for ham. But as values cannot be demonstrated, the possession of them is realized only by their possessors, hence the more evangelical the sales pitch, the more esoteric the product. I would, of course, not deny that teaching is a different activity from scholarship, and that many assertions of value are relevant to the classroom that are not relevant to the learned journal. But I think that in literature, as in other subjects, the best students are those who respond to intellectual honesty, who distrust the high priori road, and who sense that there may be some connection between limited claims and unlimited rewards.

6 CRITICISM, VISIBLE AND INVISIBLE

There is a distinction, certainly as old as Plato and possibly as old as the human mind, between two levels of understanding. I say levels, because one is nearly always regarded as superior to the other, whether in kind or in degree. Plato calls them, in his discussion of the divided line in the *Republic*, the level of *nous* and the level of *dianoia*, knowledge of things and knowledge about things. Knowledge about things preserves the split between subject and object which is the first fact in ordinary consciousness. 'I' learn 'that': what I learn is an objective body of facts set over against me and essentially unrelated to me. Knowledge of things, on the other hand, implies some kind of identification or essential unity of subject and object. What is learned and the mind of the learner become interdependent, indivisible parts of one thing.

Three principles are involved in this conception. First, learning about things is the necessary and indispensable prelude to the knowledge of things: confrontation is the only possible beginning of identity. Second, knowledge about things is the limit of teaching. Knowledge of things cannot be taught: for one thing, the possibility that there is some principle of identity that can link the knower and the known in some essential relation is indemonstrable. It can only be accepted, unconsciously as an axiom or deliberately as an act of faith. He who knows on the upper level knows that he knows, as a fact of his experience, but he cannot impart this knowledge directly. Third, *nous* is (or is usually considered to be) the same knowledge as *dianoia*: it is the relation between knower and known that is different. The difference is that something conceptual has become existential: this the the basis of the traditional contrast between knowledge and wisdom.

This distinction is of great importance in religion: Maritain's *Degrees of Knowledge* is one of many attempts to distinguish a lower comprehension from a higher apprehension in religious experience. When St Thomas Aquinas remarked on his death-bed that all his work seemed to him so much straw, he did not mean that his books were worthless, but that he himself was passing from the *dianoia* to the *nous* of what he had been writing about. I mention the religious parallel only to emphasize a principle which runs through all education: that what Plato calls *nous* is attainable only through something analogous to faith, which implies habit or consistent will, the necessary persistence in pursuing the goals of the faith.

I am dealing here, however, only with the application of the principle of two levels of knowledge to the ordinary learning process. Here the clearest illustration is that of a manual skill. In beginning to learn a skill like driving a car, a conscious mind comes into contact with an alien and emotionally disturbing object. When the skill is learned, the object ceases to be objective and becomes an extension of the personality, and the learning process has moved from the conscious mind to something that we call unconscious, subconscious, instinctive, or whatever best expresses to us the idea of unmediated unity. We think of this subconscious, usually, as more withdrawn, less turned outward to the world, than the consciousness: yet it is far less solipsistic. It is the nervous novice who is the solipsist: it is the trained driver, with a hidden skill that he cannot directly impart to others, who is in the community of the turnpike highway, such as it is.

Literature presents the same distinction. There is the *dianoia* of literature, or criticism, which constitutes the whole of what can be directly taught and learned about literature. I have explained elsewhere that it is impossible to teach or learn literature: what one teaches and learns is criticism. We do not regard this area of direct teaching and learning as an end but as a means to another end. A person who is absorbed wholly by knowledge about something is what we ordinarily mean by a pedant. Beyond this is the experience of literature itself, and the goal of this is something that we call vaguely the cultivated man, the person for whom literature is a possession, a possession that cannot be directly transmitted, and yet not private, for it belongs in a community. Nothing that we can teach a student is an acceptable substitute for the faith that a higher kind of contact with literature is possible, much less for the persistence in that faith which we call the love of reading. Even here there is the possibility of pedantry: literature is an essential part of the cultivated life, but not the whole of it, nor is the form of the cultivated life itself a literary form.

The great strength of humanism, as a conception of teaching literature, was that it accepted certain classics or models in literature, but directed its attention beyond the study of them to the possession of them, and insisted on their relevance to civilized or cultivated life. We spoke of pedantry, and there was undoubtedly much pedantry in humanism, especially at the level of elementary teaching, but not enough to destroy its effectiveness. Browning's grammarian was not a pedant, because he settled *hoti*'s business and based *oun* in the light of a blindingly clear vision of a community of knowledge. The act of faith in literary experience which humanism defended was closely associated with a more specific faith in the greatness of certain Greek and Latin classics. The classics were great, certainly, and produced an astonishingly fertile progeny in the vernaculars. But the conception of literature involved tended to be an aristocratic one, and had the limitations of aristocracy built into it. It saw literature as a hierarchy of comparative greatness, the summit of which provided the standards for the critics.

In the philologists of the nineteenth century, dealing with the vernaculars themselves, one sometimes detects a late humanistic pedantry which takes the form of critical arrogance. All too often the philologists, one feels, form an initiated clique, with literary standards and models derived (at several removes) from the 'great' poets, which are then applied to the 'lesser' ones. Old-fashioned books on English literature which touch on 'lesser' poets, such as Skelton and Wyatt in the early sixteenth century, maintain an attitude toward them of slightly injured condescension. Criticism of this sort had to be superseded by a democratizing of literary experience, not merely to do justice to underrated poets, but to revise the whole attitude to literature in which a poet could be judged by standards derived from another poet, however much 'greater'. Every writer must be examined on his own terms, to see what kind of literary experience he can supply that no one else can supply in quite the same way. The objection 'But Skelton isn't as great a poet as Milton' may not be without truth, but it is without critical point. Literary experience is far more flexible and varied than it was a century ago, but hierarchical standards still linger, and the *subjection* of the critic to the uniqueness of the work being criticized is still not a wholly accepted axiom. Also, the relevance to criticism of what used to be regarded as sub-literary material, primitive myths and the like, is still resisted in many quarters.

All teaching of literature, which is literary *dianoia* or criticism, must point beyond itself, and cannot get to where it is pointing. The revolution in the teaching of English associated with the phrase 'new criticism' began by challenging the tendency (less a tendency of teachers, perhaps, than of examination-haunted students) to accept knowledge about literature as a substitute for literary experience. The new critics set the object of literary experience directly in front of the student and insisted that he grapple with it and not try to find its meaning or his understanding of it in the introduction and footnotes. So far, so good. No serious teaching of literature can ever put the object of literary experience in any other position. But new criticism was criticism too: it developed its own techniques of talking about the work, and providing another critical counterpart of the work to read instead. No method of criticism, as such, can avoid doing this. What criticism can do, to point beyond itself, is to try to undermine the student's sense of the ultimate objectivity of the literary work. That, I fear, is not a very intelligible sentence, but the idea it expresses is unfamiliar. The student is confronted by an alien structure of imagination, set over against him, strange in its conventions and often in its values. It is not to remain so: it must become possessed by and identified with the student. Criticism cannot make this act of possession for the student; what it can do is weaken those tendencies within criticism that keep the literary work objective and separated. Criticism, in order to point beyond itself, needs to be actively iconoclastic about itself.

The metaphor of 'taste' expresses a real truth in criticism, but no metaphor is without pitfalls. The sense of taste is a contact sense: the major arts are based on the senses of distance, and it is easy to think of critical taste as a sublimation, the critic being an astral gourmet and literature itself being, as Plato said of rhetoric, a kind of disembodied cookery. This gastronomic metaphor is frequently employed by writers, for instance at the opening of *Tom Jones*, though when recognized as a metaphor it is usually only a joke. It suggests that the literary work is presented for enjoyment and evaluation, like a wine. The conception of taste is a popular one because it confers great social prestige on the critic. The man of taste is by definition a gentleman, and a critic who has a particular hankering to be a gentleman is bound to attach a good deal of importance to his taste. A generation ago the early essays of Eliot owed much of their influence and popularity to their cavalierism, their suggestion that the social affinities of good poetry were closer to the landed gentry than to the Hebrew prophets. Taste leads to a specific judgement: the metaphor of the critic as 'judge' is parallel to the metaphor of taste, and the assumption underlying such criticism is usually that the test of one's critical ability is a value-judgement on the literary work.

If this is true, the critic's contribution to literature, however gentlemanly, seems a curiously futile one, the futility being most obvious with negative judgements. Ezra Pound, T. S. Eliot, Middleton Murry, F. R. Leavis, are only a few of the eminent critics who have abused Milton. Milton's greatness as a poet is unaffected by this: as far as the central fact of his importance in literature is concerned, these eminent critics might as well have said nothing at all. A journal interested in satire recently quoted a critic as saying that satire must have a moral norm, and that Fielding's *Jonathan Wild* was a failure because no character in it represented a moral norm. The question was referred to me, and I said, somewhat irritably, that of course a moral norm was essential to satire, but it was the reader and not the satirist who was responsible for supplying it. My real objection, however, was to the critical procedure involved in the 'X is a failure because' formula. No critical principle can possibly follow the 'because' which is of any importance at all compared to the fact of *Jonathan Wild*'s position in the history of satire and in eighteenth-century English culture. The fact is a fact about literature, and, as I have tried to show elsewhere, nothing can follow 'because' except some kind of pseudo-critical moral anxiety. Thus: 'King Lear is a failure because it is indecorous to represent a king on the stage as insane.' We recognize this statement to be nonsense, because we are no longer burdened with the particular social anxiety it refers to, but all such anxieties are equally without content. Matthew Arnold decided that 'Empedocles on Etna' was a failure because its situation was one 'in which the suffering finds no vent in action; in which a continuous state of mental distress is prolonged, unrelieved by incident, hope, or resistance; in which there is everything to be endured, nothing to be done'. These phrases would exactly describe, for instance, Eliot's 'Prufrock', one of the most penetrating poems of our time, or a good deal of Arnold's contemporary, Baudelaire. We cannot question Arnold's sincerity in excluding his poem from his 1853 volume, but all he demonstrated by excluding it was his own anxious fear of irony.

The attitude that we may call critical dandyism, where the operative conceptions are vogue words of approval or the reverse, like 'interesting' or 'dreary', is an extreme but logical form of evaluating criticism, where the critic's real subject is his own social position. Such criticism belongs to the wrong side of Kierkegaard's 'either-or' dialectic: it is an attitude for which the work of art remains permanently a detached object of contemplation, to be admired because the critic enjoys it or blamed because he does not. Kierkegaard himself was so impressed by the prevalence of this attitude in art that he called it the aesthetic attitude, and tended to identify the arts with it. We do not escape from the limitations of the attitude by transposing its judgements from an aesthetic into a moral key. F. R. Leavis has always commanded a good deal of often reluctant respect because of the moral intensity he brings to his criticism, and because of his refusal to make unreal separations between moral and aesthetic values. Reading through the recent reprint of *Scrutiny*, one feels at first that this deep concern for literature, whether the individual judgements are right or wrong, is the real key to literary experience, and the real introduction that criticism can make to it. But as one goes on one has the feeling that this concern, which is there and is a very real virtue, gets deflected at some crucial point, and is prevented from fully emerging out of the shadow-battles of anxieties. Perhaps what the point is is indicated by such comments of Leavis himself as 'the poem is a determinate thing: it is *there*', and, 'unappreciated, the poem isn't *there*.' An insistence on the 'thereness' or separation of critic and literary work forces one, for all one's concern, to go on playing the same 'aesthetic' game. The paradox is that the 'aesthetic' attitude is not a genuinely critical one at all, but social: concern makes the social reference more impersonal, but does not remove it.

Evaluating criticism is mainly effective as criticism only when its valuations are favourable. Thus Ezra Pound, in the middle of his *Guide to Kulchur*, expresses some disinterested admiration for the lyrical elegies of Thomas Hardy, and the effect, in that book, is as though a garrulous drunk had suddenly sobered up, focused his eyes, and begun to talk sense. But, of course, if my argument suggests that everything which has acquired some reputation in literature should be placed 'beyond criticism', or that histories of literature should be as bland and official as possible, I should merely be intensifying the attitude I am attacking, turning the verbal icon into a verbal idol. My point is a very different one, and it begins with the fact that the work of literature is 'beyond criticism' now: criticism can do nothing but lead into it.

There are two contexts in which a work of literature is potential, an internal context and an external one. Internally, the writer has a potential theme and tries to actualize it in what he writes. Externally, the literary work, actualized in itself, becomes a potential experience for student, critic, or reader. A 'bad' poem or novel is one in which, so the critic feels, a potential literary experience has not been actualized. Such a judgement implies a consensus: the critic speaks for all critics, even if he happens to be wrong. But an actualized work of literature may still fail to become an actualized experience for its reader. The judgement here implies withdrawal from a consensus: however many critics may like this, I don't. The first type of judgement belongs primarily to the critical reaction to contemporary literature, reviewing and the like, where a variety of new authors are struggling to establish their authority. The second type belongs primarily to the tactics of critical pressure groups that attempt to redistribute the traditional valuations of the writers of the past in order to display certain new writers, usually including themselves, to better advantage. There is no genuinely critical reason for 'revaluation'. Both activities correspond in the sexual life to what Freud calls the 'polymorphous perverse', the preliminaries of contact with the object. Judicial criticism, or reviewing, is necessarily incomplete: it can never free itself from historical variables, such as the direct appeal of certain in-group conventions to the sophisticated critic. The kind of criticism that is expressed by the term 'insight', the noticing of things in the literary work of particular relevance to one's own experience, is perhaps the nearest that criticism can get to demonstrating the value of what it is dealing with. Insight criticism of this kind, however, is a form of divination, an extension of the principle of *sortes*

Virgilianae: it is essentially random both in invention and in communication.

In short, all methods of criticism and teaching are bad if they encourage the persisting separation of student and literary work: all methods are good if they try to overcome it. The tendency to persistent separation is the result of shifting the critical attention from the object of literary experience to something else, usually something in the critic's mind, and this deprives criticism of content. I know that I have said this before, but the same issues keep turning up every year. This year the issue was raised by Professor Rowse's book on Shakespeare. The questions usually asked about Shakespeare's sonnets, such as who was W. H., have nothing to do with Shakespeare's sonnets or with literary criticism, and have only been attached to criticism because, owing to Shakespeare's portentous reputation, critics have acquired an impertinent itch to know more about his private life than they need to know. It seemed to Professor Rowse that such questions were properly the concern of a historian, and he was quite right. True, he had no new facts about the sonnets and added nothing to our knowledge of this alleged subject, but his principle was sound. But Professor Rowse went further. It occurred to him that perhaps literary criticism was not a genuine intellectual discipline at all, and that there could be no issues connected with it that could not be better dealt with by someone who did belong to a genuine discipline, such as history. One of his sentences, for instance, begins: 'A real writer understands better than a mere critic.' Literary criticism ought to be profoundly grateful to Professor Rowse for writing so bad a book: it practically proves that writing a good book on Shakespeare is a task for a mere critic. Still, the fact that a responsible scholar in a related field could assume, in 1964, that literary criticism was a parasitic pseudo-subject with no facts to build with and no concepts to think with, deserves to be noted.

I do not believe, ultimately, in a plurality of critical methods, though I can see a division of labour in critical operations. I do not believe that there are different 'schools' of criticism today, attached to different and irreconcilable metaphysical assumptions: the notion seems to me to reflect nothing but the confusion in critical theory. In particular, the notion that I belong to a school or have invented a school of mythical or archetypal criticism reflects nothing but confusion about me. I make this personal comment with some hesitation, in view of the great generosity with which my books have been received, but everyone who is understood by anybody is misunderstood by somebody. It is true that I call the elements of literary structure myths, because they are myths; it is true that I call the elements of imagery archetypes, because I want a word which suggests something that changes its context but not its essence. James Beattie, in *The Minstrel*, says of the poet's activity:

> From Nature's beauties, variously compared
> And variously combined, he learns to frame
> Those forms of bright perfection

and adds a footnote to the last phrase: 'General ideas of excellence, the immediate archetypes of sublime imitation, both in painting and in poetry.' It was natural for an eighteenth-century poet to think of poetic images as reflecting 'general ideas of excellence'; it is natural for a twentieth-century critic to think of them as reflecting the same images in other poems. But I think of the term as indigenous to criticism, not as transferred from Neoplatonic philosophy or Jungian psychology. However, I would not fight for a word, and I hold to no 'method' of criticism beyond assuming that the structure and imagery of literature are central considerations of criticism. Nor, I think, does my practical criticism illustrate the use of a patented critical method of my own, different in kind from the approaches of other critics.

The end of criticism and teaching, in any case, is not an aesthetic but an ethical and participating end: for it, ultimately, works of literature are not things to be contemplated but powers to be absorbed. This completes the paradox of which the first half has already been given. The 'aesthetic' attitude, persisted in, loses its connection with literature as an art and becomes socially or morally anxious: to treat literature seriously as a social and moral force is to pass into the genuine experience of it. The advantage of using established classics in teaching, the literary works that have proved their effectiveness, is that one can skip preliminary stages and clear everything out of the way except understanding, which is the only road to possession. At the same time it is easy for understanding to become an end in itself too. The established classics are, for the most part, historically removed from us, and to approach them as new works involves a certain historical astigmatism: but to consider them as historical documents only is again to separate student and literary work. In teaching manual skills, such as car-driving, an examination can test the skill on the higher level; but an examination in English literature cannot pass beyond the level of theoretical knowledge. We may guess the quality of a student's literary experience from the quality of his writing, but there is no assured way of telling from the outside the difference between a student who knows literature and a student who merely knows about it.

Thus the teaching of literature, an activity of criticism which attempts to cast its bread on the waters without knowing when or how or by whom it will be picked up, is involved in paradox and ambiguity. The object of literary experience must be placed directly in front of the student, and he should be urged to respond to it and accept no substitutes as the end of his understanding. Yet it does not matter a tinker's curse what a student thinks and feels about literature until he can think and feel, which is not until he passes the stage of stock response. And although the cruder forms of stock response can be identified and the student released from them, there are subtler forms that are too circular to be easily refuted. There is, for instance, critical narcissism, or assuming that a writer's 'real' meaning is the critic's own attitude (or the opposite of it, if the reaction is negative). There is no 'real' meaning in literature, nothing to be 'got out of it' or abstracted from the total experience; yet all criticism seems to be concerned with approaching such a meaning. There is no way out of these ambiguities: criticism is a phoenix preoccupied with constructing its own funeral pyre, without any guarantee that a bigger and better phoenix will manifest itself as a result.

A large part of criticism is concerned with commentary, and a major work of literature has a vast amount of commentary attached to it. With writers of the size of Shakespeare and Milton, such a body of work is a proper and necessary part of our cultural heritage; and so it may be with, say, Melville or Henry James or Joyce or T. S. Eliot. The existence of a large amount of commentary on a writer is a testimony to the sense of the importance of that writer among critics. As the first critic in *The Pooh Perplex* says, on the opening page of the book: 'Our ideal in English studies is to amass as much commentary as possible upon the literary work, so as to let the world know how deeply we respect it.' An important critical principle is concealed in this remark. It is an illusion that only great literature can be commented on, and that the existence of such commentary proves or demonstrates its greatness. It is a writer's merits that make the criticism on him rewarding, as a rule, but it is not his merits that make it possible. The techniques of criticism can be turned loose on anything whatever. If this were not so, a clever parody like *The Pooh Perplex* could hardly make its point. Hence a mere display of critical dexterity or ingenuity, even as an act of devotion, is not enough: criticism, to be useful both to literature and to the public, needs to contain some sense of the progressive or the systematic, some feeling that irrevocable forward steps in understanding are being taken. We notice that all the contributors to *The Pooh Perplex* claim to be supplying the one essential thing needed to provide this sense of progress, though of course none of them does. Thus the piling up of commentary around the major writers of literature may in itself simply be another way of barricading those writers from us.

Yeats tells us that what fascinates us is the most difficult among things not impossible. Literary criticism is not in so simple a position. Teaching literature is impossible; that is why it is difficult. Yet it must be tried, tried constantly and indefatigably, and placed at the centre of the whole educational process, for at every level the understanding of words is as urgent and crucial a necessity as it is on its lowest level of learning to read and write. Whatever is educational is also therapeutic. The therapeutic power of the arts has been intermittently recognized, especially in music since David played his harp before Saul, but the fact that literature is essential to the mental health of society seldom enters our speculations about it. But if I am to take seriously my own principle that works of literature are not so much things to be studied as powers to be possessed, I need to face the implications of that principle.

I wish all teachers of English, at every level, could feel that they were concerned with the whole of a student's verbal, or in fact imaginative, experience, not merely with the small part of it that is conventionally called literary. The incessant verbal bombardment that students get from conversation, advertising, the mass media, or even such verbal games as Scrabble or cross-word puzzles, is addressed to the same part of the mind that literature addresses, and it does far more to mould their literary imagination than poetry or fiction. It often happens that new developments in literature meet with resistance merely because they bring to life conventions that the critics had decided were sub-literary. Wordsworth's *Lyrical Ballads* met with resistance of this kind, and in our day teachers and critics who think literature should be a matter of direct feeling and are prejudiced against the verbal puzzle find that their students, unlike themselves, are living in the age of *Finnegans Wake*. There is a real truth, for all of what has been said above, in the belief that the critic is deeply concerned with evaluation, and with separating the good from the bad in literature. But I would modify this belief in three ways. First, as just said, the area of literature should not be restricted to the conventionally literary, but expanded to the entire area of verbal experience. Hence the evaluating activity should not be concerned solely with civil wars in the conventionally literary field. Second, the distinction of good and bad is not a simple opposing of the conventionally literary to the conventionally sub-literary, a matter of demonstrating the superiority of Henry James to Mickey Spillane. On the contrary, it seems to me that an important and neglected aspect of literary teaching is to illustrate the affinities in structure and imagery between the 'best' and the 'worst' of what every young person reads or listens to.

Third, if I am right in saying that literature is a power to be possessed, and not a body of objects to be studied, then the difference between good and bad is not something inherent in literary works themselves, but the difference between two ways of using literary experience. The belief that good and bad can be determined as inherent qualities is the belief that inspires censorship, and the attempt to establish grades and hierarchies in literature itself, to distinguish what is canonical from what is apocryphal, is really an 'aesthetic' form of censorship. Milton remarked in *Areopagitica* that a wise man would make a better use of an idle pamphlet than a fool would of Holy Scripture, and this, I take it, is an application of the gospel principle that man is defiled not by what goes into him but by what comes out of him. The question of censorship takes us back to the metaphor of taste by a different road, for censorship is apparently based on an analogy between mental and physical nourishment, what is censorable being inherently poisonous. But there is something all wrong with this analogy: it has often been pointed out that the censor himself never admits to being adversely affected by what he reads. We need to approach the problem that censorship fails to solve in another way.

In primitive societies art is closely bound up with magic: the creative impulse is attached to a less disinterested hope that its products may affect the external world in one's favour. Drawing pictures of animals is part of a design to catch them; songs about bad weather are partly charms to ensure good weather. The magical attachments of primitive art, though they may have stimulated the creative impulse, also come to hamper it, and as society develops they wear off or become isolated in special ritual compartments. Many works of art, including Shakespeare's *Tempest*, remind us that the imaginative powers are released by the renunciation of magic. In the next stage of civilization the magical or natural attachment is replaced by a social one. Literature expresses the preoccupations of the society that produced it, and it is pressed into service to illustrate other social values, religious or political. This means that it has an attachment to other verbal structures in religion or history or morals which is allegorical. Here, too, is something that both hampers and stimulates the creative impulse. Much of Dante's *Commedia* and Milton's *Paradise Lost* is concerned with political and religious issues that we regard now as merely partisan or superstitious. The poems would never have been written without the desire to raise these issues, and as long as we are studying the poems the issues are relevant to our study. But when we pass from the study to the possession of the poems, a dialectical separation of a permanent imaginative structure from a mass of historical anxieties takes place. This is the critical principle that Shelley was attempting to formulate in his *Defence of Poetry*, and in fact the Romantic movement marks the beginning of a third stage in the attachments of the arts, and one that we are still in.

This third stage (to some extent 'decadent', as the first one is primitive, though we should be careful not to get trapped by the word) is both social and magical, and is founded on the desire to make art act kinetically on other people, startling, shocking, or otherwise stimulating them into a response of heightened awareness. It belongs to an age in which kinetic verbal stimulus, in advertising, propaganda, and mass media, plays a large and increasing role in our verbal experience. Sometimes the arts try to make use of similar techniques, as the Italian Futurist movement did, but more frequently the attempt is to create a kind of counter-stimulus. In the various shocking, absurd, angry, and similar conventions in contemporary art one may recognize a strong kinetic motivation. Even in the succession of fashions there is something of this, for the succession of vogues and movements in the arts is part of the economy of waste. Most cultivated people realize that they should overlook or ignore these attachments in responding to the imaginative product itself, and meet all such assaults on their sense of decorum with a tolerant aplomb that sometimes infuriates the artist still more. Here again, the attachment begins as a stimulus and may eventually become a hindrance, unless the artist is astute enough to detach himself at the point where the hindrance begins.

It is the critic's task, in every age, to fight for the autonomy of the arts, and never under any circumstances allow himself to be seduced into judging the arts, positively or negatively, by their attachments. The fact that, for instance, Burroughs's *Naked Lunch* is written in the convention of the psychological shocker does not make it either a good or a bad book, and the fashion for pop-art painting is neither good because painters ought to rediscover content nor bad because they ought not. But an essential part of the critic's strategy, to the extent that the critic is a teacher, is in leading his students to realize that in responding to art without attachments they are at the same time building up a resistance to kinetic stimulus themselves. Literary education is not doing the whole of its proper work unless it marshals the verbal imagination against the assaults of advertising and propaganda that try to bludgeon it into passivity. This is a battle that should be fought long before university, because university comes too late in a student's life to alter his mental habits more than superficially. I think of a public school teacher I know who got his grade-eight students to analyse the rhetorical devices in a series of magazine advertisements. The effect was so shattering that he thought at first he must be working with too young an age group: children who were contemptuous of Santa Claus and the stork were still not ready to discover that advertising was no more factual than the stories they told their parents. Eventually, however, he realized that he was right, and that he had uncovered a deeper level of literary response than literature as such can ordinarily reach at that age.

The direct response to a verbal kinetic stimulus persists into adult life, and is, of course, what makes the propaganda of totalitarian states effective for their own people. Such response is not an inability to distinguish rhetorical from factual statement, but a will to unite them. Even though a Communist, for example, understands the difference between what is said and the political necessity of saying it, he has been conditioned to associate rhetoric and fact when they are produced in a certain area of authority, not to separate them. In the democracies we are not trained in this way, but we are continually being persuaded to fall into the habit, by pressure groups trying to establish the same kind of authority, and by certain types of entertainment in which the kinetic stimulus is erotic. I recently saw a documentary movie of the rock-and-roll singer Paul Anka. The reporter pried one of the squealing little sexballs out of the audience and asked her what she found so ecstatic about listening to Anka. She said, still in a daze: 'He's so *sincere*.' The will to unite rhetorical and direct address is very clear here.

The central activity of criticism, which is the understanding of literature, is essentially one of establishing a context for the works of literature being studied. This means relating them to other things: to their context in the writer's life, in the writer's time, in the history of literature, and above all in the total structure of literature itself, or what I call the order of words. Relation to context accounts for nearly the whole of the factual basis of criticism, the aspect of it that can progress through being verified or refuted by later criticism. This central activity itself has a further context, a lower and an upper limit, with which I have been mainly concerned in this paper. On the lower limit is criticism militant, a therapeutic activity of evaluation, or separating the good from the bad, in which good and bad are not two kinds of literature, but, respectively, the active and the passive approaches to verbal experience. This kind of criticism is essentially the defence of those aspects of civilization loosely described as freedom of speech and freedom of thought. On the higher limit is criticism triumphant, the inner possession of literature as an imaginative force to which all study of literature leads, and which is criticism at once glorified and invisible.

We remember the discussion in Joyce's *Portrait* in which the characteristics of beauty are said to be *integritas, consonantia,* and *claritas*; unity, harmony, and radiance. Poet and critic alike struggle to unify and to relate; the critic, in particular, struggles to demonstrate the unity of the work of literature he is studying and to relate it to its context in literature. There remains the peculiar *claritas* or intensity, which cannot be demonstrated in either literature or criticism, though all literature and criticism point toward it. No darkness can comprehend any light; no ignorance or indifference can ever see any *claritas* in literature itself or in the criticism that attempts to convey it, just as no saint in ordinary life wears a visible gold plate around his head. All poet or critic can do is to hope that somehow, somewhere, and for someone, the struggle to unify and to relate, because it is an honest struggle and not because of any success in what it does, may be touched with a radiance not its own.

7 ELEMENTARY TEACHING AND ELEMENTAL SCHOLARSHIP

I start with the obvious starting-point: the gap between teaching and scholarship. For the most part, the conceptions of the arts and sciences which are presented to children in school are not those that contemporary scholars regard as being, in fact, the elementary principles of those subjects as now conceived. I think it was the mathematicians who first realized that the elementary mathematics taught in schools reflected conceptions of the subject that were centuries out of date. They have begun to do something about this, and to try to develop a curriculum for mathematics which will present, in a logical sequence, a contemporary view of what mathematics is. Other subjects, including English, remain unco-ordinated, based on what are at best *ad hoc* principles. At one end there are the techniques for teaching children to read, which are said to be very efficient when they work, and at the other there are the survey courses of the first year in university, designed to give a student some notion of the chronological order in which the great classics were written. I think it should be possible to work out a curriculum for the intervening stages which will treat literature as a progressive and systematic study, and which will furnish the student with something of tangible and permanent value at whatever stage he drops out of it. It seems to me that, as with mathematics, the first procedure is to make sure that the literary sequence makes sense in itself, regardless of its relations with other subjects, even in elementary school. The relation with other subjects is certainly important and essential, but must come later in consideration.

It has been said that this is an age of criticism: it is certainly an age of great self-consciousness about critical methods. A good many new 'schools' of criticism have developed in recent years, seeming to have little in common beyond the ability to disagree with each other, and to provoke positive and negative responses which seem equally confused. I think myself that we shall see much more unity in contemporary criticism when we realize that most of these new schools are also new teaching methods, each of them finding its own centre of gravity at some stage of teaching. Students of linguistics, for example, naturally develop a special interest in the beginning stages of a language, and we notice that a significant number of scholars in this and related fields have devoted attention to kindergarten and grade one reading programmes. The so-called 'new' critics seem to have a particular centre of gravity in the upper years of high school and the lower undergraduate years, to which such textbooks as Brooks and Warren's *Understanding Poetry* naturally belong. My own interest, for the last dozen years, has been in a synoptic theory of criticism. I have been trying to relate the different techniques of criticism to one another, and if you read my *Anatomy of Criticism* you will see that one of the first things I complain about in that book is the absence of a coherent teaching programme for English. But I have also a more specific interest, derived from my study of Blake, in criticism by means of myths and archetypes, which leads to a special emphasis on conventions, genres, and the principles of literary structure and imagery. I think that this approach also has a particular centre of gravity in the teaching programme, one which comes somewhere between the end of elementary school and the beginning of high school. Some of my students have carried my critical principles into the teaching of English in schools, and they seem agreed that the logical place to begin studying myths and archetypes systematically is grade nine. One of my colleagues[1] at Victoria College has written a handbook on mythology designed for grade nine, the reception of which seems to establish the point.

It is obvious that random patching of the existing curricula, though it may have a practical look, is no longer practical. The only thing that is practical now is to gain a new theoretical conception of literature. The source of this new theoretical conception is contemporary criticism; the application of it to an articulated English programme still awaits us. Most of our difficulties in teaching English result from an immature scholarship that has not properly worked out its own elementary teaching principles: most of the difficulties in our scholarship result, even more obviously, from deficiencies in the teaching programme. The establishing of a coherent curriculum for literature, and for English in particular, would give us a fully revived art of rhetoric, corresponding to the humanistic and Classical training that most of our great poets have had in the past. I hardly need to emphasize the benefit this would be to writers, in making them more secure in their techniques and more readily communicable to their public. Its effect on criticism itself will be even happier, as it will make rather less of it necessary to read.

This last is not altogether a joke. The coming population explosion of students is a serious problem, certainly, but it is trifling compared to the real horror that awaits us in the immediate future: the population explosion in scholarship. With the greatly increasing numbers of university presses developing, of critical journals being subsidized, of bright young people eager to write for both, of a growing number of elementary- and secondary-school teachers taking a more academic interest in their subject, it will be essential to develop a literary education which can deal with this more selectively. Even granting that the motive for scholarly production in the immediate future will be the desire to become better known and attract better offers, rather than the necessity of feeding one's wife and children, still the new journals and publishers' lists must be filled somehow, and deans will continue to want lists of publications to base promotions on. There will, of course, always be a steady flow of genuinely new research and information, and of genuinely new critical insights. The young scholar and critic can never be in the happy position of the young poet, not feeling any compulsion to read anything except his own works and those of his close friends. But for a critic trained early in all the essential critical methods, not every academic exercise in criticism will be something to 'keep up with' or list in a bibliography for students; and the better one's own literary education, the more quickly one can see how much of contemporary scholarly production one already knows. One would also hope to see the field of scholarship itself become more decentralized, as new techniques of criticism grow to maturity. The rigidly *Wissenschaft* framework of the Ph.D. is no longer applicable for many of the critical methods that are now appealing to students of literature; and the provision of alternative degrees in graduate schools would probably save a great deal of time and heartbreak for many such students.

The first thing that university teachers want to know is: what is important in the pre-university study of literature? Most of us, when we complain about our freshmen, base our complaints on the theme of information or memorized knowledge: our students don't know enough; they haven't read enough; the chronology of literature is a vague haze in their minds; some of them could hardly distinguish Chaucer from Tennyson except by the spelling, and so on. But if students don't have enough information, it is a simple enough matter to supply it or provide the sources of supply. The trouble is that what they learn they learn within a mental structure of habits and assumptions, and university comes much too late in a student's life to alter that structure. For example: many students come to university assuming that convention is the opposite of originality, and is a sign that a poet is superficial and insincere. If they are writing poetry themselves, they are apt to get bristly and aggressive about this assumption. They can't be writing in a convention that all their friends are writing in: they must be conveying unique experiences, because their poems say that they are. Here is a result of illiterate teaching that makes the most scrambled nonsense out of all literary values, yet nothing can really be done about it. We tell them at university that literary sincerity is quite different from personal sincerity, that it can only be developed by craftsmanship working within a convention, and that it is the function of convention to set free the power of expressing emotions, not to provide formulas for ready-made emotions, though it may do this for dull writers. They listen; they understand; they may even believe; but the effect on their mental habits is very like the effect of schoolmarm English on the little boy: 'Dar ain't no "ain't you", is dey? It's "aren't you", ain't it?'

Or, again, I am at an educational conference listening to a speech by a high authority in the field. I know him to be a good scholar, a dedicated servant of society, and an admirable person. Yet his speech is a muddy river of clichés, flowing stickily into a delta of banalities at the peroration. The content of the speech does not do justice to his mind: what it does reflect is the state of his literary education. It is not that he has never read good literature, for he has the literary tastes that one would expect a cultivated man to have. But he has never been trained to think rhetorically, to visualize his abstractions, to subordinate logic and sequence to the insights of metaphor and simile, to realize that figures of speech are not the ornaments of language, but the elements of both language and thought. And because his main scholarly interests lie outside literature, he has never been compelled to make up for these deficiencies himself. The result is that he is fluent without being articulate, and cannot break out of an armour of ready-made phrases when he tries to express his real convictions. Once again, nothing can now be done for him: there are no courses in remedial metaphor.

The greatest fallacy in the present conception of literary education is the notion that prose is the normal language of ordinary speech, and should form the centre and staple of literary teaching. From prose in this sense we move out to utilitarian English on one side and to the more specialized literary study of poetry on the other. Few subjects can be more futile than a prose-based approach to poetry, an approach which treats poems as documents, to be analysed or summarized or otherwise translated into the language of communication. The root of the fallacy is the assumption that prose represents the only valid form of thought, and that poetry, considered as thought, is essentially decorated or distorted prose. When we suggest that young people try writing poetry, what most of them immediately produce are discontinuous prose statements about their emotions, or what they think their emotions ought to be, when confronted with the outside world. This is not merely because they have been taught to read poetry as a series of statements of this kind – 'all that guff about nature', as one freshman expressed it – it is rather that they assume that all verbal expression derives from the attempt to describe something, and that poetry differs from prose, as a mode of thought, in being an attempt to describe subjective emotions.

The main principles of a coherently organized curriculum are simple enough, but very different from the one just mentioned. Poetry should be at the centre of all literary training, and literary prose forms the periphery. In a properly constructed curriculum there would be no place for 'effective communication' or for any form of utilitarian English. We still have textbooks on effective writing produced by people who have no notion how to write, mainly because they are trying to be effective about it, but one hopes that the market for them will disappear in our time. The styles employed by journalists and advertisers are highly conventionalized rhetorics, in fact practically trade jargons, and have to be learned as separate skills, without much direct reference to literature at all. A literary training is a considerable handicap in trying to understand, for example, the releases of public relations counsels. I am not saying this just to be ironic: I am stating a fact. I remember a *New Yorker* cartoon of a milkman who found the notice 'no milk' on a doorstep, and woke up the householder at four in the morning to enquire whether he meant that he had no milk or that he wanted no milk. I suspect that the milkman was a retired teacher of English: certainly he reflects the disadvantages of being sensitive to the nuances of expression. A literary person confronted with most of the verbal technologies of our time is in the position of a genuinely intelligent student confronted with an intelligence test which grossly oversimplifies its categories and calls for an arbitrary choice of half-truths. He is sure to fail the test simply because he is more intelligent than the creature who designed it. The primary function of education is to make one maladjusted to ordinary society; and literary education makes it more difficult to come to terms with the barbarizing of speech, or what *Finnegans Wake* calls the jinglish janglage.

The connections of literature are with the imagination, not with the reason, hence the ideal in literature is one of intensity and power rather than of precision or accuracy, as in science. There can be no intensity without precision, but to aim directly at precision is trying to seize the shadow. Poetry is one of the creative arts, in the context of music and painting, or rhythm and pattern. The rhythmical energy of poetry, its intimate connection with song and dance, is the elementary basis of its appeal, and the primary aspect of it to be presented to children, along with its affinity with the concrete and the sensational, its power of making things vivid by illustration, which has traditionally been expressed in the formula *ut pictura poesis*.

I am certainly no expert on the teaching of children, but it seems obvious that all such teaching has to follow the child's own rhythm of thought and development, and not project on him some half-baked adult mystique, whether that mystique claims to derive from the anti-intellectual left or the anti-anti-intellectual right. And it is clear that children recapitulate, as we should expect them to do, the experience of primitive literature, and turn most naturally and easily to the abstract and conventionalized, to riddles, conundrums, and stylized jingles. The authors of *The Lore and Language of Schoolchildren* quote an unremarkable verse:

> Mrs White had a fright
> In the middle of the night,
> She saw a ghost eating toast
> Half-way up the lamp post

and append the comment of a nine-year-old critic: 'I think what's so clever about this is the way it all rhymes.' Later, in speaking of the child's fondness for tongue twisters and multiple puns, they remark: 'It takes children a long time before they cease to be amazed that one word can have more than one meaning.' One would hope that this amazement would last the rest of their lives. The speech of a small child is full of chanting and singing, and it is clear that the child understands what many adults do not, that verse is a more direct and primitive way of conventionalizing speech than prose is.

This principle, that the physical energy and concrete vividness of verse should normally be presented earlier than the more complex and adulterated rhythm of prose, affects the training in both reading and writing. It is difficult to know how a child thinks, but it is less difficult to know how he talks, once one has gained his confidence, and how he talks might afford an educational clue. Any child who has talked to me has addressed me in an uninhibited stream of burble for which the nearest literary counterpart is the last chapter of *Ulysses*. This chapter has no punctuation, and neither has a child's speech. Surely in teaching writing one should begin by trying to channel this free current of verbal energy and start giving it some precision as it goes along. To teach a child to write as though he were deciphering something from linear B, proceeding from word to phrase, from phrase to sentence, from sentence to paragraph, is to ensure that what he eventually writes will be a dead language. Good writing has to be based on good speech, and good speech is a logical, though complex, development from natural speech. It is a striking feature of our culture that so much creative activity in literature, as in music and painting, should be either explicitly academic or explicitly resistant to education, a culture either of Brahmins or of Dharma bums. In Canada these two aspects of literary culture have reached a curious schizophrenia in which a constant polemic against academic poetry is carried on by poets who are nearly all employed by universities. It seems to me that the source of the feeling that education inhibits spontaneity may be somewhere in the region I have just indicated: in the reversal of the natural rhythms of thought and expression which a prose-based literary education is only too apt to produce.

In its concrete and sensational vocabulary, in its use of simile and metaphor, in its functional employment of pun, ambiguity, and assonance, poetry is a method of thought as well as a means of expression. It is a primitive and archaic method of thought in many ways, but for that very reason needs to come early in one's education. One of the most obvious features of poetic thought is that it is categorical. Primitive poetry delights in catalogues, long lists of strange names, the names which are potent in magic, which are the keys to history, which summon up the deeds and loves of heroes and gods. This love of lists and catalogues runs through English literature from *Widsith* to Tolkien, and is something we find recurring in the history plays of Shakespeare, in *Paradise Lost*, in the Blake prophecies, in Whitman and Melville. It seems to me that there is much in the child's mind which responds to this primitive appeal of unlocking the word-hoard. A Canadian poet, James Reaney, has written a series of twelve eclogues in imitation of Spenser, in which the speakers are geese. The July eclogue is a dialogue between a goose named Anser who is a progressive educator and consequently hates and distrusts all education, and an older goose named Valancy, named after a nineteenth-century mythopoeic Canadian poet, who tries to explain, in imagery derived from an unlikely mixture of the examination room and the Resurrection, what the kind of education he has had has meant to him:

Valancy
When I was a gosling he taught me to know the most wonderful list of things. You could play games with it; whenever you were bored or miserable what he had taught you was like a marvellous deck of cards in your head that you could shuffle through and turn over into various combinations with endless delight. At the end of the year we each made ourselves little huts of burdock leaves, lay down on our backs with large stones on our bellies and recited the whole thing over to ourselves forwards and backwards. Some of the poorer students were in those huts till November

but even those to whom it was agony, when they at length did know that they knew all that a young goose was supposed to know, the moment when they rolled the stone away and climbed out of their burdock hut – it was as joyous a moment as if they had been reborn into another world.

Anser

Well, well, well. Might I ask just what this reviving curriculum was?

Valancy

Who are the children of the glacier and the earth?
Esker and hogsback, drumlin and kame.
What are the four elements and the seven colours,
The ten forms of fire and the twelve tribes of Israel?
The eight winds and the hundred kinds of clouds,
All of Jesse's stem and the various ranks of angels?
The Nine Worthies and the Labours of Hercules,
The sisters of Emily Brontë, the names of Milton's wives?
The Kings and England and Scotland with their Queens,
The names of all those hanged on the trees of law
Since this province first cut up trees into gallows.
What are the stones that support New Jerusalem's wall?
Jasper and sapphire, chalcedony, emerald,
Sard, sardius, chrysolite, beryl, topaz,
Chrysoprasus, hyacinthine and amethyst.

What this passage also indicates is that these lists of names do not remain merely lists, as they did in the mind of the Major-General in *The Pirates of Penzance*, 'in order categorical'. They become the elements by which the imagination learns to control the natural world. The teacher needs to have the principle clearly in his mind that it is the function of literature to assimilate the natural world to the human world, chiefly through the associations of analogy and identity, the two modes of thought that reappear in literature as the simile and the metaphor. This is why poetry has so deep-rooted an affinity to correspondences and cosmological constructs of all kinds: to a universe where seven planets breed seven metals in the soil, where there must be twelve months of the year because there are twelve signs of the zodiac: four elements, and therefore four gospels, four points of the compass, and four quartets. Categories of this kind are neither obsolete science nor exploded superstition, but structural principles of literature. A keen student who discovers at university some such book as Tillyard's

Eli₂abethan World-Picture may well feel that the Elizabethans possessed some kind of key to poetic language and thought that we have lost because we have lost sight of the gate it would open. But the world of *The Faerie Queene* is not essentially different from the world of Dylan Thomas or Yeats or Eliot, and there is no reason why the poetic world-picture should not be equally accessible to our own time. In the Middle Ages and the Renaissance these schematic constructs had religious, philosophical, and some scientific validity as well. Since the Romantic movement, they have had more troglodytic connections with occultism, comparative religion, and more recently with certain branches of anthropology and psychology. One very important principle that contemporary criticism can contribute to the teaching of English, I think, is the principle that these constructs are part of the structure of literature itself, are an essential part of the teaching of it, but do not need to be projected on or derived from any other aspect of thought or culture.

There is an odd paradox in the teaching process which sounds, at first, as though teaching were an art of noble hypocrisy, like the noble lie of Plato's state. There can be no sense of excitement or discovery, no glimpsing of new worlds of the mind, without dramatizing for the student a mental attitude that is inductive and empirical, putting the learner into the same psychological position as the most original of thinkers. Yet the teacher, while he presents his material to his students inductively, needs to have a deductive scheme in his mind to which his inductive presentation is related. In the teaching of science, for instance, nobody questions that a student should be trained in experimental methods and encouraged to experiment for himself at every stage. Still, the actual principles of science taught on at least pre-university levels are principles so solidly established that the experiments simply illustrate them: in other words the teacher of science thinks of his subject deductively, though he does not so present it, at least at first.

So with the teaching of English. In teaching writing the inductive process appears as the feeling of self-expression, the power of developing a new skill, the growing sense of mastery in making all those strange new words say what one means. The teacher's role is to encourage this feeling while at the same time keeping a deductive frame of reference behind it. The teacher may, and should, have had some training in linguistics, and may share the purely descriptive and empirical attitude which that subject quite rightly takes to language. But learning to write is also a deductive and normative process: it requires a knowledge of systematic grammar and of the niceties and distinctions of verbal expression. In a world of vague speech where, as has been said, a disinterested judge is one who goes to sleep on the bench, the teacher of English must fight for and defend these inherited subtleties of language. Not to do so is to betray the subject, and both teacher and student need the support of a proper dictionary, one that says, loudly and frequently, 'Most people get this wrong.' I do not know what role the nomenclature of grammar plays in the study of it, at what stage it should be learned, or how much of it is really essential, but of its central importance there cannot be any real question.

When I was an undergraduate I was continually answering examination questions about style. When examiners ran out of other things to ask, they demanded that we discuss with specific examples the style of Spenser or Sir Thomas Browne, and the desperate appeal to be specific did not conceal from us the fact that this was what we called a 'shovelling' question. Today we are less concerned with style because we know more about the real basis of style in rhetoric and the principle of decorum. In the secondary school I should hope to see the study of grammar expand into the study of rhetoric, in the traditional sense of that word, the advance of the power of expression keeping pace with the growing realization that there is a finite number of rhetorical devices and of ways of constructing a sentence. I often think of the enthusiasm with which E. K., Spenser's editor, seized on the line from *January*, 'I love a lass (alas, why do I love ?)', and called it 'a pretty epanorthosis and withal a paronomasia'. It cannot be said too often that it was this kind of technical interest and competence in rhetoric that made Elizabethan literature possible, and created a public for it. Here again, I do not know what role nomenclature, which is a formidable aspect of rhetoric, should play in the study of it. I know only that there ought to be enough words to think with. As Wallace Stevens says, 'Progress in any aspect is a movement through changes of terminology.'[2] But even without an elaborate terminology, it should be a simple matter for grade ten to analyse the rhetorical devices in any highly conventionalized writer, such as James Thurber or S. J. Perelman.

As for the teaching of literature, it is obvious that a good deal of it should consist in reading and listening to stories. The stories of Biblical and Classical mythology should clearly have a central place in all elementary teaching of literature, so that the student is thoroughly familiar with them, as stories, before he embarks on the more systematic study of mythology that I have assumed would begin with high school. I suppose that incorporating Biblical myths into a comparative study of mythology in general might, in some parts of the country, mean circumventing or ignoring the screams of superstitious voters.[3] In any case, all through elementary school a student should become gradually aware that stories come in certain conventional shapes. I think of stories as divisible into four *mythoi* or generic plots, the romantic, the comic, the tragic, and the ironic, and I hope that this division would be useful here, or some more adequate one. It seems to me that comic and romantic stories are the ones to stress in elementary school, and that tragic and ironic ones, which are most easily understood as divergences, reversals, or parodies of the other two, should be reserved for later study. It seems to me also that the analogies and resemblances that the young student finds in all his literary experience from Shakespeare to television are what should be stressed: they are more fun to identify[4] and easier to remember than differences. Besides, the differences are mainly in value, and value-judgements can wait. In fact, they must wait, because they cannot be taught.

When the student has reached high school he should be aware of the recurring or conventional images of poetry, or what I call archetypes. There are two great structures underlying poetic imagery, the cyclical and the dialectic. The cycle of nature, running through the phases of the day, the year, the circulation of water, the generations of human life, and the like, stretches like a backbone across the whole of literature. The separation of images into the contrasting worlds or states of mind that Blake calls innocence and experience, and that religions call heaven and hell, is the dialectical framework of literature, and is the aspect of it that enables literature, without moralizing, to create a moral reality in imaginative experience. The full understanding of these two structures is complicated for the teacher, but their elementary principles are exceedingly simple, and can be demonstrated to any class of normally intelligent fifteen-year-olds. Analysis of this simple kind is, in my opinion, the key to understanding, not merely the conventions and the major genres of literature, but the much more important fact that literature, considered as a whole, is not the aggregate of all the works of literature that have got written, but an order of words, a coherent field of study which trains the imagination quite as systematically and efficiently as the sciences train the reason. If the teacher can communicate this principle, he will have done all he can for his student.

The reason for studying myths, in a course in literature, is that myths represent the structural principles of literature: they are to literature what geometrical shapes are to painting. The reason for studying mythology is that mythology as a whole provides a kind of diagram or blueprint of what literature as a whole is all about, an imaginative survey of the human situation from the beginning to the end, from the height to the depth, of what is imaginatively conceivable. This is ultimately the kind of deductive framework that, ideally, the teacher should have in mind. It seems clear too that the study of theme and structure is simpler, more fundamental, and logically earlier than the study of texture and ambiguity, which can easily lose sight of its controlling principles if it is begun too early.

On looking over an anthology of poetry used in Ontario high schools, I notice that it gives a prominence to such poets as Masefield, Gordon Bottomley, Wilfred Scawen Blunt, and others which is absurdly out of proportion to their actual importance as poets. The reason is, of course, that they are the talky poets, who write versified prose, and therefore, it is assumed, students brought up to believe that prose is normal verbal utterance will find them easier to understand. I should hope that students of the future would be brought up on ballads, Elizabethan songs, Shakespeare sonnets, Donne, Blake, Emily Dickinson (the Grandma Moses of poetry), Wordsworth's Lucy poems, and similar foolproof introductions to poetic experience, so that they would regard vigorous rhythm and metaphorical thought as the simple and direct form of utterance. The anthologist obviously believes that genuinely modern poetry is too difficult because it has moved too far from the ordinary public. What he ought to believe is that the ordinary public is difficult to reach because it has moved too far from the simplicity of poetry.

However, the anthology I am looking at also contains a poem by Campion:

> There is a garden in her face
>   Where roses and white lilies grow;
> A heavenly paradise is that place,
>   Wherein all pleasant fruits do flow.
>   There cherries grow which none may buy
>   Till 'Cherry-ripe' themselves do cry . . .
>
> Her eyes like angels watch them still;
>   Her brows like bended bows do stand,
> Threat'ning with piercing frowns to kill
>   All that attempt with eye or hand
>   Those sacred cherries to come nigh,
>   Till 'Cherry-ripe' themselves do cry.

The note in the back of the book says only that this is an example of the strained and exaggerated language that love poets of that day used. I would have students trained to realize, by the time they got to this poem, that it was about the Garden of Eden and the Garden of the Hesperides, and that it was written in a convention which had been identifying gardens with female bodies for centuries. Also that every detail in the imagery, such as the roses and lilies of the second line, belonged to a standard poetic language to be found in literally thousands of other poems. I should hope, too, that they would understand this, not as esoteric information, but as a normal part of the grammar of poetic expression, as the way poets write when they know their business, whatever age they happen to live in.

Again, I do not know where or at what stage the chronology of English literature should be mastered by a high-school student. Certainly it is difficult to remember that Milton influenced Keats unless one possesses the inference that Milton came earlier. But there is a complicating factor in modern education which hardly existed even a decade ago. It used to be that English literature was thought of as a cultural heritage which stretched back to *Beowulf*, and to Homer before that, and that the tradition of this inheritance was central in the understanding of it. So it is. But the perspective changes when we realize that Chinese and Arabic and Indian poets also use the language of the imagination, the same language except that they might speak of a lotus where a French or Italian poet would speak of a rose. In a world like ours the expansion of one's literary culture is not necessarily into our own tradition at all. This fact makes it even more essential to learn the grammar of the imagination which all literature employs. As Thomas Traherne says: 'Men do mightily wrong themselves when they refuse to be present in all ages.'[5] A generation ago the sense of tradition in literary culture was so strong that there seemed almost to be a necessary connection between literature and the conservative temperament, or at least some nostalgia for the past. Tradition is as important now as it ever was, but it is less exclusive: the vast shadow of a total human consensus in the imagination is beginning to take shape behind it.

I am not worried about how students are going to find time to learn about the conceptions of literature that criticism is developing. For every hour of new knowledge we can get rid of at least another hour of wasted time. I am not competent either to discuss a much more serious question: where and how we are going to find teachers able to teach literature in a genuinely systematic and progressive way. All I can say is, first, that the difficulties, however enormous, are no reason for abandoning the attempt, and second, that giving some sequence and coherence to the literary curriculum is in the long run a simplifying rather than a complicating process, of more benefit to the mediocre as well as to the inspired teacher. Certainly the best teachers, at least, will not remain any longer than they can help out of touch with contemporary views of their own subject.

What I do urge, as a final word, is that teachers should understand something of the practicality of literary training, at every stage of development. We begin by teaching children to read and write, on the ground that that is the most practical subject in the world, illiteracy being a problem on the same plane as starvation and exposure. But when we get to literature we tend to talk about it as though it were one of the ornaments of life, necessary for the best life, but a luxury for the ordinary one. It is essential for the teacher of literature, at every level, to remember that in a modern democracy a citizen participates in society mainly through his imagination. We often do not realize this until an actual event with some analogy to literary form takes place; but surely we do not need to wait for a president to be assassinated before we can understand what a tragedy is and what it can do in creating a community of response. Literature, however, gives us not only a means of understanding, but a power to fight. All around us is a society which demands that we adjust or come to terms with it, and what that society presents to us is a social mythology. Advertising, propaganda, the speeches of politicians, popular books and magazines, the clichés of rumour, all have their own kind of pastoral myths, quest myths, hero myths, sacrificial myths, and nothing will drive these shoddy constructs out of the mind except the genuine forms of the same thing. We all know how important the reason is in an irrational world, but the imagination, in a society of perverted imagination, is far more essential in making us understand that the phantasmagoria of current events is not real society, but only the transient appearance of real society. Real society, the total body of what humanity has done and can do, is revealed to us only by the arts and sciences; nothing but the imagination can apprehend that reality as a whole, and nothing but literature, in a culture as verbal as ours, can train the imagination to fight for the sanity and the dignity of mankind.

Part Two ∽ APPLICATIONS

8 VARIETIES OF LITERARY UTOPIAS

There are two social conceptions which can be expressed only in terms of myth. One is the social contract, which presents an account of the origins of society. The other is the utopia, which presents an imaginative vision of the *telos* or end at which social life aims. These two myths both begin in an analysis of the present, the society that confronts the mythmaker, and they project this analysis in time or space. The contract projects it into the past, the utopia into the future or some distant place. To Hobbes, a contemporary of the Puritan Revolution, the most important social principle was the maintenance of *de facto* power; hence he constructs a myth of contract turning on the conception of society's surrender of that power. To Locke, a contemporary of the Whig Revolution, the most important social principle was the relation of *de facto* power to legitimate or *de jure* authority; hence he constructs a myth turning on society's delegation of power. The value of such a myth as theory depends on the depth and penetration of the social analysis which inspires it. The social contract, though a genuine myth which, in John Stuart Mill's phrase, passes a fiction off as a fact, is usually regarded as an integral part of social theory. The utopia, on the other hand, although its origin is much the same, belongs primarily to fiction. The reason is that the emphasis in the contract myth falls on the present facts of society which it is supposed to explain. And even to the extent that the contract myth is projected into the past, the past is the area where historical evidence lies; and so the myth preserves at least the gesture of making assertions that can be definitely verified or refuted.

The utopia is a *speculative* myth; it is designed to contain or provide a vision for one's social ideas, not to be a theory connecting social facts together. There have been one or two attempts to take utopian constructions literally by trying to set them up as actual communities, but the histories of these communities make melancholy reading. Life imitates literature up to a point, but hardly up to *that* point. The utopian writer looks at his own society first and tries to see what, for his purposes, its significant elements are. The utopia itself shows what society would be like if those elements were fully developed. Plato looked at his society and saw its structure as a hierarchy of priests, warriors, artisans, and servants – much the same structure that inspired the caste system of India. The *Republic* shows what a society would be like in which such a hierarchy functioned on the principle of justice, that is, each man doing his own work. More, thinking within a Christian framework of ideas, assumed that the significant elements of society were the natural virtues, justice, temperance, fortitude, prudence. The *Utopia* itself, in its second or constructive book, shows what a society would be like in which the natural virtues were allowed to assume their natural forms. Bacon, on the other hand, anticipates Marx by assuming that the most significant of social factors is technological productivity, and his *New Atlantis* constructs accordingly.

The procedure of constructing a utopia produces two literary qualities which are typical, almost invariable, in the genre. In the first place, the behaviour of society is described *ritually*. A ritual is a significant social act, and the utopia-writer is concerned only with the typical actions which are significant of those social elements he is stressing. In utopian stories a frequent device is for someone, generally a first-person narrator, to enter the utopia and be shown around it by a sort of Intourist guide. The story is made up largely of a Socratic dialogue between guide and narrator, in which the narrator asks questions or thinks up objections and the guide answers them. One gets a little weary, in reading a series of such stories, of what seems a pervading smugness of tone. As a rule the guide is completely identified with his society and seldom admits to any discrepancy between the reality and the appearance of what he is describing. But we recognize that this is inevitable given the conventions employed. In the second place, rituals are apparently irrational acts which become *rational* when their significance is explained. In such utopias the guide explains the structure of the society and thereby the significance of the behaviour being observed. Hence, the behaviour of society is presented as rationally motivated.

It is a common objection to utopias that they present human nature as governed more by reason than it is or can be. But this rational emphasis, again, is the result of using certain literary conventions. The utopian romance does not present society as governed by reason; it presents it as governed by ritual habit, or prescribed social behaviour, which is explained rationally.

Every society, of course, imposes a good deal of prescribed social behaviour on its citizens, much of it being followed unconsciously, anything completely accepted by convention and custom having in it a large automatic element. But even automatic ritual habits are explicable, and so every society can be seen or described to some extent as a product of conscious design. The symbol of conscious design in society is the city, with its abstract pattern of streets and buildings, and with the complex economic cycle of production, distribution, and consumption that it sets up. The utopia is primarily a vision of the orderly city and of a city-dominated society. Plato's Republic is a city-state, Athenian in culture and Spartan in discipline. It was inevitable that the utopia, as a literary genre, should be revived at the time of the Renaissance, the period in which the medieval social order was breaking down again into city-state units or nations governed from a capital city. Again, the utopia, in its typical form, contrasts, implicitly or explicitly, the writer's own society with the more desirable one he describes. The desirable society, or the utopia proper, is essentially the writer's own society with its unconscious ritual habits transposed into their conscious equivalents. The contrast in value between the two societies implies a satire on the writer's own society, and the basis for the satire is the unconsciousness or inconsistency in the social behaviour he observes around him. More's *Utopia* begins with a satire on the chaos of sixteenth-century life in England and presents the Utopia itself as a contrast to it. Thus the typical utopia contains, if only by implication, a satire on the *anarchy* inherent in the writer's own society, and the utopia form flourishes best when anarchy seems most a social threat. Since More, utopias have appeared regularly but sporadically in literature, with a great increase around the close of the nineteenth century. This later vogue clearly had much to do with the distrust and dismay aroused by extreme *laissez-faire* versions of capitalism, which were thought of as manifestations of anarchy.

Most utopia-writers follow either More (and Plato) in stressing the legal structure of their societies, or Bacon in stressing its technological power. The former type of utopia is closer to actual social and political theory; the latter overlaps with what is now called science fiction. Naturally, since the Industrial Revolution a serious utopia can hardly avoid introducing technological themes. And because technology is progressive, getting to the utopia has tended increasingly to be a journey in time rather than space, a vision of the future and not of a society located in some isolated spot on the globe (or outside it: journeys to the moon are a very old form of fiction, and some of them are utopian). The growth of science and technology brings with it a pro-digious increase in the legal complications of existence. As soon as medical science identifies the source of a contagious disease in a germ, laws of quarantine go into effect; as soon as technology produces the automobile, an immense amount of legal apparatus is imported into life, and thousands of non-criminal citizens become involved in fines and police-court actions. This means a corresponding increase in the amount of ritual habit necessary to life, and a new ritual habit must be conscious, and so constraining, before it becomes automatic or unconscious. Science and technology, especially the latter, introduce into society the conception of directed social change, change with logical consequences attached to it. These consequences turn on the increase of ritual habit. And as long as ritual habit can still be seen as an imminent possibility, as something we may or may not acquire, there can be an emotional attitude toward it either of acceptance or repugnance. The direction of social change may be thought of as exhilarating, as in most theories of progress, or as horrible, as in pessimistic or apprehensive social theories. Or it may be thought that whether the direction of change is good or bad will depend on the attitude society takes toward it. If the attitude is active and resolute, it may be good; if helpless and ignorant, bad.

A certain amount of claustrophobia enters this argument when it is realized, as it is from about 1850 on, that technology tends to unify the whole world. The conception of an *isolated* utopia like that of More or Plato or Bacon gradually evaporates in the face of this fact. Out of this situation come two kinds of utopian romance: the straight utopia, which visualizes a world-state assumed to be ideal, at least in comparison with what we have, and the utopian satire or parody, which presents the same kind of social goal in terms of slavery, tyranny, or anarchy. Examples of the former in the literature of the last century include Bellamy's *Looking Backward*, Morris's *News from Nowhere*, and H. G. Wells's *A Modern Utopia*. Wells is one of the few writers who have constructed both serious and satirical utopias. Examples of the utopian satire include Zamiatin's *We*, Aldous Huxley's *Brave New World* and George Orwell's *1984*. There are other types of utopian satire which we shall mention in a moment, but this particular kind is a product of modern technological society, its growing sense that the whole world is destined to the same social fate with no place to hide, and its increasing realization that technology moves toward the control not merely of nature but of the operations of the mind. We may note that what is a serious utopia to its author, and to many of its readers, could be read as a satire by a reader whose emotional attitudes were different. *Looking Backward* had, in its day, a stimulating and emancipating influence on the social thinking of the time in a way that very few books in the history of literature have ever had. Yet most of us today would tend to read it as a sinister blueprint of tyranny, with its industrial 'army', its stentorian propaganda delivered over the 'telephone' to the homes of its citizens, and the like.

The nineteenth-century utopia had a close connection with the growth of socialist political thought and shares its tendency to think in global terms. When Engels attacked 'utopian' socialism and contrasted it with his own 'scientific' kind, his scientific socialism was utopian in the sense in which we are using that term, but what he rejected under the category of 'utopian' was the tendency to think in terms of a delimited socialist society, a place of refuge like the phalansteries of Fourier. For Engels, as for Marxist thinkers generally, there was a world-wide historical process going in a certain direction; and humanity had the choice either of seizing and directing this process in a revolutionary act or of drifting into greater anarchy or slavery. The goal, a classless society in which the state had withered away, was utopian; the means adopted to reach this goal were 'scientific' and anti-utopian, dismissing the possibility of setting up *a* utopia within a pre-socialist world.

We are concerned here with utopian literature, not with social attitudes; but literature is rooted in the social attitudes of its time. In the literature of the democracies today we notice that utopian satire is very prominent (for example, William Golding's *Lord of the Flies*), but that there is something of a paralysis of utopian thought and imagination. We can hardly understand this unless we realize the extent to which it is the result of a repudiation of Communism. In the United States particularly the attitude toward a definite social ideal as a planned goal is anti-utopian: such an ideal, it is widely felt, can produce in practice only some form of totalitarian state. And whereas the Communist programme calls for a revolutionary seizure of the machinery of production, there is a strong popular feeling in the democracies that the utopian goal can be reached only by allowing the machinery of production to function by itself, as an automatic and continuous process. Further, it is often felt that such an automatic process tends to decentralize authority and break down monopolies of political power. This combination of an anti-utopian attitude toward centralized planning and a utopian attitude toward the economic process naturally creates some inconsistencies. When I was recently in Houston, I was told that Houston had no zoning laws: that indicates a strongly anti-utopian sentiment in Houston, yet Houston was building sewers, highways, cloverleaf intersections, and shopping centres in the most uninhibited utopian way.

There is, however, something of a donkey's carrot in attaching utopian feelings to a machinery of production largely concerned with consumer goods. We can see this if we look at some of the utopian romances of the last century. The technological utopia has one literary disadvantage: its predictions are likely to fall short of what comes true, so that what the writer saw in the glow of vision we see only as a crude version of ordinary life. Thus Edgar Allan Poe has people crossing the Atlantic in balloons at a hundred miles an hour one thousand years after his own time. I could describe the way I get to work in the morning, because it is a form of ritual habit, in the idiom of a utopia, riding on a subway, guiding myself by street signs, and the like, showing how the element of social design conditions my behaviour at every point. It might sound utopian if I had written it as a prophecy a century ago, or now to a native of a New Guinea jungle, but it would hardly do so to my present readers. Similarly with the prediction of the radio (called, as noted above, the telephone, which had been invented) in

Bellamy's *Looking Backward* (1888). A slightly earlier romance, said to be the original of Bellamy's book, is *The Diothas*, by John MacNie (1883).* It predicts a general use of a horseless carriage, with a speed of twenty miles an hour (faster downhill). One passage shows very clearly how something commonplace to us could be part of a utopian romance in 1883:

> 'You see the white line running along the centre of the road,' resumed Utis. 'The rule of the road requires that line to be kept on the left, except when passing a vehicle in front. Then the line may be crossed, provided the way on that side is clear.'

But while technology has advanced far beyond the wildest utopian dreams even of the last century, the essential quality of human life has hardly improved to the point that it could be called utopian. The real strength and importance of the utopian imagination, both for literature and for life, if it has any at all, must lie elsewhere.

The popular view of the utopia, and the one which in practice is accepted by many if not most utopia-writers, is that a utopia is an ideal or flawless state, not only logically consistent in its structure but permitting as much freedom and happiness for its inhabitants as is possible to human life. Considered as a final or definitive social ideal, the utopia is a static society; and most utopias have built-in safeguards against radical alteration of the structure. This feature gives it a somewhat forbidding quality to a reader not yet committed to it. An imaginary dialogue between a utopia-writer and such a reader might begin somewhat as follows: Reader: 'I can see that this society might work, but I wouldn't want to live in it.' Writer: 'What you mean is that you don't want your present ritual habits disturbed. My utopia would feel different from the inside, where the ritual habits would be customary and so carry with them a sense of freedom rather than constraint.' Reader: 'Maybe so, but my sense of freedom right now is derived from *not* being involved in your society. If I were, I'd either feel constraint or I'd be too unconscious to be living a fully human life at all.' If this argument went on, some compromise might be reached: the writer might realize that freedom really depends on a sense of constraint, and

---

* I owe my knowledge of *The Diothas*, and much else in this paper, to the admirable collection *The Quest for Utopia, An Anthology of Imaginary Societies* by Glenn Negley and J. Max Patrick (New York: Schuman, 1952).

the reader might realize that a utopia should not be read simply as a description of a most perfect state, even if the author believes it to be one. Utopian thought is imaginative, with its roots in literature, and the literary imagination is less concerned with achieving ends than with visualizing possibilities.

There are many reasons why an encouragement of utopian thinking would be of considerable benefit to us. An example would be an attempt to see what the social results of automation might be, or might be made to be; and surely some speculation along this line is almost essential to self-preservation. Again, the intellectual separation of the 'two cultures' is said to be a problem of our time, but this separation is inevitable, it is going steadily to increase, not decrease, and it cannot possibly be cured by having humanists read more popular science or scientists read more poetry. The real problem is not the humanist's ignorance of science or vice versa, but the ignorance of both humanist and scientist about the society of which they are both citizens. The quality of an intellectual's social imagination is the quality of his maturity as a thinker, whatever his brilliance in his own line. In the year that George Orwell published *1984*, two other books appeared in the utopian tradition, one by a humanist, Robert Graves's *Watch the North Wind Rise*, the other by a social scientist, B. F. Skinner's *Walden Two*. Neither book was intended very seriously: they reflect the current view that utopian thinking is not serious. It is all the more significant that both books show the infantilism of specialists who see society merely as an extension of their own speciality. The Graves book is about the revival of mother goddess cults in Crete, and its preoccupation with the more lugubrious superstitions of the past makes it almost a caricature of the pedantry of humanism. Skinner's book shows how to develop children's will-power by hanging lollipops around their necks and giving them rewards for not eating them: its Philistine vulgarity makes it a caricature of the pedantry of social science. The utopia, the effort at social imagination, is an area in which specialized disciplines can meet and interpenetrate with a mutual respect for each other, concerned with clarifying their common social context.

The word 'imaginative' refers to hypothetical constructions, like those of literature or mathematics. The word 'imaginary' refers to something that does not exist. Doubtless many writers of utopias think of their state as something that does not exist but which they wish did exist; hence their intention as writers is descriptive rather than constructive. But we cannot possibly discuss the utopia as a literary genre on this negatively ontological basis. We have to see it as a species of the constructive literary imagination, and we should expect to find that the more penetrating the utopian writer's mind is, the more clearly he understands that he is communicating a vision to his readers, not sharing a power or fantasy dream with them.

II

Plato's *Republic* begins with an argument between Socrates and Thrasymachus over the nature of justice. Thrasymachus attempts, not very successfully, to show that justice is a verbal and rhetorical conception used for certain social purposes, and that existentially there is no such thing as justice. He has to use words to say this, and the words he uses are derived from, and unconsciously accept the assumptions of, a discussion started by Socrates. So Socrates has little difficulty in demonstrating that in the verbal pattern Thrasymachus is employing justice has its normal place, associated with all other good and real things. Others in the group are not satisfied that an existential situation can be so easily refuted by an essentialist argument, and they attempt to restate Thrasymachus' position. Socrates' argument remains essential to the end, but it takes the form of another kind of verbal pattern, a descriptive model of a state in which justice is the existential principle. The question then arises: what relation has this model to existing society?

If what seems the obvious answer is the right one, Plato's imaginary Republic is the ideal society that we do not live in, but ought to be living in. Not many readers would so accept it, for Plato's state has in full measure the forbidding quality that we have noted as a characteristic of utopias. Surely most people today would see in its rigorous autocracy, its unscrupulous use of lies for propaganda, its ruthlessly censored art, and its subordination of all the creative and productive life of the state to a fanatical military caste, all the evils that we call totalitarian. Granted all the Greek fascination with the myth of Lycurgus, the fact that Sparta defeated Athens is hardly enough to make us want to adopt so many of the features of that hideous community.

Plato admits that dictatorial tyranny is very like his state-pattern entrusted to the wrong men. But to assume much of a difference between tyranny and Plato's state we should have to believe in the perfectibility of intellectuals, which neither history nor experience gives us much encouragement to do.

We notice, however, that as early as the Fifth Book Socrates has begun to deprecate the question of the practicability of establishing his Republic, on the ground that thought is one thing and action another. And as the argument goes on there is an increasing emphasis on the analogy of the just state to the wise man's mind. The hierarchy of philosopher, guard, and artisan in the just state corresponds to the hierarchy of reason, will, and appetite in the disciplined individual. And the disciplined individual is the only free individual. The free man is free because his chaotic and lustful desires are hunted down and exterminated, or else compelled to express themselves in ways prescribed by the dictatorship of his reason. He is free because a powerful will is ready to spring into action to help reason do whatever it sees fit, acting as a kind of thought police suppressing every impulse not directly related to its immediate interests. It is true that what frees the individual seems to enslave society, and that something goes all wrong with human freedom when we take an analogy between individual and social order literally. But Plato is really arguing from his social model to the individual, not from the individual to society. The censorship of Homer and the other poets, for example, illustrates how the wise man uses literature, what he accepts and rejects of it in forming his own beliefs, rather than what society ought to do to literature. At the end of the Ninth Book we reach what is the end of the *Republic* for our purposes, as the Tenth Book raises issues beyond our present scope. There it is made clear that the *Republic* exists in the present, not in the future. It is not a dream to be realized in practice; it is an informing power in the mind:

> I understand; you speak of that city of which we are the founders, and which exists in idea only; for I do not think that there is such an one anywhere on earth.
>
> In heaven, I replied, there is laid up a pattern of such a city, and he who desires may behold this, and beholding, govern himself accordingly.

But whether there really is or ever will be such an one is of no importance to him; for he will act according to the laws of that city and of no other.

(Jowett tr.)

In Christianity the two myths that polarize social thought, the contract and the utopia, the myth of origin and the myth of *telos*, are given in their purely mythical or undisplaced forms. The myth of contract becomes the myth of creation, and of placing man in the garden of Eden, the ensuing fall being the result of a breach of the contract. Instead of the utopia we have the City of God, a utopian metaphor most elaborately developed in St Augustine. To this city men, or some men, are admitted at the end of time, but of course human nature is entirely incapable of reaching it in its present state, much less of establishing it. Still, the attainment of the City of God in literature must be classified as a form of utopian fiction, its most famous literary treatment being the *Purgatorio* and *Paradiso* of Dante. The conception of the millennium, the Messianic kingdom to be established on earth, comes closer to the conventional idea of the utopia, but that again does not depend primarily on human effort.

The church, in this scheme of things, is not a utopian society, but it is a more highly ritualized community than ordinary society; and its relation to the latter has some analogies to the relation of Plato's Republic to the individual mind. That is, it acts as an informing power on society, drawing it closer to the pattern of the City of God. Most utopias are conceived as élite societies in which a small group is entrusted with essential responsibilities, and this élite is usually some analogy of a priesthood. For in Utopia, as in India, the priestly caste has reached the highest place. H. G. Wells divides society into the Poietic, or creative, the Kinetic, or executive, the Dull, and the Base. This reads like an uncharitable version of the four Indian castes – particularly uncharitable considering that the only essential doctrine in Wells's utopian religion is the rejection of original sin. Wells's writing in general illustrates the common principle that the belief that man is by nature good does not lead to a very good-natured view of man. In any case his 'samurai' belong to the first group, in spite of their warrior name. The utopias of science fiction are generally controlled by scientists, who, of course, are another form of priestly élite.

Another highly ritualized society, the monastic community, though not intended as a utopia, has some utopian characteristics. Its members spend their whole time within it; individual life takes its pattern from the community; certain activities of the civilized good life, farming, gardening, reclaiming land, copying manuscripts, teaching, form part of its structure. The influence of the monastic community on utopian thought has been enormous. It is strong in More's *Utopia*, and much stronger in Campanella's *City of the Sun*, which is more explicitly conceived on the analogy of the church and monastery. The conception of the ideal society as a secularized reversal of the monastery, the vows of poverty, chastity, and obedience transposed into economic security, monogamous marriage, and personal independence, appears in Rabelais's scheme for the Abbey of Thélème. Something like this reappears in many nineteenth-century utopias, not only the literary ones but in the more explicitly political schemes of St Simon, Fourier, and Comte, of whose writings it seems safe to say that they lack Rabelais's lightness of touch. The government of the monastery, with its mixture of the elective and the dictatorial principles, is still going strong as a social model in Carlyle's *Past and Present*. Utopian satire sometimes introduces celibate groups of fanatics by way of parody, as in *1984* and in Huxley's *Ape and Essence*.

It is obvious from what we have said that a Christian utopia, in the sense of an ideal state to be attained in human life, is impossible: if it were possible it would be the kingdom of heaven, and trying to realize it on earth would be the chief end of man. Hence More does not present his Utopia as a Christian state: it is a state, as we remarked earlier, in which the natural virtues are allowed to assume their natural forms. In that case, what is the point of the *Utopia*, which is certainly a Christian book? Some critics feel that More could have meant it only as a *jeu d'esprit* for an in-group of humanist intellectuals. But that conception makes it something more trivial than anything that More would write or Rabelais and Erasmus much appreciate. The second book of *Utopia* must have been intended quite as seriously as the trenchant social criticism of the first.

We note that the *Utopia*, again, takes the form of a dialogue between a first-person narrator and a guide. The guide is Hythloday, who has been to Utopia, and whose description of it takes up the second book. The narrator is More himself. In the first book the social attitudes of the two men are skilfully contrasted. More is a gradualist, a reformer; he feels that Hythloday should use his experience and knowledge in advising the princes of Europe on the principles of social justice. Hythloday has come back from Utopia a convinced Communist and a revolutionary. All Europe's misery, blundering, and hypocrisy spring from its attachment to private property: unless this is renounced nothing good can be done, and as this renunciation is unlikely he sees no hope for Europe. At the end More remarks that, although he himself has not been converted to Hythloday's all-out utopianism, there are many things in Utopia that he would hope for rather than expect to see in his own society. The implication seems clear that the ideal state to More, as to Plato, is not a future ideal but a hypothetical one, an informing power and not a goal of action. For More, as for Plato, Utopia is the kind of model of justice and common sense which, once established in the mind, clarifies its standards and values. It does not lead to a desire to abolish sixteenth-century Europe and replace it with Utopia, but it enables one to see Europe, and to work within it, more clearly. As H. G. Wells says of his Utopia, it is good discipline to enter it occasionally.

There is, however, an element of paradox in More's construct that is absent from Plato's. More's state is not eutopia, the good place, but utopia, nowhere. It is achieved by the natural virtues without revelation, and its eclectic state religion, its toleration (in certain circumstances) of suicide and divorce, its married priesthood, and its epicurean philosophy all mean that it is not, like the Republic, the invisible city whose laws More himself, or his readers, would continually and constantly obey. It has often been pointed out that More died a martyr to some very un-Utopian causes. The point of the paradox is something like this: Europe has revelation, but the natural basis of its society is an extremely rickety structure; and if Europe pretends to greater wisdom than Utopia it ought to have at least something of the Utopian solidity and consistency in the wisdom it shares with Utopia. This paradoxical argument in More reappears in Montaigne's essay on the cannibals, where it is demonstrated that cannibals have many virtues we have not, and if we disdain to be cannibals we should have at least something of those virtues. Similarly Gulliver returns from the society of rational horses to that of human beings feeling a passionate hatred not of the human race, as careless readers of Swift are apt to say, but of its pride, including its pride in not being horses.

In most utopias the state predominates over the individual: property is usually held in common and the characteristic features of individual life, leisure, privacy, and freedom of movement, are as a rule minimized. Most of this is, once more, simply the result of writing a utopia and accepting its conventions: the utopia is designed to describe a unified society, not individual varieties of existence. Still, the sense of the individual as submerged in a social mass is very strong. But as soon as we adopt the principle of *paradeigma* which Plato sets forth in his Ninth Book, the relation of society to individual is reversed. The ideal state now becomes an element in the liberal education of the individual free man, permitting him a greater liberty of mental perspective than he had before.

The Republic built up by Socrates and entered into by his hearers is derived from their ability to see society on two levels, a lower natural level and an upper ideal level. What gives them the ability to perceive this upper level is education. The vision of the *Republic* is inextricably bound up with a theory of education. The bodily senses perceive the 'actual' or objective state of things; the soul, through education, perceives the intelligible world. And though not all utopia-writers are Platonists, nearly all of them make their utopias depend on education for their permanent establishment. It seems clear that the literary convention of an ideal state is really a by-product of a systematic view of education. That is, education, considered as a unified view of reality, grasps society by its intelligible rather than its actual form, and the utopia is a projection of the ability to see society, not as an aggregate of buildings and bodies, but as a structure of arts and sciences. The thought suggests itself that the paralysis in utopian imagination we have mentioned in our society may be connected with a confusion about both the objectives and the inner structure of our educational system.

It is a theory of education, in any case, that connects a utopian myth with a myth of contract. This is abundantly clear in Plato and later in Rousseau, whose *Emile* is the utopian and educational counterpart of his *Contrat social*. In the sixteenth century, Machiavelli's *Prince*,

Castiglione's *Courtier* and More's *Utopia* form a well-unified Renaissance trilogy, the first two providing a contract myth and an educational structure respectively, based on the two central facts of Renaissance society, the prince and the courtier. Other Renaissance works, such as Spenser's *Faerie Queene*, set forth a social ideal and so belong peripherally to the utopian tradition, but are based on an educational myth rather than a utopian one. For Spenser, as he says in his letter to Raleigh, the Classical model was not Plato's *Republic* but Xenophon's *Cyropaedia*, the ideal education of the ideal prince.

Both the contract myth and the utopia myth, we said, derive from an analysis of the mythmaker's own society, or at least if they do not they have little social point. The overtones of the contract myth, unless the writer is much more complacent than anyone I have read, are tragic. All contract theories, whatever their origin or direction, have to account for the necessity of a social condition far below what one could imagine as a desirable, or even possible, ideal. The contract myth thus incorporates an element of what in the corresponding religious myth appears as the fall of man. Tragedy is a form which proceeds toward an epiphany of law, or at least of something inevitable and ineluctable; and a contract myth is by definition a legal one. The *telos* myth is comic in direction: it moves toward the actualizing of something better.

Any serious utopia has to assume some kind of contract theory as the complement of itself, if only to explain what is wrong with the state of things the utopia is going to improve. But the vision of something better has to appeal to some contract behind the contract, something which existing society has lost, forfeited, rejected, or violated, and which the utopia itself is to restore. The ideal or desirable quality in the utopia has to be *recognized*, that is, seen as manifesting something that the reader can understand as a latent or potential element in his own society and his own thinking. Thus Plato's *Republic* takes off from a rather gloomy and cynical contract theory, adapted apparently from the sophists by Glaucon and Adeimantus for the pleasure of hearing Socrates refute it. But the vision of justice which Socrates substitutes for it restores a state of things earlier than anything this contract theory refers to. This antecedent state is associated with the Golden Age in the *Laws* and with the story of Atlantis in the two sequels to the *Republic*, the *Timaeus* and the *Critias*. In the Christian myth, of course, the pre-contract ideal state is that of paradise. We have now to try to isolate the paradisal or Golden Age element in the utopian myth, the seed which it brings to fruition.

III

The utopian writer looks at the ritual habits of his own society and tries to see what society would be like if these ritual habits were made more consistent and more inclusive. But it is possible to think of a good many ritual habits as not so much inconsistent as unnecessary or superstitious. Some social habits express the needs of society; others express its anxieties. And although we tend to attach more emotional importance to our anxieties than to our needs or genuine beliefs, many anxieties are largely or entirely unreal. Plato's conception of the role of women in his community, whatever one thinks of it, was an extraordinary imaginative break from the anxieties of Athens with its almost Oriental seclusion of married women. Every utopian writer has to struggle with the anxieties suggested to him by his own society, trying to distinguish the moral from the conventional, what would be really disastrous from what merely inspires a vague feeling of panic, uneasiness, or ridicule.

So far we have been considering the typical utopia, the rational city or world-state, and the utopian satire which is a product of a specifically modern fear, the Frankenstein myth of the enslavement of man by his own technology and by his perverse desire to build himself an ingenious trap merely for the pleasure of getting caught in it. But another kind of utopian satire is obviously possible, one in which social rituals are seen from the outside, not to make them more consistent but simply to demonstrate their inconsistency, their hypocrisy, or their unreality. Satire of this kind holds up a mirror to society which distorts it, but distorts it consistently. An early example is Bishop Hall's *Mundus Alter et Idem* (1605), much ridiculed by Milton, but perhaps more of an influence on him than he was willing to admit. A more famous one is *Gulliver's Travels*, especially the first part, the voyage to Lilliput. The Lilliputian society is essentially the society of Swift's England, with its rituals looked at satirically. In the voyage to Brobdingnag the ridicule of the gigantic society is softened down, in the portrayal of the king even minimized, the satirical emphasis being thrown on Gulliver's account of his own society. The shift of emphasis indicates the close connection between this kind of satire and utopian fiction, the connection being much closer in the last part, where the rational society of the Houyhnhnms is contrasted with the Yahoos.

In Butler's *Erewhon* we have an early example of technological utopian satire: the Erewhonians are afraid of machines, and their philosophers have proved that machines will take over if not suppressed in time. We could trace this theme back to *Gulliver's Travels* itself, where the flying island of Laputa demonstrates some of the perils in combining human mechanical ingenuity with human folly and greed. But most of *Erewhon* adheres to the earlier tradition of the mirror-satire. The Erewhonians, for example, treat disease as a crime and crime as a disease, but they do so with exactly the same rationalizations that the Victorians use in enforcing the opposite procedure.

Following out this line of thought, perhaps what ails ordinary society is not the inconsistency but the multiplicity of its ritual habits. If so, then the real social ideal would be a greatly simplified society, and the quickest way to utopia would be through providing the absolute minimum of social structure and organization. This conception of the ideal society as simplified, even primitive, is of far more literary importance than the utopia itself, which in literature is a relatively minor genre never quite detached from political theory. For the simplified society is the basis of the pastoral convention, one of the central conventions of literature at every stage of its development.

In Christianity the city is the form of the myth of *telos*, the New Jerusalem that is the end of the human pilgrimage. But there is no city in the Christian, or Judaeo-Christian, myth of origin: that has only a garden, and the two progenitors of what was clearly intended to be a simple and patriarchal society. In the story which follows, the story of Cain and Abel, Abel is a shepherd and Cain a farmer whose descendants build cities and develop the arts. The murder of Abel appears to symbolize the blotting out of an idealized pastoral society by a more complex civilization. In Classical mythology the original society appears as the Golden Age, to which we have referred more than once, again a peaceful and primitive society without the complications of later ones. In both our main literary traditions, therefore, the tendency to see the ideal society in terms of a lost simple paradise has a ready origin.

In the Renaissance, when society was so strongly urban and centripetal, focused on the capital city and on the court in the centre of it, the pastoral established an alternative ideal which was not strictly utopian, and which we might distinguish by the term Arcadian. The characteristics of this ideal were simplicity and equality: it was a society of shepherds without distinction of class, engaged in a life that permitted the maximum of peace and of leisure. The arts appeared in this society spontaneously, as these shepherds were assumed to have natural musical and poetic gifts. In most utopias the relation of the sexes is hedged around with the strictest regulations, even taboos; in the pastoral, though the Courtly Love theme of frustrated devotion is prominent, it is assumed that making love is a major occupation, requiring much more time and attention than the sheep, and thus more important than the economic productivity of society.

The Arcadia has two ideal characteristics that the utopia hardly if ever has. In the first place, it puts an emphasis on the integration of man with his physical environment. The utopia is a city, and it expresses rather the human ascendancy over nature, the domination of the environment by abstract and conceptual mental patterns. In the pastoral, man is at peace with nature, which implies that he is also at peace with his own nature, the reasonable and the natural being associated. A pastoral society might become stupid or ignorant, but it could hardly go mad. In the second place, the pastoral, by simplifying human desires, throws more stress on the satisfaction of such desires as remain, especially, of course, sexual desire. Thus it can accommodate, as the typical utopia cannot, something of that outlawed and furtive social ideal known as the Land of Cockayne, the fairyland where all desires can be instantly gratified.

This last is an ideal half-way between the paradisal and the pastoral, and is seldom taken seriously. The reason is that it does not derive from an analysis of the writer's present society, but is primarily a dream or wish-fulfilment fantasy. In the fourteenth-century poem called *The Land of Cockayne*, roast geese walk around advertising their edibility: the line of descent to the shmoos of 'Li'l Abner' is clear enough. The same theme exists in a more reflective and sentimental form, where it tends to be an illusory or vanishing vision, often a childhood memory. This theme is common as a social cliché and in the popular literature which expresses social clichés: the cottage away from it all, happy days on the farm, the great open spaces of the west, and the like. A typical and well-known literary example is James Hilton's *Lost Horizon*, a neo-Kantian kingdom of both ends, so to speak, with its mixture of Oriental wisdom and American plumbing. But though the Land of Cockayne belongs to social mythology more than to the imaginative mythology of literature, it is a genuine ideal, and we shall meet other forms of it.

Spenser's *Faerie Queene*, already alluded to, is an example of the sort of courtier-literature common in the Renaissance, which had for its theme the idealizing of the court or the reigning monarch. This literature was not directly utopian, but its imaginative premisses were allied to the utopia. That is, it assumed that for mankind the state of nature is the state of society and of civilization and that, whether man is in his nature good or bad, life can be improved by improving his institutions. The pastoral, though of no importance politically, nevertheless kept open the suggestion that the state of nature and the state of society were different, perhaps opposing states. The pastoral was allied to the spirit of satire which, as in Erasmus's *Praise of Folly* and Cornelius Agrippa's *Vanity of the Arts and Sciences*, called the whole value of civilization into question.

In the eighteenth century these two attitudes both assumed political importance, and met in a head-on collision. The eighteenth-century descendant of the pastoral myth was the conception of the 'natural society' in Bolingbroke, and later in Rousseau. Here the natural state of man is thought of as distinct from and, so to speak, underlying the state of society. The state of nature is reasonable, the state of society full of anomalies and pointless inequalities. The conservative or traditional view opposed to this is, in Great Britain, most articulate in Burke, who, following Montesquieu, and in opposition to the principles of the French Revolution, asserted that the state of nature and the state of society were the same thing. The difference between the two views is primarily one of contract theory. For Burke the existing social order in any nation is that nation's real contract: for Rousseau it is essentially a corruption of its contract. The *telos* myths differ accordingly. For Burke improvement is possible only if we preserve the existing structure. This is not a utopian view, but it is not necessarily anti-utopian: it still keeps the utopian premiss of the improvability of institutions. For Rousseau the *telos* myth becomes revolutionary: only an overthrow of the existing order can manifest the natural and reasonable social order that it has disguised.

The fourth book of *Gulliver's Travels* is a pastoral satire representing the conservative opposition to the pastoral conception of a natural society. The Yahoo is the natural man, man as he would be if he were purely an animal, filthy, treacherous, and disgusting. Gulliver has more intelligence than the Yahoos, but what he learns from his sojourn with the Houyhnhnms is that his nature is essentially Yahoo nature. His intelligence, he discovers, is nothing he can take pride in, for human beings back home make 'no other use of reason than to improve and multiply those vices whereof their brethren in this country had only the share that nature allotted them'. The natural society, if it could be attained at all, could be attained only by some kind of animal like the Houyhnhnm, who possessed a genuine reason not needing the disciplines of state and church. The Houyhnhnms can live in a genuinely pastoral world; human beings have to put up with the curse of civilization.

The terms of this argument naturally changed after the Industrial Revolution, which introduced the conception of revolutionary process into society. This led to the present division of social attitudes mentioned above, between the Marxist utopia as distant end and the common American belief in the utopianizing tendency of the productive process, often taking the form of a belief that utopian standards of living can be reached in America alone. This belief, though rudely shaken by every disruptive historical event at least since the stock market crash of 1929, still inspires an obstinate and resilient confidence. The popular American view and the Communist one, superficially different as they are, have in common the assumption that to increase man's control over his environment is also to increase his control over his destiny. The refusal to accept this assumption is the principle of modern utopian satire.

Whatever utopian thought and imagination has survived this state of affairs in democratic literature has been much more affected by pastoral or Arcadian themes than by the utopian conception of the rational city. Both Plato and More lay stress on limiting the city-state to what would now be called an 'optimum' size. And almost anyone today, considering the problems of present-day society, would soon find himself saying 'too many people'. He could hardly visualize a utopia without assuming some disaster that would reduce the population – at least, those who did not survive might reasonably consider it a disaster. Thus Don Marquis, in *The Almost Perfect State*, speaks of a United States with a total population of five million. The assumption that a more desirable society must be a greatly simplified one marks the influence of the pastoral tradition.

We do find, in fact, a type of utopian satire based on the theme of cyclical return: contemporary civilization goes to pieces with an appalling crash, and life starts again under primitive conditions like those of some earlier period of history. The best story of this type I know is Richard Jeffries's *After London*, but the theme enters the Robert Graves book referred to earlier and is a common one in science fiction (for example, Walter Miller's *A Canticle for Leibowitz* and some of John Wyndham's stories, especially *Re-Birth*). And even in the nineteenth-century industrial utopias, with their clicking machinery and happy factory crowds and fast-talking interpreters, an occasional one, such as W. H. Hudson's *A Crystal Age*, takes a different tone, and reminds us that ideals of peace, dignity, and quiet are too important to be squeezed into a few intervals of bustling routine.

Of the famous utopias, the one which shows pastoral influence most consistently is William Morris's *News from Nowhere*. This work was, significantly, written as a reaction to Bellamy's *Looking Backward*, and, even more significantly, it scandalized the Communist associates of Morris's magazine, *The Commonweal*, in which it appeared. It was an attempt to visualize the ultimate utopian goal of Communism after the classless society had been reached, and the reader is not asked whether he thinks the social conception practicable, but simply whether or not he likes the picture. The picture is considerably more anarchist than Communist: the local community is the sole source of a completely decentralized authority, and the centralizing economic tendencies have disappeared along with the political ones. There is, in other words, a minimum of industrial and factory production. Morris started out, not with the Marxist question 'Who are the workers?' but with the more deeply revolutionary question 'What is work?' It is perhaps because Socrates never asked this question, but simply took the agenda of the work done in his own society as the basis of his definition of justice, that Plato's *Republic* is the authoritarian structure it is. Morris was influenced by Carlyle, who, though he tended to imply that all work was good, and unpleasant work particularly beneficial to the moral fibre, still did succeed, in *Sartor Resartus*, in distinguishing work from drudgery as well as from idleness. Ruskin, though also with a good deal of dithering, followed this up, and established the principle that Morris never departed from: work is creative act, the expression of what is creative in the worker. Any work that falls short of this is drudgery, and drudgery is exploitation, producing only the mechanical, the ugly, and the useless. We notice that in Morris we need an aesthetic, and hence imaginative, criterion to make any significant social judgement. According to Morris the pleasure in craftsmanship was what kept the medieval workers from revolution: this leads to the unexpected inference that, in an exploiting society, genuine work is the opiate of the people. In the society of the future, however, work has become a direct expression of the controlled energy of conscious life.

In Morris's state 'manufacture' has become hand work, and the basis of production is in what are still called the minor or lesser arts, those that are directly related to living conditions. In terms of the societies we know, Morris's ideal is closer to the Scandinavian way of life than to the Russian or the American. To make craftsmanship the basis of industry implies an immense simplification of human wants – this is the pastoral element in Morris's vision. The population has stabilized because people have stopped exploiting their sexual instincts as well as each other's work. England has become a green and pleasant land – something even seems to have happened to the climate – with a great deal of fresh air and exercise. The pastoral theme of the unity of man and physical nature is very prominent. Around the corner, perhaps, looms the spectre of endless picnics and jolly community gatherings and similar forms of extroverted cheer; but the sense of this is hardly oppressive even to a cynical reader. There is a certain anti-intellectual quality, perhaps, in the rather childlike inhabitants, their carefree ignorance of history and their neglect of the whole contemplative side of education. It is briefly suggested at the end that perhaps this society will need to mature sufficiently to take account of the more contemplative virtues if it is to escape the danger of losing its inheritance, as Adam did, through an uncritical perverseness of curiosity. In the meantime we are indebted to the most unreligious of the great English writers for one of the most convincing pictures of the state of innocence.

The social ideal is an essential and primary human ideal, but it is not the only one, nor does it necessarily include the others. Human fulfilment has a singular and a dual form as well as a plural one. Marvell's 'The Garden' speaks of an individual and solitary fulfilment in which one is detached from society and reaches a silent incorporation into nature which the poet symbolizes by the word 'green'. It is further suggested that this solitary apotheosis was the genuine paradisal state, before a blundering God created Eve and turned Eden into a suburban development of the City of God. Yet the creation of Eve, in itself, introduced a sexual fulfilment which, as long as man remained unfallen, had no objective beyond itself. Theoretically, the higher religions recognize and provide for these dreams of lost solitary and sexual paradises; in practice, being socially organized, they tend to be socially obsessed. Christianity is opposed to Communism and other forms of state-worship, but church and family are equally social units. Traditionally, Christianity frowns on the sexual relationship except as a means of producing the family, and on the solitary illumination except as a variety of socially accepted belief. If even religion tends to divide human impulses into the social and the anti-social, we can hardly expect more tolerance from ordinary society, which is a neurotically jealous mistress, suspicious and resentful of any sign of preferring a less gregarious experience.

Yet less socialized ideals continue to hover around the locked gates of their garden, trying to elude the angels of anxiety and censorship. Through the pastoral they achieve some imaginative expression, and it is largely its connection with the pastoral that makes Thoreau's *Walden* so central and so subversive a book in American culture. The theme of the sage who makes a voluntary break with society in order to discover his genuine self in a context of solitude and nature is common in the Orient and has been a major influence on the arts there, but it is rare in the West. Even Wordsworth, though he has much of the theory, speaks, at the opening of the *Prelude* and elsewhere, more as someone on sabbatical leave from society than as someone aloof from it. Thoreau achieves a genuine social detachment, and has the sensitive, loving kinship with nature that characterizes the pastoral at its best. What makes him relevant to a paper on utopias is the social criticism implied in his book. He sets out to show how little a man actually needs for the best life, best in the sense of providing for the greatest possible amount of physical and mental well-being. And while one may quarrel over the details of his experiment in economy, there is no doubt that he makes his main point.

Man obviously needs far less for the best life than he thinks he needs; and civilization as we know it is grounded on the technique of complicating wants. In fact, this technique is widely believed, in America, to be the American way of life par excellence. Thoreau says: 'The only true America is that country where you are at liberty to pursue such a mode of life as may enable you to do without these, and where the state does not endeavour to compel you to sustain the slavery, and war, and other superfluous expenses which directly or indirectly result from the use of such things.' The pastoral revolutionary tradition is still at work in this remark, still pointing to the natural and reasonable society buried beneath the false one. For Thoreau the place of human identity is not the city or even the community, but the home. In constructing his cabin he remarks: 'It would be worth the while to build still more deliberately than I did, considering, for instance, what foundation a door, a window, a cellar, a garret, have in the nature of man.' Whatever the standards and values are that make a social ideal better than the reality, they cannot appear unless the *essence* of society has been separated from non-essentials. It is its feeling for what is socially essential that makes the pastoral convention central to literature, and no book has expressed this feeling more uncompromisingly than *Walden*.

Walden devotes itself to the theme of individual fulfilment: its social criticism is implicit only and the complications in human existence caused by the sexual instinct are not dealt with at all. The attempt to see the sexual relationship as something in itself, and not merely as a kind of social relationship, is something that gives a strongly pastoral quality to the work of D. H. Lawrence. For him the sexual relation is natural in the sense that it has its closest and most immediate affinities with the physical environment, the world of animals and plants and walks in the country and sunshine and rain. The idyllic sense of this world as helping to protect and insulate true love from the noisy city-world of disembodied consciousness runs through all Lawrence's work from the early *White Peacock* to the late *Lady Chatterley's Lover*. People complain, Lawrence says, that he wants them to be 'savages', but the gentian flowering on its coarse stem is not savage. Lawrence has been a major influence on the social attitude which has grown up in the United States since the Second World War, and which may be described as a development of Freudianism. Like the Marxism of which it is, to some extent, a democratic counterpart, it is a revolutionary attitude, but unlike Marxism it imposes no specific social obligations on the person who holds it. The enemy is still the bourgeois, not the bourgeois as capitalist, but the bourgeois as 'square', as the representative of repressive morality. Freud himself had little hope that society would ever cease to be a repressive anxiety-structure, but some of the most uninhibited utopian thinking today comes from such Freudians as Norman O. Brown (*Life Against Death*) and Herbert Marcuse (*Eros and Civilization*), who urge us at least to consider the possibility of a non-repressive society.

In literature, some manifestations of this quasi-Freudian movement, like the beatniks, are rigidly conventionalized social ones, but what is relevant to us at present is rather the literature of protest, the theme of vagabondage and the picaresque in Kerouac and Henry Miller, the cult of violence in Mailer, the exploration of drugs and perversions, the struggle for a direct asocial experience which is apparently what the interest in Zen Buddhism symbolizes. The motto of all this is that of the starling in Sterne: 'I can't get out': it expresses the claustrophobia of individual and sexual impulses imprisoned by the alien social consciousness that has created civilization. This sounds as though the contemporary literature of protest was intensely anti-utopian, and so in many respects it is. It is, however, for the most part a militant or 'Luddite' pastoralism, trying to break the hold of a way of life which has replaced the perspective of the human body with the perspective of its mechanical extensions, the extensions of transportation and social planning and advertising which are now turning on the body and strangling it as the serpents did Laocoon.

The great classical utopias derived their form from city-states, and, though imaginary, were thought of as being, like the city-states, exactly locatable in space. Modern utopias derive their form from a uniform pattern of civilization spread over the whole globe, and so are thought of as world-states, taking up all the available space. It is clear that if there is to be any revival of utopian imagination in the near future, it cannot return to the old-style spatial utopias. New utopias would have to derive their form from the shifting and dissolving movement of society that is gradually replacing the fixed locations of life. They would not be rational cities evolved by a philosopher's dialectic: they would be rooted in the body as well as in the mind, in the unconscious as well as the conscious, in forests and deserts as well as in highways and buildings, in bed as well as in the symposium. Do you not agree, asks Socrates in the *Republic*, that the worst of men is the man who expresses in waking reality the character of man in his dreams? But modern utopias will have to pay some attention to the lawless and violent lusts of the dreamer, for their foundations will still be in dreamland. A fixed location in space is 'there', and 'there' is the only answer to the spatial question 'where?' Utopia, in fact and in etymology, is not a place; and when the society it seeks to transcend is everywhere, it can only fit into what is left, the invisible non-spatial point in the centre of space. The question 'Where is utopia?' is the same as the question 'Where is nowhere?' and the only answer to that question is 'Here'.

9 THE REVELATION TO EVE

Dreams are of great importance in the Classical epics, where they may be true or deceitful, and may descend through the gate of ivory or of horn. An epic designed to justify the ways of God to men would have to be especially careful in its treatment of dreams: in Homer Zeus himself may send a deceiving dream as well as a true one, but in *Paradise Lost* the two gates must be as wide apart as the gates of heaven and hell themselves.

The creation of Adam is associated with two dreams: first a dream of the trees of Paradise, then a dream of Eve. In both cases Adam awakes to find the dream true. Keats was later to see in these dreams a symbol of the imagination of the poet, which tries to realize a world that others can understand and live in, and is therefore a fully creative and not merely a subjective or fantastic power. Milton's meaning is different but not wholly dissimilar. Adam's dreams are prompted by appetite in its two main forms of food and sexual love. In the unfallen state appetite is good, being a part of God's creation, and what Adam calls 'mimic Fancy' is aligned with reason. What Adam wants, in short, is what Adam has: desire in the unfallen state is completely satisfied by the appropriate object. Eve's dreams, like Adam's, are very close to her waking experience, and help to bind together her sense of time in a world too happy to have much history: 'Works of day pass't, or morrows next designe' (V, 33). The Satan-inspired dream of Eve, on the other hand, uses the kind of symbolism that we now think of as typical of a dream. Because she is unfallen, such a dream can only come from outside her, though, like Bunyan's Christian in the Valley of the Shadow, she is troubled to think that it may have proceeded from her own mind. She is right by anticipation: since the fall, inner desires which are excessive by nature and can never be satisfied have taken root in us, and

produce the wish-fulfilment fantasies of lust and greed, which are the
two appetites in their fallen form. They are the reflection in us of what
Satan describes as (IV, 509-11)

> fierce desire,
> Among our other torments not the least.
> Still unfulfilld.

After the fall, Adam, fully awake and conscious, receives from
Michael his second revelation, the tremendous Biblical vision of the
future, stretching from Cain to the Last Judgement, with which the
great poem reaches its close. From the previous revelation of Raphael
Eve had absented herself, in order to hear it later from Adam alone. But
now Adam is less trustworthy as a medium of revelation: while he
wakes to hear the revelation, Eve is put to sleep, as Adam was when
she was created, the little symmetry in the design being called to our
attention (XI, 369). Eve is given dreams which are inspired this time
by God instead of by Satan, and which constitute a revelation that is
distinctively hers. We are told very little about these dreams, except
that their central subject is the defeat of the serpent by a redeemer descended from her.

The famous, or notorious, line in *Paradise Lost* (IV, 299) about the
relations of Adam and Eve, 'Hee for God only, shee for God in him',
illustrates a central problem in reading the poem. This is the problem
of the language of analogy. The statement is made of the unfallen
Adam and Eve, and so is not literally true of men and women as we
know them. Fallen life shows an analogy to unfallen life, and the analogy accounts for the social supremacy of men over women that we
find assumed in the Bible, from the account of the fall itself in Genesis
(Gen. 3:16; *PL*, X, 195-6) to St Paul's directives for the primitive
church. But obviously no fallen son of Adam can represent God in the
way that the unfallen Adam could. The example of the unfallen Adam
merely puts a heavier responsibility on his male descendants to be
worthy of what ought to be a purely spiritual authority. Similarly, monogamous marriage arises in the world as a fallen analogy of the divinely
sanctioned union of Adam and Eve, and a prejudice in favour of the
permanence of all marriages is therefore justifiable. But, for Milton, to
prohibit divorce altogether is to ignore the fact that the relation of

ordinary to paradisal marriage is analogous only, and that the realities of unfallen life are ideals, not always attainable ones, in this world. The analogy also extends in the other direction. The relation of man to woman symbolizes, or dramatizes, the relation of creator to creature. God speaks of himself as male, and his revelation uses the terms Father and Son, although in most contexts, apart from the Incarnation, we can hardly ascribe literal sex to the Deity. We think of God as male primarily because he is the Creator: we think of Nature as female, not merely as a mother from whose body we are born, but as a creature of God. Human souls, including male souls, are symbolically female when thought of as creatures: the redeemed souls of men and women, who are aware of their status as creatures, make up a female church or Bride of Christ. Among spirits, whether fallen or unfallen, sex is not functional: spirits can be of what sex they please (I, 423-4). But in human life the sexes represent the polarizing of man's existence between God and Nature, creation and creature. Man is set above woman to remind him of the rightful places that God and Nature respectively should hold in his life. Adam's substance, so to speak, is in the God who created him: in himself, apart from God, he is only the shadow of himself. Similarly Eve's substance is in Adam, as her formation from his rib indicates.

Being cut off or 'alienated' (IX, 9) from God puts one into the state of pride. This state is subjective, and needs an object, which is normally an idol, idolatry being the worshipping of something created instead of the creator. For Adam, once turned away from God, the most immediate idol is the fallen Eve, the fairest of creatures, and for his descendants idolatry becomes a debased form of woman-worship, or taking woman, along with the Mother Nature to which in this context she belongs, to be numinous instead of a creation ranking below man on the chain of being. For Eve, on the other hand, the root of idolatry is self-worship. There is nothing wrong with her admiring her own image in the water, but the episode suggests, again by anticipation, the story of Narcissus, who fell in love with his image – that is, exchanged his real or divine self for his own subjective shadow. The direction of the fallen Narcissus is also Satan's, as his 'daughter' Sin indicates when she says to him (II, 764-5):

> Thy self in me thy perfect image viewing,
> Becam'st enamourd.

But the fact that man is capable of idolatry is connected with the peculiar role of sex in human life. The devils are not, strictly speaking, idolators: they are atheists or fatalists. They assert that they were not created by God, and originated directly from nature, but they have no occasion to associate nature with anything feminine.

In Classical mythology there is a pervasive sexual symbolism which points to a blurred memory on the part of fallen man of the relation of God to his creation. The chief of gods in this mythology is a male sky-god, Jupiter, who, where the context is appropriate, may be spoken of by a Christian poet in terms recalling the Christian God without violation of decorum. But the fact that Jupiter has a consort who is also his sister – *et soror et coniunx*, as Virgil says – shows that the original Jupiter is, like Juno, a deified spirit of nature, not a creator qualitatively distinct from his creation. Classical myth, vaguely aware that a spirit of nature, when deified, is a devil, also said that his rule was a usurpation, and that before him there was a golden age of Saturn and Rhea, when, as Milton ingeniously suggests in *Il Penseroso* (23–6), incestuous unions might have been innocent. The myth of the golden age takes us one step nearer to the authentic revelation of the original state of man. One very brief passage in the *Argonautica* picked up by Milton (X, 580–4) hints that Saturn and Rhea in their turn succeeded a still more primitive pair, Ophion and Eurynome. The word Ophion, serpent, indicates that we here are very close to a genuine memory of the real beginnings of idolatry. Eurynome means wide-ruling: Milton's gloss, 'the wide-Encroaching Eve perhaps', is somewhat puzzling, but it seems to say that the memory of the fallen Eve is the source, for the heathen, of the myth of a great mother-goddess from whom all deified principles in nature have ultimately descended, even though their fathers are the fallen angels.

Classical mythology does not clearly separate creator and creature, but it does contain a sexual symbolism which, as we should expect, puts the male above and the female below. Milton himself uses this symbolism in both Classical and Christian contexts. The male principle in nature is associated with the sky, the sun, the wind, or the rain. The specifically female part of nature is the earth, and the imagery of caves, labyrinths, and waters issuing from underground recall the process of birth from a womb. Trees and shady spots generally, and more particularly flowers, are also feminine, and so is the moon, the lowest heavenly body. The imagery of the labyrinth or maze is associated sometimes with meandering rivers, sometimes with a tangle of shrubs or trees. A forest so dense that the (male) sky is shut out, as in the 'branching elm star-proof' of *Arcades*, may be a symbol of natural virginity, the abode of Diana. The sexual union of sun and earth is celebrated with great exuberance and power in Milton's *Fifth Elegy*, on the coming of spring. In *Paradise Lost* Adam smiles on Eve (IV, 499–501):

> as Jupiter
> On *Juno* smiles, when he impregns the Clouds
> That shed *May* Flowers,

an allusion which places Jupiter and Juno definitely in the category of deified nature-spirits. Similarly Adam's voice calls to Eve 'Milde, as when *Zephyrus* on *Flora* breathes' (V, 16).

In Biblical symbolism, too, the earth or fertile land is often in a feminine relation to its ruler or owner, representing what Milton calls 'the holy covenant of union and marriage between the king and his realm', meaning in this context Charles I, though he was later to ridicule the same king for thinking of his parliament as 'but a female'. The land of Israel is called 'married' (Beulah) by Isaiah, and the 'black but comely' bride of the Song of Songs is also associated with the fertile land ruled by King Solomon. When Adam awakens Eve in Book V he addresses her in language prefiguring (or, for the reader, recalling) the aubade of the bride in the Song of Songs. It is also the Song of Songs that introduces the image of the female body as an enclosed garden (*hortus conclusus*) which had an extensive religious and poetic later life. We are not surprised to find the garden of Eden in *Paradise Lost* described in feminine imagery, with its river rising from underground and running 'With mazie error under pendent shades' (IV, 39), and where a vine 'gently creeps', in an image later associated with Eve's hair. The newly created Eve awakens 'Under a shade (i.e. tree) of flours', and the first thing she sees is her reflection in a lake 'Of waters issu'd from a Cave' (IV, 450–4). The contrast with Adam awakening in the sunlight and inspecting first of all his own body is clearly deliberate.

The fallen forms of the two human appetites are lust and greed: in a more demonic context they become force and fraud, the two weapons of

Satan. Satan finds that he is unable to destroy the world by force. God displays the scales, the symbol of created order in a significant place in the sky, between the Virgin of divine justice and the scorpion, and Satan, then as later in *Paradise Regained* able to read the future in the 'Starry Rubric' (*PR*, IV, 393), does not try to fight. The scales prefigure the later rainbow, which guarantees the permanence of the natural order after the deluge. Satan's only effective weapon, then, is fraud, and fraud creates an evil analogy to the good. The greatest good for Eve is knowledge of God through Adam: Satan presents her with a dream of attaining knowledge, and eventually god-head, for herself, under the image of suddenly rising from the earth into the air, where she is just as suddenly abandoned. The sexual sensations of flying and falling, and the orgasm rhythm of the whole dream, show that Satan's symbolism is as eloquent as his rhetoric. This demonic surge upward to the sky suggests two other images: the Gunpowder Plot and the struggles of rebellious Titans bound under exploding volcanoes, both of which enter the imagery of *Paradise Lost*. We have also the Limbo of Vanities, the upward sweep of those who try to take heaven by force or fraud. After the flood, when man settles down systematically to idolatry, a more solid image of demonic pride, the Tower of Babel, is set up.

Eve rises into the air, where she sees 'The Earth outstretcht immense, a prospect wide' (V, 88). The air is, later, Satan's headquarters, as Satan appears to realize already ('in the air, as we,' he says). From there, it is further suggested, she may rise to heaven if she likes, and see what the gods are doing. She seems to be symbolically at the point, usually represented by a mountain-top under the moon, which is the boundary between terrestrial and celestial worlds in Dante's *Purgatorio*, Spenser's *Mutabilitie Cantoes*, several poems of Yeats, and elsewhere, and would also have been the top of the Tower of Babel if that point had ever been reached. The imagery of Eve's dream of ascent is echoed in the later elevation of Adam, who is taken to a hill (XI, 378–80):

> Of Paradise the highest, from whose top
> The Hemisphere of Earth in cleerest ken
> Stretched out to amplest reach of prospect lay

where Michael's vision is displayed to him. Eve at this time is placed on a much lower level to receive her dreams – another example of the curious antithetical symmetry which pervades the poem. The elevation of Adam in its turn is explicitly compared to Satan's placing of Christ on a mountain-top during the temptation (though in *Paradise Regained* the climactic temptation was shifted to the pinnacle of the temple, following Luke's order). We can understand the link between Satan's temptation of Eve and his temptation of Christ, but why should God's purely benevolent design of imparting prophetic knowledge to Adam be included in the same complex of imagery?

The reason is that Satan is not the only one who can construct analogies. God constantly frustrates Satan by turning to good what Satan intended to be evil. Adam's new knowledge of good and evil, 'That is to say, of knowing good by evil', is placed in its proper context of the revelation of God to man which is later recorded in the Bible. Even outside Christianity the same principle operates. The word 'fall' is a spatial metaphor: we are now 'down', and any effort to better ourselves must take us 'up'. Leaving Christianity out of account for the moment, there are both good and bad men in the world; both wish to go 'up', and both have to start from the same point. The bad man recognizes no God except what he considers to be his own good, and his life is a structure of pride like the Tower of Babel. The good man – let us say a virtuous heathen – recognizes the existence of a good that is not himself, and attempts to seek for it. One conspicuous result of such imaginative virtue is the structure of Classical poetry and philosophy, a natural and reasonable human analogy of revelation – not itself revelation, of course, or possessing any final authority, but an impressive monument, none the less, of the wisdom which still remains implanted by God in the human mind. This structure is a kind of virtuous Tower of Babel: there is a considerable confusion of tongues in it, but it represents man dreaming of his Creator, and following the impulse to return to his Creator which is an original part of his nature. We may call it the anabasis of Eros. Love awakes in the soul, is attracted first by objects of sense, and then by more abstract and conceptual elements until it begins to draw nearer to God. Once Christianity appears in the world, this analogical structure of love is not abolished but becomes a supplement to its revelation. As such it forms the basis for the imagery of a good deal of Milton's own poetry, including the bulk of his earlier poetry. A pedagogical version of it is the model for Milton's ideal curriculum of education.

The lower part of this analogical structure is composed of Classical mythology. Classical myths, the fables of the heathen, are almost literally dreams, blurred and distorted versions, created partly by memory and partly by fancy, of what the Bible presents, in Milton's view, so much more simply and plainly. They are dreams of man as a child of Eve rather than of Adam, and are dominated by female images and personalities. Mother Nature, and more particularly Mother Earth, appear as the great *diva triformis*, the goddess of the moon, the forest, and the lower world, all symbolically female regions, or as Venus, the goddess of sexual love who personates the 'God' (X, 145) that Eve became to Adam at the moment of his fall. Venus has two male figures subordinated to her, Eros and Adonis, the gods of love and death, the poles of Mother Nature's cycle. The Spenserian image of the Gardens of Adonis, with Venus presiding over her wounded lover, appears at the end of *Comus*, a kind of erotic Pietà, as Venus with the infant God of Love is a kind of erotic Nativity. The dying-god flowers, the anemone and the hyacinth particularly, appear in the Latin elegies, and again in *Naturam non pati senium*, as ornaments of the Earth. Tammuz (Adonis) himself, in both the *Nativity Ode* and *Paradise Lost*, is introduced as the object of a female cult. The image of a mother hiding or shrouding a male child, as the Earth hides the seeds of new life, is associated with the Garden of Eden, with the references to Amalthea hiding her 'florid son' Dionysus, and to the Abyssinian princes in their prison-Paradise (IV, 275–80). The female images of labyrinth, cave, flowers, shade, thicket, and moonlit night partake of the darkness, mystery, lost direction, and concealment characteristic of religions of nature without the daylight of revelation.

It is within this shrouding and enclosing female Nature that the imagination of the poet awakens. In *Ad patrem* Milton speaks of his poetry as dreams in a secluded cave. The poet at this stage is psychologically close to the lover, and what he loves, at first, is simply the senuous beauty and delight of nature in general, like the narrator of the First and Seventh Elegies admiring all the pretty girls he sees on the streets. The minor poet may remain at this stage of uncommitted, or temporarily committed, attraction, sporting with Amaryllis in the shade or with the tangles of Neaera's hair – again we notice the thematic feminine words 'shade' and 'tangles'. If the poet-lover becomes more serious he may go in either a right or a wrong direction. The wrong direction is that of the courtly love convention of unquestioning obedience to a mistress and the acceptance of the frustration that her whims and coyness may cause. Milton shows a consistent dislike of this convention and a reluctance to write within it: for him it is the purest expression of 'man's effeminate slackness' (XI, 634) which allows a woman, and hence the created nature which she represents, to have rule over him. The right direction, of course, is marriage, the wedded love which in *Paradise Lost* is contrasted with the frustration of 'the starved lover' and the jealousy which is 'the injured lover's hell' (IV, 769; V, 450). This is a rational state in which the man is normally the superior, and its prototype in Classical mythology is the union of love and the soul represented by the Cupid and Psyche story in Apuleius.

It is conventional in courtly love poetry for the poet to abandon sensuous love at a certain point and turn to ideal, philosophical, or religious forms of love. Milton is unusual, however, in the promptness with which he makes the break. For him, as man continues to ascend the scale of his own nature, the Adam within him awakes, and progressively dominates the element of Eve. Man's attitude to the world around him then becomes less sensuous and more rational. He begins to think of nature less as a mother or mistress and more as an intelligently designed and created order. Nature is coming to represent less herself and more the wisdom of God which the virtuous man is seeking. On the upper levels of natural religion, one tends to become a Platonist, thinking in terms of a lower world of the body and a higher world of the soul, which may become released from the lower world as from a prison. In Milton's earlier poems we meet flights in the air which may be purely demonic like Eve's dream, as notably in *In quintum Novembris*; or the symbolism may be that of the soul escaping from the body and seeking its natural element in a higher world, as in the elegy on the Bishop of Ely.

The lower part of the analogy of Eros is the world of sense, where nature, the objective world, appears mainly in feminine images to the perceiver. There are thus two levels of nature, though there are also different ways of conceiving these two levels. One way is that of the simple physical contrast of winter and summer. Nature in this context exists as a cyclical movement between life and death. The earth rises to pour out her treasures of life in the spring as the sun awakens her, and sinks back to sleep in the winter. The image of Proserpine, spending half the year below the ground with her secret lover, and rising above the ground for the other half, appears in *Paradise Lost* as a poignant anticipation of Eve, driven from her natural habitat of Eden to the cursed wilderness below. Arethusa, the nymph of the underground river who rises with her lover Alpheus in Proserpine's land of Sicily, is a similar image, appearing in both *Arcades* and *Lycidas*. In the *Nativity Ode* Nature has stopped her sexual activities partly out of respect for her Creator and partly because it is too cold, or rather because the sun is, and reposes in a sterility which assumes innocence.

These two levels of nature modulate into a more conceptual relation in *Paradise Lost* as a lower level of chaos or the abyss, 'The womb of Nature, and perhaps her grave' (II, 911), and an upper level of cosmos or creation proper, which comes into being after the abyss has been made pregnant by a male Spirit of God, who in natural imagery would be associated with birds or the wind. The difference in this perception of the two levels of nature is connected with the difference between two views of death. Sensibly and objectively, death is annihilation, a return to the underworld of chaos; rationally, it is the separation from the sensible body that enables one's immortal soul to live in the world appropriate to it.

As we rise to a still more penetrating vision of nature, its two levels take on the Platonic aspect just mentioned. Here we have a lower physical and sensible aspect and a higher intellectual one: nature as attractive object and nature as designed object or creature. The imagery of these two levels might be called the 'allegro' and the 'penseroso' imagery. The former is that of the earthly Paradise, as expressed in the fables of the Elysian fields and the gardens of the Hesperides; the latter is that of the music of the spheres, the sense of harmonious design that conveys to us the intuition that nature is not just there, as a mother is just there to a small child, but has been intelligently and purposefully put there by a power superior to her.

The poet in nature is thus placed in a far more comprehensive situation than singing the praises of pretty girls would ever reveal to him. Even in his most sensuous poetry, the poet feels links drawing him, not merely to nature, but to the hidden powers of nature, to whatever it is that can 'keep unsteady nature to her law', in the words of *Arcades*. In the poem to Salzilli, Milton speaks of the poet's song as having the power to prevent floods: this is the image of the poet as a benevolent magician controlling nature by the 'sweet compulsion' of his song, of which the archetype is Orpheus. This image frequently appears in Shakespeare, especially in *A Midsummer Night's Dream* and *The Tempest*, which one suspects were the favourite plays of L'Allegro. In these two comedies the spirits of the elements represent powers of nature which are linked to human activity. Milton does not, like the later Romantics, make much of the metaphor of the poet as 'creator', participating in the creative activity of God by producing poems, but he could certainly have understood what Coleridge meant by calling the poet a tamer of chaos. The poet identifies himself with the created order, with the law of unsteady nature against the annihilation into which by herself nature would plunge. The Salzilli image, with its affinities to magic and the figure of Orpheus, is thus connected with the imagery of the permanence of the created order which was reaffirmed after the flood, and confirmed by the emblem of the rainbow.

The poet, if he is following rightly his innate impulse to rise from nature to God, will not look in nature for anything numinous: the so-called gods of nature are devils. The elemental spirit, like Shakespeare's Puck or Ariel, is a more accurate image because such a spirit is, even when mischievous or unwilling, amenable to rational control. The Christian poet finds his identity with nature, not by looking for gods in it, but through a feeling of protection and security in nature which is ultimately a sense of the providence of God as revealed through nature. The symbol of this hidden beneficent design is the Genius, whether of the wood, as in *Arcades*, or of the shore, as in *Lycidas*. The Attendant Spirit and Sabrina in *Comus* are elemental spirits who take on this role of good Genius or guiding daimon in the lower world. The image of the Genius is Virgilian, but Milton indicates a larger background for it in the *Apology for Smectymnuus* when he speaks of 'having read of heathen Philosophers, some to have taught, that whosoever would but use his eare to listen, might hear the voice of his guiding *Genius* ever before him, calling, and as it were pointing to that way which is his part to follow' (*Prose Works*, I, 904). The Lady's 'Echo' song in *Comus* helps to bring out this identity of human and physical nature as common creatures of God.

The poet's art is a musical one, in the Platonic sense: verse is closely allied to voice, and poems are generally described in musical metaphors as sung or played on a reed. The music that we know is a subordinate art to the verbal music of poetry, as Milton indicates in a parenthesis in *Paradise Lost*: 'For Eloquence the Soul, Song charms the Sense' (II, 556). The curious context of this remark – he is speaking of the arts of the devils in hell – reminds us that the analogy of Eros is, outside Christianity, pervaded by demonic inspiration, and rooted in it. The greater human art is, however, the more obviously it becomes the praise of God, and as praise of God it forms a part of the response to the Creator by the creature which it what is meant, symbolically, by 'harmony'. Harmony includes both the music of the spheres in nature and 'That undisturbed song of pure consent' in heaven referred to in *At a Solemn Music*.

As the poet gains in the understanding of the meaning of his own art, he realizes that his art is on the side, not merely of order as against chaos, but of life as against death. The supreme effort of Orpheus as poet was not to charm the trees, but to raise Eurydice from the lower world, his failure representing the inadequacy of unaided human art (cf. III, 17 ff.). Prospero in Shakespeare claims that his magic was able to raise the dead, and the poet's music is at least 'consent' with a life-giving power: 'Dead things with inbreathed sense able to pierce.' The metaphors here extend into medicine: in the Shakespearean romance of *Pericles* a doctor raises the dead (or what amounts to that) by music, and Asclepius as well as Orpheus haunts Milton's Latin elegies (especially, of course, the one on the death of the Vice-Chancellor, who was a doctor). In the *Apology for Smectymnuus*, again, Milton speaks of what Comus carries in his glass as 'a thick intoxicating potion, which a certain Sorceresse, the abuser of loves name, carries about' (*Prose Works*, I, 892). The antidote for this, a healing drug or herb which leads one to knowledge and virtue, is mentioned in the *Second Elegy* and enters *Comus* as the mysterious 'haemony', which is compared to the Homeric moly. The Biblical archetypes of the narcotic potion and haemony are, of course, the fruits of the trees of knowledge and life respectively.

If we may associate the Attendant Spirit with the musician Henry Lawes, it may be reasonable to associate his shepherd friend with the poet Milton, and see in this haemony something closely connected with the poet's art. Haemony is a dark inconspicuous plant which bears a flower in 'another country' (*Comus* 630–2), and in *Lycidas* the image of a plant that does not grow here but bears its flower in another world is associated specifically with the poet's desire for fame. It is explained in *Lycidas* that fame, the love of which is an impetus powerful enough to make a poet 'scorn delights and live laborious days', has nothing to do with Virgil's *fama* or rumour, but is a secular counterpart of what in Christian revelation is the hope of immortality. In *Paradise Lost* this image of the exotic flower appears as the amaranth (III, 353), which represents the genuine form of immortality, and originally bloomed beside the Tree of Life.

In writing within the analogy of Eros, the poet is elaborating and articulating a dream of man which is neither the dream that Satan gave Eve nor the dream that God gave her later, but something in between: a dream about God based on the fallen knowledge of good and evil, in which, though the knowledge of evil may be primary, there is a great deal of good, and in the good a great deal of genuine pleasure. The pleasure is at its most eloquent, of course, in *L'Allegro* and *Il Penseroso*. The tone of *L'Allegro* is pastoral, the pastoral being the expression of the heightened pleasure that comes from simplifying one's wants and moderating one's desires, so that lust and greed subside into something more like their proper forms, 'unreprovèd pleasures free'. As night falls we encounter an expected series of images: elemental spirits recalling Puck and Queen Mab; Hymen, the spirit of wedded love; an erotic (Lydian) music expressly described as a maze or labyrinth, and finally an Elysian world. This is a world of (129–30)

> Such sights as youthful Poets dream
> On Summer eeves by haunted stream.

The word 'haunted', in a context like this, has usually in it a sense of the gentler presences that impel us to associate Nature with feminine pronouns.

The imagery of *Il Penseroso* is even more explicitly feminine, from the 'secret shades' where the goddess of Melancholy is born, to the moon wandering in the maze of the sky. Here also the poet is a Platonist, speculating about the world inhabited by the soul when freed from the body, and about the spirits (95–6)

> Whose power hath a true consent
> With Planet or with Element.

'Consent' is again the musical metaphor, linked to the music sent by the 'Genius of the wood' to the poet hiding from 'day's garish eye' and sleeping in the lap of nature. The analogy of Eros stretches (at least in the poetic convention assumed) far back beyond Plato to the ancient teaching of the 'thrice great Hermes', and continues through the magical imagery of medieval and Renaissance romance – the modern reader can see it continuing in Shelley and Yeats. Religious images also form a part of the 'penseroso' dream: we notice, first, that they are images of 'high church' practice – cloisters, stained glass, organ music, Gothic architecture – and, secondly, that they are appreciated on purely aesthetic grounds. The Nonconformist poet sees these tendencies in Christianity as a part of the analogy of Eros, to be enjoyed and appreciated in some contexts and condemned in others. Melancholy herself is a nun, not a Christian nun, of course, but a vestal virgin, being a daughter of Vesta.

Both she and Mirth take their poet to the upper limits of their dreaming analogy world. Mirth leads him to the earthly Paradise, an Elysium where Orpheus lies dreaming, and where he might be awakened, by the music the poet hears, to complete the redemption of Eurydice. The poem of melancholy, mentioning Orpheus in passing, leads to a hermitage where the poet learns the secrets of the inner harmony of nature, and comes 'To something like Prophetic strain' (174) – that is, to an aesthetic analogy of religious experience. In these poems we are in substantially the same cosmos that the poet outlines in the *Vacation Exercise* poem, where, in language oddly anticipating Eve's first dream, he can 'look in' to the world of the gods, and comes to rest in the palace of Alcinous, whose gardens are another type of the earthly Paradise, and where music or poetry once again is an erotic maze of 'willing chains and sweet captivitie' (35–52).

Of course, one does not move upward effortlessly in this ascent of Eros. Every man, within Christianity or outside it, is faced in the world with a moral challenge. He cannot simply live on the unmoral level of plants and animals: he must either go downwards to sin or upwards to virtue. Mother Nature must ultimately become either the evil enchantress Circe or Hecate, or turn into some kind of *ewig-weibliche* inspiration like the Muse Urania or the Queen in *Arcades*. The first line of defence against Circe is reason, for the alliance of nature and reason is the key to the fact that Nature is a designed order, a fellow creature of God. As Milton says, 'they expresse nature best, who in their lives least wander from her safe leading, which may be called regenerate reason' (*Prose Works*, I, 874). But reason in this world is a limited monarchy, and the great leap from the sensible to the intellectual world can result only from a moral revolution in the soul. Just as Eden was the home of man only as long as man remained unfallen, so nature in its purity, as the order God created and saw to be good, is perceptible only to the pure, the perception being symbolized by hearing the music of the spheres. Hence a need for purity in the major poet, a principle with an obvious personal application to Milton himself, which anyone but Milton might have found embarrassing. Even in that very light-hearted poem the *First Elegy*, there is a reference to the moly which may preserve the young poet from the enchantments of Circe, and in the Sixth Elegy there is a much more solemn statement of the contrast between the poet who remains on the sensuous level, celebrating wine and women in his song, and the poet who becomes what is described, still in Classical imagery, as the augur or priest of the gods. For the latter a rigid chastity is prescribed – chastity less as a virtue than as a necessary kind of discipline, like an athlete's training. We see that the impulse we have called Eros can develop away from the love of the sensuous toward the love of God so that nothing of the sexually 'erotic' is left in it. This is not a paradox to any student of Plato, as Milton well understood, though Milton's fullest exposition of Plato's Eros, in *The Doctrine and Discipline of Divorce*, applies it mainly to wedded love.

The Lady in *Comus* has reached the pinnacle of the ascent of Eros, and has gone as far as natural virtue can go. Her chastity is virginity as well – an identification which is traditional in magic and romance, but in Milton indicates the non-Christian setting of the imagery. In an explicitly Christian poem chastity would not exclude marriage. In any case the Lady's chastity draws her away from the sensible world toward the world of the angels, who (456–62)

> in cleer dream, and solemn vision
> Tell her of things that no gross ear can hear,
> Till oft convers with heav'nly habitants
> Begin to cast a beam on th' outward shape,
> The unpolluted temple of the mind,
> And turns it by degrees to the souls essence,
> Till all be made immortal.

Immortality here is spoken of in Platonic terms as natural, the essence of the soul as distinct from the mortal body. Such a conception of it is, for Milton, not actually Christian but part of the 'divine philosophy' of the brothers, which has hermetic, Platonic, and Neoplatonic affinities. Of course Milton in *Comus* is dealing with the conventions of poetry, not with the doctrines of religion or the facts of life, but even so the upper levels of virtue are not reached by the Lady entirely through her own efforts, hence the providential guidance given her by the Attendant Spirit. The further up one goes toward one's Creator, the more clearly the demonic element in Nature, its pollution by Sin and Death, becomes revealed. We are no longer, in *Comus*, within the world of 'unreprovèd pleasures free', where Bacchus has begotten Mirth on Venus, but in a world of 'grots and caverns shagged with horrid shades', where Bacchus has begotten Comus on Circe. The feminine images of darkness, the forest, the labyrinth, the moon, the charm, the entanglement, are here all connected with Hecate and Circe and the kind of sensual degradation symbolized by Circe's beasts and the sexual emblems borne by Comus, the enchanting rod and the cup or glass.

The conflict in *Comus* is, like all of Milton's temptations, a dialectical one in which the genuine and perverted versions of the same ideas are separated. Comus and his followers claim to 'imitate the starry quire', and therefore among other things to represent the genuine design of nature. The Lady is tempted by the suggestion that innocence is both amoral and natural, as the sex life of animals proves. The Lady's resistance separates the humanly natural and innocent from its opposite. There is a structural parallel with *The Tempest*, where Prospero creates a humanly natural society out of what is thrown on his island. His agent is Ariel, a spirit natural but not human: there is no place for Ariel in the new society, and he has to be set free in his own element. The Lady has, without realizing it, been making use of the Attendant Spirit, an elemental spirit of the upper air, as her protector, and when she is freed, the Attendant Spirit, like Ariel, returns to his own world. That world is nature in its pure or original form, symbolized, not by the 'penseroso' heavenly spheres to which the Lady is attuned, but by the 'allegro' earthly-Paradise figures of Cupid and Psyche, their offspring Youth and Joy, and the Gardens of Adonis. Again, it is a central point in Milton's ethic that when man has done all he can, God accepts what he does and strengthens man's power. After Jesus has, *quasi homo*, done all he can, God's power enables him miraculously to stand on the pinnacle of the temple: after Samson has done all he can, God's power takes over his will and sends him to the Philistine temple for his triumphant martyrdom. Sabrina represents a similar extra power granted to the Lady, and the poem closes with the inevitably accurate lines (1021–2):

> Or, if Vertue feeble were,
> Heav'n it self would stoop to her.

An explicitly Christian poem, like the *Nativity Ode*, would naturally have a different direction of imagery. The *Nativity Ode* deals, not with the anabasis of Eros, but with the katabasis of Agape, with the descent of divine love to man[1]. Consequently, the images of *Comus* appear in roughly the reverse order. First comes the music of the spheres, in counterpoint to the song of the angels, unconscious and explicit praises of God respectively, then a vision of Nature in her original creation before the fall. The true gods, that is, the angels and the personified virtues, are a part of this vision, as is the reference to the 'age of gold'. Astraea, the goddess of justice, returns to the earth 'Orbed in a rainbow', the rainbow, like the scales which are also an emblem of justice, being a recurrent image of the permanence in the order of nature. Fallen nature is now, of course, full of false gods, most of whom traditionally assume male forms. But we notice feminine imagery reappearing whenever there is any feeling of regret or nostalgia for the passing of the older order. Nobody regrets the passing of Moloch, but we feel differently about the nymphs who 'in twilight shade of tangled thickets mourn' (the two thematic words again), about the Genius driven out of 'haunted spring and dale', about the fairies obliged to leave, in the last phrase associated with the gods and spirits of nature, their 'moon-loved maze'. Finally we reach the Mother and Son in their genuine forms, while the feminine 'youngest teemed star' has over-tones partly of Psyche, the bride of Eros, and partly of the wise virgins of the Bridegroom's wedding. Here as elsewhere we notice how the fact that Milton is unaccustomed to the word 'its' (although it does occur once in this poem), and substitutes 'his' or 'her' instead, gives grammatical gender, and hence a trace of sexual feeling, to the imagery. Thus hell is referred to as 'her', which perhaps indicates that hell is to Satan what the Church is to Christ, the society he leads and the environment he lives in.

It is obvious that in Milton, as in most Christian poets, the same images can be used in innocent or demonic contexts, and that the tone depends a good deal on whether the theme is implicitly or explicitly Christian. We have already met this principle in *Il Penseroso* and in the Genius, who may be part of the apotheosis of Lycidas or part of the retinue of false gods in the *Nativity Ode*. The fairy world, again, suggests the free play of the imagination in *L'Allegro* and the illusions of Satanic evil at the end of the first book of *Paradise Lost* and in *Comus*. Another Virgilian and magical image of the enchantress charming the moon may be used in a demonic context in *Paradise Lost*, where the labouring moon eclipses at the night-hag's charms, or it may be used playfully, in the context of the poetic Eros convention, as it is in one of the Italian sonnets (*Diodati, e te'l diro*):

> E'l cantar che di mezzo l'hemispero
> Traviar ben può la faticosa Luna.

In this context the image is an analogy of the conception of harmony descending into chaos and forming a creation out of it, so central to Milton's view of creation, the creation being the primary example of what we have called the katabasis of Agape. It is also in connection with a singer that Milton makes a use, very rare for him, of this des-cending Agape image in a secular context. The singer Leonora, it is suggested, sings with the voice of the descending Spirit of God, which pervades all things, and which teaches us through her to become accustomed to the more rarefied music of immortality.

Comus depicts the victory of innocence, and the help of Sabrina shows that the Lady's innocence has been recognized by 'Heaven'. The analogy between Sabrina's sprinkling of the Lady and the rite of baptism, the introduction to revelation, is clear enough. *Paradise Regained* is a song of experience, beginning after baptism and recognition, and, in terms of the sexual symbolism, it is a man's vision of the powers behind nature, not a woman's dream of them. God made nature and is the real power behind it, but the visible part of nature, the part that corresponds to our dying bodies, has been usurped by Satan. Christ is, in our terms, the incarnation of Agape, to whom Satan exhibits the analogy of Eros as his domain. For the whole chain of being so far as we can see it, from chaos to man, and including the spirits of the elements, is Satan's, or so he claims (*PR*, IV, 200-3):

> What both from Men and Angels I receive,
> Tetrarchs of fire, air, flood, and on the earth
> Nations besides from all the quarter'd winds,
> God of this world invok't, and world beneath.

The claim is considerably oversimplified, but it is true that the analogy of Eros is pervaded with a demonic element, and that it is Christ's task to recognize and reject that element. In *Paradise Regained* Christ descends, like Spenser's Guyon in the cave of Mammon, to a lower world, nature in its aspect as Satan's visible world displayed, where, unlike Proserpine, he refuses to eat so much as a pomegranate seed, rejecting every iota of it and making a complete break with it in order to ground himself wholly on the prophetic Hebrew tradition. Because he did this, we may say, speaking from Milton's point of view, the author of *L'Allegro* and *Il Penseroso* is able to be the most liberal and humane of poets, and the analogy of Eros is now safeguarded, not only by the providence of God, as in *Comus*, but by the Gospel as well.

We first enter the wilderness of Satan's kingdom, much the same world as the demonic forest of *Comus*, being a 'woody maze' and 'A pathless Desert dusk with horrid shades', parts of it being also (*PR*, II, 296-7)

> To a Superstitious eye, the haunt
> Of Wood-Gods and Wood-Nymphs.

The suppression of explicit sexual imagery is connected with the fact that Satan realizes the uselessness of a sexual temptation of Jesus, as urged by Belial in a scrambled echo of the Song of Songs (*PR*, II, 159-62):

> Virgin majesty with mild
> And sweet allay'd, yet terrible to approach,
> Skill'd to retire, and in retiring draw
> Hearts after them tangl'd in Amorous Nets.

Satan is always lying, even when talking to other devils or to himself, and his rejection of Belial's suggestion means that he is really adopting it, but in disguised and sublimated forms. His first major attack, after the failure of the first temptation, is on the two appetites, for food and for sexual experience. The emphasis is on food for obvious reasons, but the banquet he summons up is served by beautiful nymphs recalling the 'faery damsels met in forest wide' of medieval romance. As Christ refuses one temptation after another, Satan is compelled to go further and further up the ladder of Eros, and in the temptations of Parthia and Rome he moves from passive to active sensuality. The forces of Parthia remind the poet again of the faery damsels of romance, specifically the Angelica of Boiardo and Ariosto, and the vision of the Emperor Tiberius hints at more elementary delights than purely administrative ones. Jesus' answer, with its echo of the 'gold cup' of the Great Whore, who is the symbol of the persecuting Roman Emperors, indicates how clearly he sees the sexual cup of Comus in what Satan is offering (*PR*, IV 116-19):

> (For I have also heard, perhaps have read)
> Their wines of *Setia, Cales,* and *Falerne,*
> *Chios* and *Creet,* and how they quaff in Gold,
> Crystal, and Myrrhine cups, embossed with Gems
> And studs of Pearl.

Satan gradually realizes, with increasing contempt, that Jesus does not want the sublimated eroticism of power. What he must want, then, Satan assumes, is the kind of wisdom that Yeats calls the property of the dead, a wisdom involving a retreat from the world, or what we should now think of as a kind of return to the womb. Such a desire could be readily satisfied in the city which is under the patronage of the virgin goddess of wisdom (*PR*, IV, 240-50):

Athens, the eye of *Greece*, Mother of Arts
And Eloquence, native to famous wits
Or hospitable, in her sweet recess,
City or Suburban, studious walks and shades;
See there the Olive Grove of *Academe*,
Plato's retirement, where the *Attic* bird
Trills her thick-warbl'd notes the summer long;
There, flowrie hill, *Hymettus*, with the sound
Of Bees industrious murmur, oft invites
To studious musing; there Ilissus rouls
His whispering stream.

The overtones of a shrouding female *hortus conclusus* are unmistakable, and the whole passage reads like a feeble parody of *Il Penseroso*. Satan, as usual, has the right explanation of Jesus' attitude in a perverted form. In the temptation, Jesus fulfils the law in the wilderness and becomes the true Joshua, or conqueror of the Promised Land, which is also the feminine garden of Eden (*PR*, I, 7). In the Passion and Resurrection, Christ fulfils the prophecy made to Adam; by overcoming the temptation he fulfils the dream of Eve. The Virgin Mary, the 'second Eve', is very prominent in the poem, and the typology of the whole temptation is summed up, from our present point of view, in the final line: 'Home to his mother's house private returned.'

We may notice in passing how Satan perverts even the genuine elements of the civilization he displays. What was really impressive about Greek culture, for Milton, was 'the liberty of Greece' (*PL*, X, 307) that Xerxes tried to yoke. The philosophy of Plato and Socrates was a product of liberty, not, as Satan presents it, an escape from the world or a means of getting entangled in sophisticated arguments. 'The Mountain Nymph, sweet Liberty' which appears in *L'Allegro* is certainly liberty in a different context, but it is not a wholly different kind of liberty. Satan's temptation of Athens ends 'These rules will render thee a king complete', and Christ's answer ends 'These only, with our Law, best form a king.' Two conceptions of cyropedia, of education as the training of a prince, are colliding here. One leads to the conception of the king as a temporal ruler, who, if not a tyrant, would be the philosopher-king of Plato's 'airy burgomasters', in Milton's phrase. The other is the institute of a Christian prince, leading to the king who is a spiritual ruler or prophet, a herald of freedom. A social and political aspect of Milton's analogical and sexual imagery is implied, and one which is set out in the prose works.

Jesus returns to his mother's house at the end of the temptation, but leaves it again to be about his father's business when he starts on his ministry, or work in the world proper. Here the female principle complementing Jesus is not the mother but the redeemed Bride or Church. Consequently it is semantically dangerous for Christians to think in terms of a Mother Church: it implies a regression to the law. 'But mark, readers,' says Milton, 'the crafty scope of these prelates; they endeavour to impress deeply into weak and superstitious fancies the awful notion of a mother, that hereby they might cheat them into a blind and implicit obedience to whatsoever they shall decree or think fit' (*Prose Works*, I, 727–8). Christians should think of their Church as a bride, a young virgin, still under tutelage. 'For of any age or sex, most unfitly may a virgin be left to an uncertain and arbitrary education. . . . In like manner the Church bearing the same resemblance, it were not reason to think she should be left destitute of that care which is as necessary and proper to her as instruction' (*Prose Works*, I, 755). This last means that the relation of Christ and the Church ought to be precisely the relation of Adam to Eve in the unfallen state. The conception is Pauline, but the interpretation of Paul involved is, of course, a left-wing Protestant one. The Word, the male principle, should have 'absolute rule'; the Church has only to murmur 'unargued I obey'. The autonomous Church, who claims the authority to teach the Word herself, is in the position of the unfaithful bride or harlot identified with Israel and frequently denounced by the prophets, or else a man-made counterfeit of the Church, 'Like that air-borne Helena in the fables'.

Similarly society is in a female relationship to the prophet, the speaker of the Word, the possessor of Adam's spiritual authority. Delilah, like Job's wife, represents the threat of the forces of social inertia and habit to the voice of genuine leadership, or prophecy. There are two degrees of female recalcitrance in the Bible: there is Israel as the disobedient harlot of Hosea and Ezekiel, who is eventually forgiven and brought back to repentance, and who is represented in Christian tradition by the story of Mary Magdalene, and there is the Great

Whore, the consolidated form of social apostasy, Delilah as Philistine. They correspond respectively to the fallen Eve and her demonic shadow in nature, the aspect of her that tempted Adam to fall too. Here we see the relevance of the theme of divorce in Milton to his sexual imagery. Milton's arguments for divorce do not concern us here; but behind these arguments is a larger symbolic structure in which the intolerable wife is the symbol of the custom and error that entangles the prophet. Adam could have prevented his fall only by 'divorcing' Eve after she had fallen, and before Jesus can return to his mother's house he has to complete a parallel divorce from the entire fallen human society, which of course for Adam consisted only of Eve. This divorce of Christ, being a re-creation of man, repeats the original creation, 'when by his divorcing command the world first rose out of chaos, nor can be renewed again out of confusion, but by the separating of unmeet consorts' (*Prose Works*, II, 273).

A secular counterpart to the symbolism of Word and Church also appears in the prose. Thus we read of 'men enchanted with the Circaean cup of servitude', and mazes and labyrinths and coverts, whether of argument or of action, often have a latent suggestion of some enchantress hampering the freedom of a warfaring Christian. On the other hand, Truth in the prose is often personified in terms recalling the innocent and naked Eve. Truth and Justice, so closely associated in the *Nativity Ode*, are explicitly identified in *Eikonoklastes*. Truth for Milton is existential, being ultimately a person and not a principle or rational vision: hence Truth is also the Astraea represented by the Virgin of the zodiac, already mentioned, who is flanked with the scales symbolizing justice within its context of God's creative and ordering power. The vision of Truth in *Areopagitica* and elsewhere is thus closely associated with the insight into the harmony of created nature in *Comus* and *At a Solemn Music*. Both aspects of Truth take us upward to the Wisdom personified in the Bible as the daughter of the Creator, playing before him[1] when the world was ordered, and the exact opposite of Athene, the virgin mother of Athens whom Jesus has to abandon before he can return to the home of the genuine virgin mother. If he had not abandoned her, she would eventually have turned into Sin, the daughter who was born of Satan much as Athene is said to have been born of Zeus. Sin is described as serpentine, like the Gorgon's head on

Athene's shield: it seems strange that this image can represent a genuine ideal in the context of *Comus*, but so it is.

What we have been looking at in Milton's imagery is a particular way of relating the two great mythological structures on which the literature of our own Near Eastern and Western traditions has been founded. One structure is dominated by a male father-god, stresses the rational order of nature, and thinks of nature as an artefact, something designed and constructed. The other centres on a mother-goddess, perennially renewing the mystery of birth in the act of love. The father-god myth subordinates the female principle, making it a daughter-figure of Truth or Wisdom; the mother-goddess myth subordinates the male principle, making it the son-lover-victim figure of the dying god. The male mythology was dominant from the beginning of the Christian era down to the Romantic movement. In the medieval and Renaissance period its rival was incorporated in the Venus-Eros cult of the courtly love convention. After the Romantic movement began, the mother-centred myth gained ground. The father-myth is an inherently conservative one; the other is more naturally revolutionary, and the revolutionary emphasis in Milton shows how near he is to the mythology of Romanticism and its later by-products, the revolutionary erotic, Promethean, and Dionysian myths of Freud, Marx, and Nietzsche. The artefact myth has declined during the last two centuries partly because so many of its central elements came to be regarded as fictions, and again it is interesting to see how these elements in Milton are represented by symbols either known to be fictions, like the music of the spheres, or presented as possible fictions, like the Ptolemaic cosmos.

Milton, of course, accepted the artefact myth as primary along with the traditional ideas about how the sexual myth was to be subordinated to it. But he was also a poet who understood the claims of both on the imagination. The father-god myth has a moral principle built into it: it assumes a creator with an intelligent and purposeful Plan A for man's creation, who after Adam's defection falls back on an equally well-designed Plan B for his salvation. The mother-goddess myth has only very ambiguous moral principles: it expresses an unconditioned desire which, either as that or in its frustrated form of resentment, may go in any direction and take any form. Theoretically, as we said, Eve's dream is fulfilled in the moment that Christ is raised, as she was, to a high eminence by Satan, then left to fall, and is sustained by the power of God as Satan falls instead. But Eve had shown, even in the unfallen state, a disconcerting capacity to have her own thoughts, her own desires, her own resentments even, to arrive at her own conclusions independently of Adam's superior reason. This tendency had led her to separate herself from Adam and fall under Satan's influence. God, who made her as she was, nevertheless had her separated again, and perhaps let her dream more or less in her own way: Michael suggests that he is only establishing the general atmosphere (XII, 595-6):

> Her also I with gentle Dreams have calm'd,
> Portending good

and Eve's own account is even vaguer. It is significant that the revelation to Adam is so full and explicit, extending through most of two whole books, and the revelation to Eve so briefly, even evasively, referred to. The awakened father of mankind follows the master plan of God's salvation as it is unrolled scene by scene, and agrees to the justice, wisdom, and reason incorporated into it. We are expected to be similarly convicted and convinced, but, if the clear light of reason is ever dimmed by a passion or emotion that is not quite so sure of its objects, we may remember that, far below this rarefied pinnacle of rational vision, there lies a humiliated mother dreaming of the vengeance of her mighty son.

It will be easiest for me to begin with a personal reference. My first sustained effort in scholarship was an attempt to work out a unified commentary on the prophetic books of Blake. These poems are mythical in shape: I had to learn something about myth to write about them, and so I discovered, after the book was published, that I was a member of a school of 'myth criticism' of which I had not previously heard. My second effort, completed ten years later, was an attempt to work out a unified commentary on the theory of literary criticism, in which again myth had a prominent place. To me, the progress from one interest to the other was inevitable, and it was obvious to anyone who read both books that my critical ideas had been derived from Blake. How completely the second book was contained in embryo in the first, however, was something I did not realize myself until I recently read through *Fearful Symmetry*, for the first time in fifteen years, in order to write a preface to a new paperback edition. It seems perhaps worth while to examine what has been so far a mere assumption, the actual connecting links between my study of Blake and my study of the theory of criticism. At least the question is interesting to me, and so provides the only genuine motive yet discovered for undertaking any research.

Blake is one of the poets who believe that, as Wallace Stevens says, the only subject of poetry is poetry itself, and that the writing of a poem is itself a theory of poetry. He interests a critic because he removes the barriers between poetry and criticism. He defines the greatest poetry as 'allegory addressed to the intellectual powers', and defends the practice of not being too explicit on the ground that it 'rouzes the faculties to act'. His language in his later prophecies is almost deliberately colloquial and 'unpoetic', as though he intended his poetry to be also a work of criticism, just as he expected the critic's response to be also a creative one. He understood, in his own way, the principle later stated by Arnold that poetry is a criticism of life, and it was an uncompromising way. For him, the artist demonstrates a certain way of life: his aim is not to be appreciated or admired, but to transfer to others the imaginative habit and energy of his mind. The main work of criticism is teaching, and teaching for Blake cannot be separated from creation.

Blake's statements about art are extreme enough to make it clear that he is demanding some kind of mental adjustment to take them in. One of the Laocoon Aphorisms reads: 'A Poet, a Painter, a Musician, an Architect: the Man Or Woman who is not one of these is not a Christian.' If we respond to this in terms of what we ordinarily associate with the words used, the aphorism will sound, as Blake intended it to sound, like someone in the last stages of paranoia. Blake has an unusual faculty for putting his central beliefs in this mock-paranoid form, and in consequence has deliberately misled all readers who would rather believe that he was mad than that their own use of language could be inadequate. Thus when a Devil says in *The Marriage of Heaven and Hell*: 'those who envy or calumniate great men hate God; for there is no other God', our habitual understanding of the phrase 'great men' turns the remark into something that makes Carlyle at his worst sound by comparison like a wise and prudent thinker. When we read in the *Descriptive Catalogue*, however, that Chaucer's Parson is 'according to Christ's definition, the greatest of his age', we begin to wonder if this paradoxical Devil has really so sulphurous a smell. Similarly, Blake's equating of the arts with Christianity implies, first, that his conception of art includes much more than we usually associate with it, and, second, that it excludes most of what we do associate with it. Blake is calling a work of art what a more conventional terminology would call a charitable act, while at the same time the painting of, say, Reynolds is for him not bad painting but anti-painting. Whether we agree or sympathize with Blake's attitude, what he says does involve a whole theory of criticism, and this theory we should examine.

One feature of Blake's prophecies which strikes every reader is the gradual elimination, especially in the two later poems *Milton* and *Jerusalem* that form the climax of this part of his work, of anything resembling narrative movement. The following passage occurs in Plate 71 of *Jerusalem*:

What is Above is Within, for every-thing in Eternity is
translucent:
The Circumference is Within, Without is formed the Selfish
Center,
And the Circumference still expands going forward to
Eternity,
And the Center has Eternal States; these States we now
explore.

I still have the copy of Blake that I used as an undergraduate, and I see that in the margin beside this passage I have written the words, 'Something moves, anyhow.' But even that was more of an expression of hope than of considered critical judgement. This plotless type of writing has been discussed a good deal by other critics, notably Hugh Kenner and Marshall McLuhan, who call it 'mental landscape', and ascribe its invention to the French *symbolistes*. But in Blake we not only have the technique already complete, but an even more thoroughgoing way of presenting it.

If we read *Milton* and *Jerusalem* as Blake intended them to be read, we are not reading them in any conventional sense at all: we are staring at a sequence of plates, most of them with designs. We can see, of course, that a sequence of illustrated plates would be an intolerably cumbersome and inappropriate method of presenting a long poem in which narrative was the main interest. The long poems of other poets that Blake illustrated, such as Young's *Night Thoughts* and Blair's *Grave*, are meditative poems where, even without Blake's assistance, the reader's attention is expected to drop out of the text every so often and soar, or plunge, whichever metaphor is appropriate, although perhaps wander is even more accurate. No doubt the development of Blake's engraving technique had much to do with the plotlessness of the engraved poems. We notice that the three poems of Blake in which the sense of narrative movement is strongest – *Tiriel, The French Revolution, The Four Zoas* – were never engraved. We notice, too, that the illustration on a plate often does not illustrate the text on the same plate, and that in one copy of *Jerusalem* the sequence of plates in Part Two is slightly different. The elimination of narrative movement is clearly central to the structure of these poems, and the device of a sequence of plates is consistent with the whole scheme, not a mere accident.

The theme of *Milton* is an instant of illumination in the mind of the poet, an instant which, like the moments of recognition in Proust, links him with a series of previous moments stretching back to the creation of the world. Proust was led to see men as giants in time, but for Blake there is only one giant, Albion, whose dream is time. For Blake in *Milton*, as for Eliot in *Little Gidding*, history is a pattern of timeless moments. What is said, so to speak, in the text of *Milton* is designed to present the context of the illuminated moment as a single simultaneous pattern of apprehension. Hence it does not form a narrative, but recedes spatially, as it were, from that moment. *Jerusalem* is conceived like a painting of the Last Judgement, stretching from heaven to hell and crowded with figures and allusions. Again, everything said in the text is intended to fit somewhere into this simultaneous conceptual pattern, not to form a linear narrative. If I ever get a big enough office, I shall have the hundred plates of my *Jerusalem* reproduction framed and hung around the walls, so that the frontispiece will have the second plate on one side and the last plate on the other. This will be *Jerusalem* presented as Blake thought of it, symbolizing the state of mind in which the poet himself could say: 'I see the Past, Present & Future existing all at once Before me.' In the still later Job engravings the technique of placing the words within a pictorial unit is, of course, much more obvious.

Many forms of literature, including the drama, fiction, and epic and narrative poetry, depend on narrative movement in a specific way. That is, they depend for their appeal on the participation of the reader or listener in the narrative as it moves along in time. It is continuity that keeps us turning the pages of a novel, or sitting in a theatre. But there is always something of a summoned-up illusion about such continuity. We may keep reading a novel or attending to a play 'to see how it turns out'. But once we know how it turns out, and the spell ceases to bind us, we tend to forget the continuity, the very element in the play or novel that enabled us to participate in it. Remembering the plot of anything seems to be unusually difficult. Every member of this audience is familiar with many literary narratives, could even lecture on them with very little notice, and yet could not give a consecutive account of what happened in them, just as all the evangelical zeal of the hero of *The Way of All Flesh* was not equal to remembering the story of the resurrection of Christ in the Gospel of John. Nor does this seem particularly regrettable. Just as the pun is the lowest form of wit, so it is generally agreed, among knowledgeable people like ourselves, that summarizing a plot is the lowest form of criticism.

I have dealt with this question elsewhere, and can only give the main point here. Narrative in literature may also be seen as theme, and theme *is* narrative, but narrative seen as a simultaneous unity. At a certain point in the narrative, the point which Aristotle calls *anagnorisis* or recognition, the sense of linear continuity or participation in the action changes perspective, and what we now see is a total design or unifying structure in the narrative. In detective stories, when we find out who done it, or in certain types of comedy or romance that depend on what are now called 'gimmicks', such as Jonson's *Epicoene*, the point of *anagnorisis* is the revelation of something which has previously been a mystery. In such works Aristotle's word *anagnorisis* is best translated 'discovery'. But in most serious works of literature, and more particularly in epics and tragedies, the better translation is 'recognition'. The reader already knows what is going to happen, but wishes to see, or rather to participate in, the completion of the design.

Thus the end of reading or listening is the beginning of critical understanding, and nothing that we call criticism can begin until the whole of what it is striving to comprehend has been presented to it. Participation in the continuity of narrative leads to the discovery or recognition of the theme, which *is* the narrative seen as total design. This theme is what, as we say, the story has been all about, the point of telling it. What we reach at the end of participation becomes the centre of our critical attention. The elements in the narrative thereupon regroup themselves in a new way. Certain unusually vivid bits of characterization or scenes of exceptional intensity move up near the centre of our memory. This reconstructing and regrouping of elements in our critical response to a narrative goes on more or less unconsciously, but the fact that it goes on is what makes remembering plot so difficult.

Thus there are two kinds of response to a work of literature, especially one that tells a story. The first kind is a participating response in time, moving in measure like a dancer with the rhythm of continuity. It is typically an uncritical, or more accurately a pre-critical response. We cannot begin criticism, strictly speaking, until we have heard the author out, unless he is a bore, when the critical response starts prematurely and, as we say, we can't get into the book. The second kind of response is thematic, detached, fully conscious, and one which sees and is capable of examining the work as a simultaneous whole. It may be an act of understanding, or it may be a value-judgement, or it may be both. Naturally these two types of response overlap more in practice than I suggest here, but the distinction between them is clear enough, and fundamental in the theory of criticism. Some critics, including Professors Wimsatt and Beardsley in *The Verbal Icon*, stress the deficiencies of 'holism' as a critical theory; but we should distinguish between 'holism' as a critical theory and as a heuristic principle.

There are, of course, great differences of emphasis within literature itself, according to which kind of response the author is more interested in. At one pole of fiction we have the pure storyteller, whose sole interest is in suspense and the pacing of narrative, and who could not care less what the larger meaning of his story was, or what a critic would find in it afterwards. The attitude of such a storyteller is expressed in the well-known preface to *Huckleberry Finn*: 'Persons attempting to find a motive in this narrative will be prosecuted; persons attempting to find a moral in it will be banished; persons attempting to find a plot in it will be shot.' Motive and moral and plot certainly are in *Huckleberry Finn*, but the author, or so he says, doesn't want to hear about them. All the storyteller wants to do is to keep the attention of his audience to the end: once the end is reached, he has no further interest in his audience. He may even be hostile to criticism or anti-intellectual in his attitude to literature, afraid that criticism will spoil the simple entertainment that he designed. The lyrical poet concerned with expressing certain feelings or emotions in the lyrical conventions of his day often takes a similar attitude, because it is natural for him to identify his conventional literary emotions with his 'real' personal emotions. He therefore feels that if the critic finds any meaning or significance in his work beyond the intensity of those emotions, it must be only what the critic wants to say instead. Anti-critical statements are usually designed only to keep the critic in his place, but the attitude they represent, when genuine, is objective, thrown outward into the designing of the continuity. It is the attitude that Schiller, in his essay on *Naïve and Sentimental Poetry*, means by naïve, and which includes what we mean in English by naïve. Naïve writers' *obiter dicta* are often repeated, for consolation, by the kind of critic who is beginning to suspect that literary criticism is a more difficult discipline than he realized when he entered into it. But it is not possible for any reader today to respond to a work of literature with complete or genuine *naïveté*. Response is what Schiller calls sentimental by its very nature, and is hence to some degree involved with criticism.

If we compare, let us say, Malory with Spenser, we can see that Malory's chief interest is in telling the stories in the 'French book' he is using. He seems to know that some of them, especially the Grail stories, have overtones in them that the reader will linger with long after he has finished reading. But Malory makes no explicit reference to this, nor does one feel that Malory himself, preoccupied as he was with a nervous habit of robbing churches, would have been much interested in a purely critical reaction to his book. But for Spenser it is clear that the romance form, the quest of the knight journeying into a dark forest in search of some sinister villain who can be forced to release some suppliant female, is merely a projection of what Spenser really wants to say. When he says at the end of Book II of *The Faerie Queene*:

> Now gins this goodly frame of Temperaunce
> Fayrely to rise

it is clear that his interest is thematic, in the emergence of a fully articulated view of the virtue of Temperance which the reader can contemplate, as it were, like a statue, seeing all of its parts at once. This simultaneous vision extends over the entire poem, for Temperance is only one of the virtues surrounding the ideal Prince, and the emergence of the total form of that Prince is the thematic mould into which the enormous narrative is finally poured. The stanza in Spenser, especially the final alexandrine, has a role rather similar to the engraved design in Blake: it deliberately arrests the narrative and forces the reader to concentrate on something else.

In our day the prevailing attitude to fiction is overwhelmingly thematic. Even as early as Dickens we often feel that the plot, when it is a matter of unplausible mysteries unconvincingly revealed, is something superimposed on the real narrative, which is more like a procession of characters. In our day the born storyteller is even rather peripheral to fiction, at best a borderline case like Somerset Maugham, and the serious novelist is as a rule the novelist who writes not because he has a story to tell but because he has a theme to illustrate. One reason for this present preference of the thematic is that the ironic tone is central to modern literature. It is the function of irony, typically in Greek tragedy, to give the audience a clearer view of the total design than the actors themselves are aware of. Irony thus sets up a thematic detachment as soon as possible in the work, and provides an additional clue to the total meaning.

There may be, then, and there usually is, a kind of empathic communion set up in the reader or audience of a work of literature, which follows the work continuously to the end. The sense of empathy may be established by a story, where we read on to see what happens. Or by a pulsating rhythm, such as the dactylic hexameter in Homer, which has a surge and sweep that can carry us through even the longueurs referred to by Horace. We notice the effectiveness of rhythm in continuity more clearly in music, and most clearly in fast movements. I recall a cartoon of a tired man at a concert consulting his programme and saying: 'Well, the next movement is *prestissimo molto ed appassionato*, thank God.' Or by the fluctuating intensity of a mood or emotion, again most clearly in music and in lyrical poetry. Or by a continuous sense of lifelikeness in realistic fiction, a sense which can extend itself even to realistic painting, as the eye darts from one detail to another. All these empathic responses are 'naïve', or essentially pre-critical.

Certain forms of art are also designed to give us the strongest possible emphasis on the continuous process of creation. The sketch, for example, is often more prized than the finished painting because of the greater sense of process in it. *Tachisme* and action-painting, spontaneous improvisation in swing, jazz, or more recently electronic music, and the kind of action-poetry, often read to jazz, which evokes the ghosts of those primeval jam-sessions postulated by early critics of the ballad, are more complete examples. All forms of art which lay great stress on continuous spontaneity seem to have a good deal of resistance to criticism, even to the education which is the natural context of criticism. We are told in Professor Lord's *Singer of Tales* that the most continuous form of poetry ever devised, the formulaic epic, demands illiteracy for success on the part of the poet, and there seems to be an inevitable affinity between the continuous and the unreflecting. It is this continuity which is particularly Aristotle's imitation of an action. One's attention is completely absorbed in it: no other work of art is demanding attention at the same time, hence one has the sense of a unique and novel experience, at least as an ideal (for, of course, one may be rereading a book or seeing a familiar play). But, as in the world of action itself, one cannot participate and be a spectator at the same time. At best one is what Wyndham Lewis calls a 'dithyrambic spectator'. Lewis's disapproval of the dithyrambic spectator indicates an opposed emphasis on the detached contemplation of the entire work of art, and one so extreme that it talks of eliminating the sense of linear participating movement in the arts altogether. It would not clarify our argument to examine Lewis's very muddled polemics at this point, but they have some interest as documents in a tradition which strongly emphasized a visual and contemplative approach to art. Blake's plotless prophecies are, somewhat unexpectedly, in a similar (though by no means identical) tradition.

Just as the sense of participation in the movement of literature is absorbed, unique and novel, isolated from everything else, so the contemplative sense of its simultaneous wholeness tends to put the work of literature in some kind of framework or context. There are several such contexts, some of them indicated already. One of them is the allegorical context, where the total meaning or significance of the literary work is seen in relation to other forms of significance, such as moral ideas or historical events. A few works of literature, such as *The Pilgrim's Progress*, are technically allegories, which means that this explicit relation to external meaning is also a part of its continuity. Most literary works are not allegorical in this technical sense, but they bear a relation to historical events and moral ideas which is brought out in the kind of criticism usually called commentary. As I have explained elsewhere, commentary allegorizes the works it comments on.

We notice that Blake is somewhat ambiguous in his use of the term 'allegory'. He says in a letter to Butts, 'Allegory addressed to the Intellectual powers . . . is My Definition of the Most Sublime Poetry.' But in commenting on one of his paintings of the Last Judgement, he says: 'The Last Judgement is not Fable or Allegory, but Vision. Fable or Allegory are a totally distinct & inferior kind of Poetry.' The first use of the term recognizes the fact that 'the most sublime poetry', including his own prophecies, will demand commentary. The second use indicates that his own poems and pictures are not allegorical in the Spenserian or continuous sense, nor are they allegorical in a much more obvious and central way. They do not subordinate their literary qualities to the ideas they convey, on the assumption that the latter are more important. In the second passage quoted above Blake goes on to say with great precision: 'Fable is allegory, but what Critics call The Fable, is Vision itself.' Fable is here taken in its eighteenth-century critical sense of fiction or literary structure. Aristotle's word for intellectual content, *dianoia*, 'thought', can be understood in two ways, as a moral attached to a fable, or as the structure of the fable itself. The latter, according to Blake, contains its own moral significances by implication, and it destroys its imaginative quality to assume that some external moral attached to it can be a definitive translation of its 'thought'.

We touch here on a central dilemma of literature. If literature is didactic, it tends to injure its own integrity; if it ceases wholly to be didactic, it tends to injure its own seriousness. 'Didactic poetry is my abhorrence,' said Shelley, but it is clear that if the main body of Shelley's work had not been directly concerned with social, moral, religious, philosophical, political issues he would have lost most of his self-respect as a poet. Nobody wants to be an ineffectual angel, and Bernard Shaw, one of Shelley's most direct descendants in English literature, insisted that art should never be anything but didactic. This dilemma is partly solved by giving an ironic resolution to a work of fiction. The ironic resolution is the negative pole of the allegorical one. Irony presents a human conflict which, unlike a comedy, a romance, or even a tragedy, is unsatisfactory and incomplete unless we see in it a significance beyond itself, something typical of the human situation as a whole. What that significance is, irony does not say: it leaves that question up to the reader or audience. Irony preserves the seriousness of literature by demanding an expanded perspective on the action it presents, but it preserves the integrity of literature by not limiting or prescribing for that perspective.

Blake is clearly not an ironic writer, however, any more than he is an allegorist, and we must look for some other element in his thematic emphasis. A third context to which the theme of a literary work may be attached is its context in literature itself, or what we may call its archetypal framework. Just as continuous empathy is naïve and absorbed in a unique and novel experience, so the contemplation of a unified work is self-conscious, educated, and one which tends to classify its object. We cannot in practice study a literary work without remembering that we have encountered many similar ones previously. Hence after following a narrative through to the end, our critical response includes the establishing of its categories, which are chiefly its convention and its genre. In this perspective the particular story is seen as a *projection* of the theme, as one of an infinite number of possible ways of getting to the theme. What we have just experienced we now see to be a comedy, a tragedy, a courtly love lyrical complaint, or one of innumerable treatments of the Tristan or Endymion or Faust story.

Further, just as some works of literature are explicitly or continuously allegorical, so some works are continuously, or at least explicitly, allusive, calling the reader's attention to their relation to previous works. If we try to consider *Lycidas* in isolation from the tradition of the pastoral elegy established by Theocritus and Virgil, or *Ash Wednesday* in isolation from its relation to Dante's *Purgatorio*, we are simply reading these works out of context, which is as bad a critical procedure as quoting a passage out of context. If we read an Elizabethan sonnet sequence without taking account of the conventional nature of every feature in it, including the poet's protests that he is not following convention and is really in love with a real person, we shall merely substitute the wrong context for the right one. That is, the sonnet sequence will become a biographical allegory, as the sonnets of Shakespeare do when, with Oscar Wilde, we reach the conclusion that the profoundest understanding of these sonnets, the deepest appreciation of all their eloquence and passion and power, comes when we identify the 'man in hue' of Sonnet 20 with an unknown Elizabethan pansy named Willie Hughes.

Blake's prophecies are intensely allusive, though nine-tenths of the allusions are to the Bible. 'The Old & New Testaments are the Great Code of Art', Blake says, and he thinks of the framework of the Bible, stretching from Creation to Last Judgement and surveying the whole of human history in between, as indicating the framework of the whole of literary experience, and establishing the ultimate context for all works of literature whatever. If the Bible did not exist, at least as a form, it would be necessary for literary critics to invent the same kind of total and definitive verbal structure out of the fragmentary myths and legends and folk tales we have outside it. Such a structure is the first and most indispensable of critical conceptions, the embodiment of the whole of literature as an order of words, as a potentially unified imaginative experience. But although its relation to the Bible takes us well on toward a solution of the thematic emphasis in Blake's illuminated poetry, it does not in itself fully explain that emphasis. If it did, the prophecies would simply be, in the last analysis, Biblical commentaries, and this they are far from being.

Blake's uniqueness as a poet has much to do with his ability to sense the historical significance of his own time. Up to that time, literature and the arts had much the same educational and cultural value that they have now, but they competed with religion, philosophy, and law on what were at best equal and more usually subordinate terms. Consequently when, for example, Renaissance critics spoke of the profundity of poetry, they tended to locate that profundity in its allegorical meaning, the relations that could be established between poetry and ideas, more particularly moral and religious ideas. In the Romantic period, on the other hand, many poets and critics were ready to claim an authority and importance for poetry and the imaginative arts prior to that of other disciplines. When Shelley quotes Tasso on the similarity of the creative work of the poet to the creative work of God, he carries the idea a great deal further than Tasso did. The fact of this change in the Romantic period is familiar, but the trends that made it possible are still not identified with assurance.

My own guess is that the change had something to do with a growing feeling that the origin of human civilization was human too. In traditional Christianity it was not: God planted the garden of Eden and suggested the models for the law, rituals, even the architecture of human civilization. Hence a rational understanding of 'nature', which included the understanding of the divine as well as the physical origin of human nature, took precedence over the poetic imagination and supplied a criterion for it. The essential moral ideas fitted into a divine scheme for the redemption of man; we understand the revelation of this scheme rationally; literature forms a series of more indirect parables or emblems of it. Thus poetry could be the companion of camps, as Sidney says: it could kindle an enthusiasm for virtue by providing examples for precepts. The sense of excitement in participating in the action of the heroic narrative of, say, the Iliad was heightened by thinking of the theme or total meaning of the Iliad as an allegory of heroism. Thus, paradoxically, the Renaissance insistence on the allegorical nature of major poetry preserved the *naïveté* of the participating response. We see this principle at work wherever poet and audience are completely in agreement about the moral implications of a poetic theme, as they are, at least theoretically, in a hiss-the-villain melodrama.

Blake was the first and the most radical of the Romantics who identified the creative imagination of the poet with the creative power of God. For Blake God was not a superhuman lawgiver or the mathematical architect of the stars; God was the inspired suffering humanity of Jesus. Everything we call 'nature', the physical world around us, is sub-moral, sub-human, sub-imaginative; every act worth performing has as its object the redeeming of this nature into something with a genuinely human, and therefore divine, shape. Hence Blake's poetry is not allegorical but mythopoeic, not obliquely related to a rational understanding of the human situation, the resolution of which is out of human hands, but a product of the creative energy that alone can redeem that situation. Blake forces the reader to concentrate on the meaning of his work, but not didactically in the ordinary sense, because his meaning is his theme, the total simultaneous shape of his poem. The context into which the theme or meaning of the individual poem fits is not the received ideas of our cultural tradition, of which it is or should be an allegory. It is not, or not only, the entire structure of literature as an order of words, as represented by the Bible. It is rather the expanded vision that he calls apocalypse or Last Judgement: the vision of the end and goal of human civilization as the entire universe in the form that human desire wants to see it, as a heaven eternally separated from a hell. What Blake did was closely related to the Romantic movement, and Shelley and Keats at least are mythopoeic poets for reasons not far removed from Blake's.

Since the Romantic movement, there has been a more conservative tendency to deprecate the central place it gave to the creative imagination and to return, or attempt to return, to the old hierarchy. T. S. Eliot is both a familiar and a coherent exponent of this tendency, and he has been followed by Auden, with his Kierkegaardian reinforcements. According to Eliot, it is the function of art, by imposing an order on life, to give us the sense of an order in life, and so to lead us into a state of serenity and reconciliation preparatory to another and superior kind of experience, where 'that guide' can lead us no further. The implication is that there is a spiritually existential world above that of art, a world of action and behaviour, of which the most direct imitation in this world is not art but the sacramental act. This latter is a form of uncritical or pre-critical religious participation that leads to a genuinely religious contemplation, which for Eliot is a state of heightened consciousness with strong affinities to mysticism. Mysticism is a word which has been applied both to Blake and to St John of the Cross: in other words it has been rather loosely applied, because these two poets have little in common. It is clear that Eliot's mystical affinities are of the St John of the Cross type. The function of art, for Eliot, is again of the subordinated or allegorical kind. Its order represents a higher existential order, hence its greatest ambition should be to get beyond itself, pointing to its superior reality with such urgency and clarity that it disappears in that reality. This, however, only happens either in the greatest or the most explicitly religious art: nine-tenths of our literary experience is on the subordinate plane where we are seeing an order in life without worrying too much about the significance of that order. On this plane the naïve pre-critical direct experience of participation can still be maintained, as it is in Renaissance critical theory. The Romantics, according to this view, spoil both the form and the fun of poetry by insisting so much on the profundity of the imaginative experience as to make it a kind of portentous *ersatz* religion.

This leads us back to the aphorism of Blake with which we began, where the artist is identified with the Christian. Elsewhere he speaks of 'Religion, or Civilized Life such as it is in the Christian Church', and says that poetry, painting and music are 'the three Powers in Man of conversing with Paradise, which the flood did not Sweep away'. For Blake art is not a substitute for religion, though a great deal of religion as ordinarily conceived is a substitute for art, in that it abuses the mythopoeic faculty by creating fantasies about another world or rationalizing the evils of this one instead of working toward genuine human life. If we describe Blake's conception of art independently of the traditional myth of fall and apocalypse that embodies it, we may say that the poetic activity is fundamentally one of identifying the human with the non-human world. This identity is what the poetic metaphor expresses, and the end of the poetic vision is the humanization of reality, 'All Human Forms identified', as Blake says at the end of *Jerusalem*. Here we have the basis for a critical theory which puts such central conceptions as myth and metaphor into their proper central place. So far from usurping the function of religion, it keeps literature in the context of human civilization, yet without limiting the infinite variety and range of the poetic imagination. The criteria it suggests are not moral ones, nor are they collections of imposing abstractions like Unity, but the interests, in the widest sense, of mankind itself, or himself, as Blake would prefer to say.

In this conception of art the productive or creative effort is inseparable from the awareness of what it is doing. It is this unity of energy and consciousness that Blake attempts to express by the word 'vision'. In Blake there is no either/or dialectic where one must be either a detached spectator or a preoccupied actor. Hence there is no division, though there may be a distinction, between the creative power of shaping the form and the critical power of seeing the world it belongs to. Any division instantly makes art barbaric and the knowledge of it pedantic – a bound Orc and a bewildered Urizen, to use Blake's symbols. The vision inspires the act, and the act realizes the vision. This is the most thoroughgoing view of the partnership of creation and criticism in literature I know, but for me, though other views may seem more reasonable and more plausible for a time, it is in the long run the only one that will hold.

11 THE KEYS TO THE GATES

The criticism of Blake, especially of Blake's prophecies, has developed in direct proportion to the theory of criticism itself. The complaints that Blake was 'mad' are no longer of any importance, not because anybody has proved him sane, but because critical theory has realized that madness, like obscenity, is a word with no critical meaning. There are critical standards of coherence and incoherence, but if a poem is coherent in itself the sanity of its author is a matter of interest only to the more naïve type of biographer. Those who have assumed that the prophecies are incoherent because they have found them difficult often use the phrase 'private symbolism'. This is also now a matter of no importance, because in critical theory there is no such thing as private symbolism. There may be allegorical allusions to a poet's private life that can only be interpreted by biographical research, but no set of such allusions can ever form a poetic structure. They can only be isolated signposts, like the allusions to the prototypes of the beautiful youth, dark lady, and rival poet which historians and other speculative critics are persuaded that they see in the Shakespeare sonnets.

When I first embarked on an intensive study of Blake's prophecies, I assumed that my task was to follow the trail blazed by Foster Damon's great book, and take further steps to demonstrate the coherence of those poems. My primary interests, like Damon's, were literary, not occult or philosophical or religious. Many other writers had asserted that while the prophecies were doubtless coherent enough intellectually, they would turn out to depend for their coherence on some extra-poetic system of ideas. A student interested in Blake's prophecies as poems would have to begin by rejecting this hypothesis, which contradicts all Blake's views about the primacy of art and the cultural disaster of substituting abstractions for art. But as I went on I was puzzled and annoyed by a schematic quality in these prophecies that refused to dissolve into what I then regarded as properly literary forms. There were even diagrams in Blake's own designs which suggested that he himself attached a good deal of value to schematism, and such statements as 'I must create a system'. Perhaps, then, these critics I had begun by rejecting were right after all: perhaps Blake was not opposed to abstraction but only to other people's abstractions, and was really interested merely in expounding some conceptual system or other in an oblique and allegorical way. In any event, the schematic, diagrammatic quality of Blake's thought was there, and would not go away or turn into anything else. Yeats had recognized it; Damon had recognized it; I had to recognize it. Like Shelley, Blake expressed an abhorrence of didactic poetry, but continued to write it.

This problem began to solve itself as soon as I realized that poetic thought is inherently and necessarily schematic. Blake soon led me, in my search for poetic analogues, to Dante and Milton, and it was clear that the schematic cosmologies of Dante and Milton, however they got into Dante and Milton, were, once they got there, poetic constructs, examples of the way poets think, and not foreign bodies of knowledge. If the prophecies are normal poems, or at least a normal expression of poetic genius, and if Blake nevertheless meant to teach some system by them, that system could only be something connected with the principles of poetic thought. Blake's 'message', then, is not simply *his* message, nor is it an extra-literary message. What he is trying to say is what he thinks poetry is trying to say: the imaginative content implied by the existence of an imaginative form of language. I finished my book in the full conviction that learning to read Blake was a step, and for me a necessary step, in learning to read poetry, and to write criticism. For if poetic thought is inherently schematic, criticism must be so too. I began to notice that as soon as a critic confined himself to talking seriously about literature his criticism tightened up and took on a systematic, even a schematic, form.

The nature of poetic 'truth' was discussed by Aristotle in connection with action. As compared with the historian, the poet makes no specific or particular statements: he gives the typical, recurring, or universal event, and is not to be judged by the standards of truth that we apply to specific statements. Poetry, then, does not state historical truth, but contains it: it sets forth what we may call the *myth* of history, the kind of thing that happens. History itself is designed to record events, or, as we may say, to provide a primary verbal imitation of events. But it also, unconsciously perhaps, illustrates and provides examples for the poetic vision. Hence we feel that *Lear* or *Macbeth* or *Oedipus Rex*, although they deal almost entirely with legend rather than actual history, contain infinite reserves of historical wisdom and insight. Thus poetry is 'something more philosophical' than history.

This last observation of Aristotle's has been of little use to critics except as a means of annoying historians, and it is difficult to see in what sense Anacreon is more philosophical than Thucydides. The statement is best interpreted, as it was by Renaissance critics, schematically, following a diagram in which poetry is intermediate between history and philosophy, pure example and pure precept. It follows that poetry must have a relation to thought paralleling its relation to action. The poet does not think in the sense of producing concepts, ideas or propositions, which are specific predications to be judged by their truth or falsehood. As he produces the mythical structures of history, so he produces the mythical structures of thought, the conceptual frameworks that enter into and inform the philosophies contemporary with him. And just as we feel that the great tragedy, if not historical, yet contains an infinity of the kind of meaning that actual history illustrates, so we feel that great 'philosophical' poetry, if not actually philosophical, contains an infinity of the kind of meaning that discursive writing illustrates. This sense of the infinite treasures of thought latent in poetry is eloquently expressed by several Elizabethan critics, and there is perhaps no modern poet who suggests the same kind of intellectual richness so immediately as Blake does.

Blake, in fact, gives us so good an introduction to the nature and structure of poetic thought that, if one has any interest in the subject at all, one can hardly avoid exploiting him. There are at least three reasons why he is uniquely useful for this purpose. One is that his prophecies are works of philosophical poetry which give us practically nothing at all unless we are willing to grapple with the kind of poetic thought that they express. Another is that Blake also wrote such haunting and lucid lyrics, of which we can at first say little except that they seem to belong in the centre of our literary experience. We may not know why they are in the centre, and some readers would rather not know; but for the saving remnant who do want to know, there are the prophecies to help us understand. The third reason in Blake's quality as an illustrator of other poets. If a person of considerable literary experience is reading a poem he is familiar with, it is easy for him to fall – in fact, it is very difficult for him not to fall – into a passive habit of not really reading the poem, but merely of spotting the critical clichés he is accustomed to associate with it. Thus, if he is reading Gray's 'Ode on the Death of a Favourite Cat,' and sees the goldfish described as 'angel forms', 'genii of the stream' and with 'scaly armour', his stock response will start murmuring: 'Gray means fish, of course, but he is saying so in terms of eighteenth-century personification, Augustan artificiality, his own peculiar demure humour,' and the like. Such a reading entirely obliterates Gray's actual processes of poetic thought and substitutes something in its place that, whatever it is, is certainly not poetry or philosophy, any more than it is history. But if he is reading the poem in the context of Blake's illustrations, Blake will compel him to see the angel forms, the genii of the stream, and the warriors in scaly armour, as well as the fish, in such a way as to make the unvisualized clichés of professional reading impossible, and to bring the metaphorical structure of the poem clearly into view.

I am suggesting that no one can read Blake seriously and sympathetically without feeling that the keys to poetic thought are in him, and what follows attempts to explain how a documentation of such a feeling would proceed. I make no claim that I am saying anything here that I have not said before, though I may be saying it in less compass.

EASTERN GATE: TWOFOLD VISION

The structure of metaphors and imagery that informed poetry, through the Middle Ages and the Renaissance, arranged reality on four levels. On top was heaven, the place of the presence of God: below it was the proper level of human nature, represented by the stories of the Garden of Eden and the Golden Age; below that was the physical world, theologically fallen, which man is in but not of: and at the bottom was the world of sin, death, and corruption. This was a deeply conservative view of reality in which man, in fallen nature, was confronted with a moral dialectic that either lowered him into sin or raised him to his proper level. The raising media included education, virtue, and obedience to law. In the Middle Ages this construct was closely linked with similar constructs in theology and science. These links weakened after the sixteenth century and eventually disappeared, leaving the construct to survive only in poetry, and, even there, increasingly by inertia. It is still present in Pope's *Essay on Man*, but accompanied with a growing emphasis on the limitation of poetic objectives. This limitation means, among other things, that mythopoeic literature, which demands a clear and explicit framework of imagery, is in the age of Pope and Swift largely confined to parody.

As the eighteenth century proceeded, the imaginative climate began to change, and we can see poets trying to move toward a less conservative structure of imagery. This became a crucial problem when the French Revolution confronted the Romantic poets. No major poet in the past had been really challenged by a revolutionary situation except Milton, and even Milton had reverted to the traditional structure for *Paradise Lost*. Blake was not only older than Wordsworth and Coleridge, but more consistently revolutionary in his attitude; again, unlike most English writers of the period, he saw the American Revolution as an event of the same kind as its French successor. He was, therefore, the first English poet to work out the revolutionary structure of imagery that continues through Romantic poetry and thought to our own time.

At the centre of Blake's thought are the two conceptions of innocence and experience, 'the two contrary states of the human soul'. Innocence is characteristic of the child, experience of the adult. In innocence, there are two factors. One is an assumption that the world was made for the benefit of human beings, has a human shape and a human meaning, and is a world in which providence, protection, communication with other beings, including animals, and, in general, 'mercy, pity, peace and love', have a genuine function. The other is ignorance of the fact that the world is not like this. As the child grows up, his conscious mind accepts 'experience', or reality without any human shape or meaning, and his childhood innocent vision, having nowhere else to go, is driven underground into what we should call the subconscious, where it takes an essentially sexual form. The original innocent vision becomes a melancholy dream of how man once possessed a happy garden, but lost it for ever, though he may regain it after he dies. The following diagram illustrates the process as well as the interconnection of *Songs of Innocence and Experience, The Marriage of Heaven and Hell*, and the early political prophecies *The French Revolution* and *America* in Blake's thought:

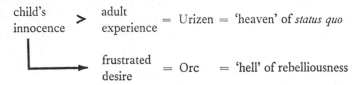

child's innocence > adult experience = Urizen = 'heaven' of *status quo*

frustrated desire = Orc = 'hell' of rebelliousness

In place of the old construct, therefore, in which man regains his happy garden home by doing his duty and obeying the law, we have an uneasy revolutionary conception of conscious values and standards of reality sitting on top of a volcano of thwarted and mainly sexual energy. This construct has two aspects, individual or psychological, and social or political. Politically, it represents an ascendant class threatened by the growing body of those excluded from social benefits, until the latter are strong enough to overturn society. Psychologically, it represents a conscious ego threatened by a sexually-rooted desire. Thus the mythical structure that informs both the psychology of Freud and the political doctrines of Marx is present in *The Marriage of Heaven and Hell*, which gives us both aspects of the Romantic movement: the reaction to political revolution and the manifesto of feeling and desire as opposed to the domination of reason.

In the associations that Blake makes with Urizen and Orc, Urizen is an old man and Orc a youth: Urizen has the counter-revolutionary colour white and Orc is a revolutionary red. Urizen is therefore associated with sterile winter, bleaching bones, and clouds; Orc with summer, blood, and the sun. The colours white and red suggest the bread and wine of a final harvest and vintage, prophesied in the fourteenth chapter of Revelation. Orc is 'underneath' Urizen, and underneath the white cliffs of Albion on the map are the 'vineyards of red France' in the throes of revolution. In a map of Palestine, the kingdom of Israel, whose other name, Jacob, means usurper, sits on top of Edom, the kingdom of the red and hairy Esau, the rightful heir. Isaiah's vision of a Messiah appearing in Edom, with his body soaked in blood from 'treading the winepress' of war, haunts nearly all Blake's prophecies. There are many other associations; perhaps we may derive the most important from the following passage in *America*:

> The terror answerd: I am Orc, wreath'd round the accursed
>   tree:
> The times are ended: shadows pass the morning gins to break;
> The fiery joy, that Urizen perverted to ten commands,
> What night he led the starry hosts thro' the wide wilderness:
> That stony law I stamp to dust: and scatter religion abroad
> To the four winds as a torn book, & none shall gather the leaves:
> But they shall rot on desart sands, & consume in bottomless
>   deeps:
> To make the desarts blossom, & the deeps shrink to their
>   fountains,
> And to renew the fiery joy, and burst the stony roof.
> That pale religious letchery, seeking Virginity,
> May find it in a harlot, and in coarse-clad honesty
> The undefil'd thro' ravish'd in her cradle night and morn:
> For every thing that lives is holy, life delights in life:
> Because the soul of sweet delight can never be defil'd.
> Fires inwrap the earthly globe, yet man is not consumd:
> Amidst the lustful fires he walks: his feet become like brass,
> His knees and thighs like silver, & his breast and head like gold.*

At various times in history there has been a political revolution symbolized by the birth or rebirth of Orc, the 'terrible boy': each one, however, has eventually subsided into the same Urizenic form as its predecessor. Orc is the human protest of energy and desire, the impulse to freedom and to sexual love. Urizen is the 'reality principle', the belief that knowledge of what is real comes from outside the human body. If we believe that reality is what we bring into existence through an act of creation, then we are free to build up our own civilization and abolish the anomalies and injustices that hamper its growth; but if we believe that reality is primarily what is 'out there', then we are condemned, in Marx's phrase, to study the world and never to change it. And the world that we study in this way we are compelled to see in the

---

* Blake's punctuation is retained.

distorted perspective of the human body with its five cramped senses, not our powers of perception as they are developed and expanded by the arts. Man in his present state is so constructed that all he can see outside him is the world under the law. He may believe that gods or angels or devils or fairies or ghosts are also 'out there', but he cannot see these things: he can see only the human and the sub-human, moving in established and predictable patterns. The basis of this vision of reality is the world of the heavenly bodies, circling around automatically and out of reach.

One early Orc rebellion was the Exodus from Egypt, where Orc is represented by a pillar of fire (the 'fiery joy') and Urizen by a pillar of cloud, or what *Finnegans Wake* calls 'Delude of Isreal'. Orc was a human society of twelve (actually thirteen) tribes; Urizen, a legal mechanism symbolized by the twelvefold Zodiac with its captive sun, which is why Urizen is said to have 'led the starry hosts' through the wilderness. The eventual victory of Urizen was marked by the establishing of Aaron's priesthood (the twelve stones in his breastplate symbolized the Zodiac as well as the tribes, according to Josephus), and by the negative moral law of the Decalogue, the moral law being the human imitation of the automatism of natural law. The final triumph of Urizen was symbolized by the hanging of the brazen serpent (Orc) on the pole, a form of the 'accursed tree', and recalling the earlier association of tree and serpent with the exile of Adam into a wilderness, as well as anticipating the Crucifixion.

Jesus was another Orc figure, gathering twelve followers and starting a new civilization. Christian civilization, like its predecessors, assumed the Urizenic form that it presented so clearly in Blake's own time. This historical perversion of Christianity is studied in *Europe*, where Enitharmon, the Queen of Heaven, summons up twelve starry children, along with Orc as the captive sun, to reimpose the cult of external reality, or what Blake calls natural religion, on Christendom. With the Resurrection, traditionally symbolized by a red cross on a white ground, Jesus made a definitive step into reality: the revolutionary apocalypse Blake hopes for in his day is a second coming or mass resurrection, which is why resurrection imagery is prominently displayed in *America*. Now, at the end of European civilization, comes another rebellion of Orc in America, bearing on its various banners a tree, a serpent, and thirteen red and white stripes. The spread of this rebellion to Europe itself is a sign that bigger things are on the way.

The Israelites ended their revolt in the desert of the moral law: now it is time to reverse the movement, to enter the Promised Land, the original Eden, which is to Israel what Atlantis is to Britain and America. The Promised Land is not a different place from the desert, but the desert itself transformed (Blake's imagery comes partly from Isaiah 35, a chapter he alludes to in *The Marriage of Heaven and Hell*). The 'deeps shrink to their fountains' because in the apocalypse there is no more sea: dead water is transformed to living water (as in Ezekiel's vision, Ezek. 47:8). The spiritual body of risen man is sexually free, an aspect symbolized by the 'lustful fires' in which he walks. Man under the law is sexually in a prison of heat without light, a volcano: in the resurrection he is unhurt by the flames, like the three Hebrews in Nebuchadnezzar's furnace who were seen walking with the son of God. According to *The Marriage of Heaven and Hell*, Jesus became Jehovah after his death, and Jehovah, not Satan, is the one who dwells in flaming fire. The risen man, then, is the genuine form of the metallic statue of Nebuchadnezzar's dream, without the feet of clay that made that statue an image of tyranny and the cycle of history.

The Resurrection rolled the stone away covering the tomb ('burst the stony roof'). The stone that covers the tomb of man under the law is the vast arch of the sky, which we see as a concave 'vault of paved heaven' (a phrase in the early 'Mad Song') because we are looking at it from under the 'stony roof' of the skull. The risen body would be like the shape of one of Blake's Last Judgement paintings, with an 'opened centre' or radiance of light on top, in the place which is the true location of heaven. Finally, the entire Bible or revelation of the divine in and to man can be read either as the charter of human freedom or as a code of restrictive and negative moral commands. Orc proposes to use Urizen's version of the holy book as fertilizer to help make the desert blossom: what he would do, in other words, is to internalize the law, transform it from arbitrary commands to the inner discipline of the free spirit.

NORTHERN GATE: SINGLE VISION

The optimistic revolutionary construct set up in Blake's early prophecies

is found again in Shelley, whose Prometheus and Jupiter correspond to Orc and Urizen. But in later Romanticism it quickly turns
pessimistic and once more conservative, notably in Schopenhauer,
where the world as idea, the world of genuine humanity, sits on top of a
dark, threatening, and immensely powerful world as will. A similar
construct is in Darwin and Huxley, where the ethical creation of human
society maintains itself precariously against the evolutionary force
below it. In Freud, civilization is essentially an anxiety-structure, where
the 'reality principle', Blake's Urizen, must maintain its ascendancy
somehow over the nihilistic upthrusts of desire. It may permit a certain
amount of expression to the 'pleasure principle', but not to the extent
of being taken over by it. And in Blake, if every revolt of Orc in history
has been 'perverted to ten commands', the inference seems to be that
history exhibits only a gloomy series of cycles, beginning in hope and
inevitably ending in renewed tyranny. In Blake's later prophecies, we
do find this Spenglerian view of history, with a good many of Spengler's
symbols attached to it.

The cyclical movement of history is summarized by Blake in four
stages. The first stage is the revolutionary birth of Orc; the second, the
transfer of power from Orc to Urizen at the height of Orc's powers,
accompanied by the binding or imprisoning of Orc; the third, the
consolidating of 'natural religion' or the sense of reality as out there,
symbolized by Urizen exploring his dens; the fourth, a collapse and
chaos symbolized by the crucifixion of Orc, the hanging of the serpent
on the dead tree. This fourth stage is the one that Blake sees his own
age entering, after the triumph of natural religion or 'Deism' in the
decades following Newton and Locke. It is an age characterized by
mass wars (Isaiah's treading of the winepress), by technology and
complex machinery, by tyranny and 'empire' (imperialism being the
demonic enemy of culture), and by unimaginative art, especially in
architecture. The central symbol of this final phase is the labyrinthine
desert in which the Mosaic exodus ended. Jesus spent forty days in the
desert, according to Mark, 'with the wild beasts': the passage from
empire to ruin, from the phase of the tyrant to the phase of the wild
beast, is symbolized in the story of Nebuchadnezzar, whose metamorphosis is illustrated at the end of *The Marriage of Heaven and Hell*. The
figure of Ijim in *Tiriel* has a parallel significance.

As Blake's symbolism becomes more concentrated, he tends to generalize the whole cycle in the conception of 'Druidism'. The Druids, according to Blake's authorities, worshipped the tree and the serpent, the Druid temple of Avebury, illustrated on the last plate of *Jerusalem*, being serpent-shaped; and they went in for orgies of human sacrifice which illustrate, even more clearly than warfare, the fact that the suppression or perversion of the sexual impulse ends in a death wish (I am not reading modern conceptions into Blake here, but following Blake's own symbolism). This 'Druid' imagery is illustrated in the following passage from *Europe*, describing the reaction of the tyrannical 'King' or guardian angel of the reactionary Albion and his councillors to the American revolution and kindred portents of apocalyptic disaffection:

> In thoughts perturb'd they rose from the bright
> ruins silent following
> The fiery King, who sought his ancient temple
> serpent-form'd
> That stretches out its shady length along the
> Island white.
> Round him roll'd his clouds of war; silent the
> Angel went,
> Along the infinite shores of Thames to golden
> Verulam.
> There stand the venerable porches that high-
> towering rear
> Their oak-surrounded pillars, form'd of massy
> stones, uncut
> With tool: stones precious: such eternal in
> the heavens,
> Of colours twelve, few known on earth, give
> light in the opake,
> Plac'd in the order of the stars, when the five
> senses whelm'd
> In deluge o'er the earth-born man: then turn'd
> the fluxile eyes
> Into two stationary orbs, concentrating all
> things.

> The ever-varying spiral ascents to the heavens
>   of heavens
> Were bended downward, and the nostrils golden
>   gates shut,
> Turn'd outward barr'd and petrify'd against the
>   infinite . . .
>
> Now arriv'd the ancient Guardian at the southern
>   porch.
> That planted thick with trees of blackest leaf,
>   & in a vale
> Obscure, inclos'd the Stone of Night; oblique
>   it stood, o'erhung
> With purple flowers and berries red: image of
>   that sweet south
> Once open to the heavens and elevated on the
>   human neck,
> Now overgrown with hair and cover'd with a
>   stony roof:
> Downward 'tis sunk beneath th' attractive north,
>   that round the feet
> A raging whirlpool draws the dizzy enquirer to
>   his grave.

It is an intricate passage, but it all makes sense. The serpent temple of Avebury is identified with the white-cliffed Albion in its final Druid phase. It is centred at Verulam, which, as the site of a Roman camp, a 'Gothic' cathedral, and the baronial title of Bacon, takes in the whole cycle of British civilization. As we approach the temple, it appears to be a Stonehenge-like circle of twelve precious stones, 'plac'd in the order of the stars', or symbolizing the Zodiac. The imagery recalls the similar decadence of Israel in the desert: the twelve Zodiacal gems of Aaron's breastplate have been mentioned, and the Israelites also built megalithic monuments on which they were forbidden to use iron (Jos. 8:31), hence 'uncut with tool', iron being in Blake the symbol of Los the blacksmith, the builder of the true city of gems (Isa. 54:16).

The central form of Druid architecture is the trilithic cromlech or dolmen, the arch of three stones. According to Blake, the two uprights of this arch symbolize the two aspects of creative power, strength and beauty, or sublimity and pathos, as he calls them in the *Descriptive Catalogue*, the horizontal stone being the dominant Urizenic reason. Human society presents this arch in the form of an 'Elect' class tyrannizing over the 'Reprobate', the unfashionable artists and prophets who embody human sublimity, and the 'Redeemed', the gentler souls who are in the company of the beautiful and pathetic. This trilithic structure appears in such later militaristic monuments as the Arch of Titus: in its 'Druid' form, it is illustrated with great power in *Milton*, Plate 6, and *Jerusalem*, Plate 70. In the former, the balancing rock in front may represent the 'Stone of Night' in the above passage. To pass under this arch is to be subjugated, in a fairly literal sense, to what is, according to the *Descriptive Catalogue*, both the human reason and the 'incapability of intellect', as intellect in Blake is always associated with the creative and imaginative. Another form of tyrannical architecture characteristic of a degenerate civilization is the pyramid[1], representing the volcano or imprisoning mountain under which Orc lies. Blake connects the pyramids with the servitude of the Israelites among the brick-kilns and the epithet 'furnace of iron' (I Kings 8:51) applied to Egypt in the Bible. The association of pyramids and fire is as old as Plato's pun on the word πύρ.

The temple of Verulam is a monument to the fall of man, in Blake the same event as the deluge and the creation of the world in its present 'out there' form. This form is that of the law, the basis of which is revolution in its mechanical sense of revolving wheels, the symbol of which is the *ouroboros*, the serpent with its tail in its mouth (indicated in a passage omitted above). We see the world from individual 'opake' centres, instead of being identified with a universal Man who is also God, who created what we see as alien to us, and who would consequently see his world from the circumference instead of the centre, the perspective reinstated in man by the arts. Such a God-Man would be 'full of eyes', like the creatures of Ezekiel's vision, and by an unexpected but quite logical extension of the symbolism, Blake makes him full of noses too. Burning meat to gods on altars, after all, does assume that gods have circumferential noses.

The 'Stone of Night', the opposite of the 'lively stones' (I Pet. 2:5) of the genuine temple, is an image of the human head, the phrase 'stony roof' being repeated from the passage in *America* quoted above.

It is in the south because the south is the zenith, the place of the sun in full strength in Blake's symbolism. Now it is covered with purple flowers and red berries, probably of the nightshade: the colours are those of the dying god, which is what Orc (usually Luvah in this context) comes to be in Blake's later poems. The Stone of Night has fallen like a meteor through the bottom or nadir of existence, represented by the north, and now has the same relation to its original that a gravestone has to a living body. We may compare the 'grave-plot' that Thel reached when she passed under the 'northern bar', and the black coffin which is the body of the chimney sweep (and the enslaved Negro, who also belongs in the 'southern clime'). Blake's imagery of the north combines the magnetic needle and the legend of the northern maelstrom, the latter supplying a demonic parody of the ascending spiral image on the altar.

From the perspective of single vision, then, our original diagram of buried innocence trying to push its way into experience has to be completed by the death in which all life, individual or historical, ends. Death in Blake's symbolism is Satan, the 'limit of Opacity', reduction to inorganic matter, who operates in the living man as a death wish or 'accuser' of sin. His source in the outer world is the sky, Satan being the starry dragon of Revelation 12:4. Blake identifies this dragon with the Covering Cherub of Ezekiel 28, and the Covering Cherub again with the angel trying to keep us out of the Garden of Eden. Thus the sky is, first, the outward illusion of reality that keeps us out of our proper home; second, the macrocosmic Stone of Night, the rock on top of man's tomb designed to prevent his resurrection; and third, the circumference of what Blake calls the 'Mundane Shell', the world as it appears to the embryonic and unborn imagination. Thus:

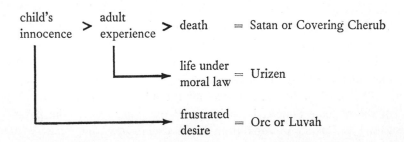

Ordinary human life, symbolized in Blake first by 'Adam' and later by 'Reuben', oscillates between the two submerged states.

The conception of Druidism in Blake, then, is a conception of human energy and desire continuously martyred by the tyranny of human reason, or superstition. The phrase 'dying god' that we have used for Luvah suggests Frazer, and Blake's Druid symbolism has some remarkable anticipations of Frazer's *Golden Bough* complex, including the mistletoe and the oak. The anticipations even extend to Frazer's own unconscious symbolism: the colours of the three states above are, reading up, red, white, and black; and Frazer's book ends with the remark that the web of human thought has been woven of these three colours, though the status of the white or scientific one in Blake is very different. The following passage from *Jerusalem* 66 illustrates Blake's handling of sacrificial symbolism:

> The Daughters of Albion clothed in garments of
> needle work
> Strip them off from their shoulders and bosoms,
> they lay aside
> Their garments, they sit naked upon the Stone of
> trial.
> The knife of flint passes over the howling Victim:
> his blood
> Gushes & stains the fair side of the fair Daughters
> of Albion.
> They put aside his curls: they divide his seven
> locks upon
> His forehead: they bind his forehead with thorns
> of iron,
> They put into his hand a reed, they mock,
> Saying: Behold
> The King of Canaan, whose are seven hundred chariots
> of iron!
> They take off his vesture whole with their Knives
> of flint:
> But they cut asunder his inner garments: searching
> with
> Their cruel fingers for his heart, & there they
> enter in pomp,

In many tears: & there they erect a temple & an
        altar:
They pour cold water on his brain in front, to
        cause
Lids to grow over his eyes in veils of tears: and
        caverns
To freeze over his nostrils, while they feed his
        tongue from cups
And dishes of painted clay.

The imagery combines the mockery and passion of Jesus with features
from Aztec sacrifices, as Blake realizes that the two widely separated
rituals mean essentially the same thing. In the Mexican rites, the 'ves-
ture whole' is the skin, not the garment, and the heart is extracted from
the body, not merely pierced by a spear as in the Passion. As the passage
goes on, the victim expands from an individual body into a country:
that is, he is beginning to embody not merely the dying god, but the
original universal Man, Albion, whose present dead body is England.
The veils and caverns are religious images derived from analogies between the human body and the landscape. Serpent worship is for Blake a
perennial feature of this kind of superstition, and the victim is fed from
dishes of clay partly because, as Blake says in *The Everlasting Gospel*,
'dust & Clay is the Serpent's meat'. An early Biblical dying-god figure
is that of Sisera, the King of Canaan, whose murder at the hands of Jael
suggests the nailing down of Jesus and Prometheus; and the reference
to 'needle work' in the first line also comes from Deborah's war song.
The role given to the Daughters of Albion shows how clearly Blake
associates the ritual of sacrifice, many features of which are repeated
in judicial executions, with a perversion of the erotic instinct; and, in
fact, Blake is clearer than Frazer about the role of the 'white goddess'
in the dying god cult, the Cybele who decrees the death of Attis.

SOUTHERN GATE: THREEFOLD VISION

The conception of a cycle common to individual and to historical life
is the basis of the symbolism of several modern poets, including Yeats,
Joyce in *Finnegans Wake*, and Graves in *The White Goddess*. In its
modern forms, it usually revolves around a female figure. *The Marriage*

of Heaven and Hell prophesies that eventually the bound Orc will be set free and will destroy the present world in a 'consummation', which means both burning up and the climax of a marriage. When the marriage is accomplished 'by an improvement of sensual enjoyment', the world of form and reason will be their 'outward bound or circumference' instead of a separate and therefore tyrannizing principle. One would think then that a female figure would be more appropriate for the symbolism of the world of form than the aged and male Urizen.

In traditional Christian symbolism, God the Creator is symbolically male, and all human souls, whether of men or of women, are creatures, and therefore symbolically female. In Blake, the real man is creating man; hence all human beings, men or women, are symbolically male. The symbolic female in Blake is what we call nature, and has four relations to humanity, depending on the quality of the vision. In the world of death, or Satan, which Blake calls Ulro, the human body is completely absorbed in the body of nature – a 'dark Hermaphrodite', as Blake says in *The Gates of Paradise*. In the ordinary world of experience, which Blake calls Generation, the relation of humanity to nature is that of subject to object. In the usually frustrated and suppressed world of sexual desire, which Blake calls Beulah, the relation is that of lover to beloved, and in the purely imaginative or creative state, called Eden, the relation is that of creator to creature. In the first two worlds, nature is a remote and tantalizing 'female will'; in the last two she is an 'emanation'. Human women are associated with this female nature only when in their behaviour they dramatize its characteristics. The relations between man and nature in the individual and historical cycles are different, and are summarized in *The Mental Traveller*, a poem as closely related to the cyclical symbolism of twentieth-century poetry as Keats's *La Belle Dame Sans Merci* is to pre-Raphaelite poetry.

The Mental Traveller traces the life of a 'Boy' from infancy through manhood to death and rebirth. This Boy represents humanity, and consequently the cycle he goes through can be read either individually and psychologically, or socially and historically. The latter reading is easier, and closer to the centre of gravity of what Blake is talking about. The poem traces a cycle, but the cycle differs from that of the single vision in that the emphasis is thrown on rebirth and return instead of on death. A female principle, nature, cycles in contrary motion against the Boy, growing young as he grows old and vice versa, and producing four phases that we may call son and mother, husband and wife, father and daughter, ghost (Blake's 'spectre'), and ghostly bride (Blake's 'emanation'). Having set them down, we next observe that not one of these relations is genuine: the mother is not really a mother, nor the daughter really a daughter, and similarly with the other states. The 'Woman Old', the nurse who takes charge of the Boy, is Mother Nature, whom Blake calls Tirzah, and who ensures that everyone enters this world in the mutilated and imprisoned form of the physical body. The sacrifice of the dying god repeats this symbolism, which is why the birth of the Boy also contains the symbols of the Passion (we should compare this part of *The Mental Traveller* with the end of *Jerusalem* 67).

As the Boy grows up, he subdues a part of nature to his will, which thereupon becomes his mistress: a stage represented elsewhere in the Preludium to *America*. As the cycle completes what Yeats would call its first gyre, we reach the opposite pole of a 'Female Babe' whom, like the newborn Boy, no one dares touch. This female represents the 'emanation' or accumulated form of what the Boy has created in his life. If she were a real daughter and not a changeling, she would be the Boy's own permanent creation, as Jerusalem is the daughter of Albion, 'a City, yet a Woman'; and with the appearance of such a permanent creation, the cycle of nature would come to an end. But in this world all creative achievements are inherited by someone else and are lost to their creator. This failure to take possession of one's own deepest experience is the theme of *The Crystal Cabinet* (by comparing the imagery of this latter poem with *Jerusalem* 70 we discover that the Female Babe's name, in this context, is Rahab). The Boy, now an old man at the point of death, acquires, like the aged King David, another 'maiden' to keep his body warm on his death-bed. He is now in the desert or wilderness, which symbolizes the end of a cycle, and his maiden is Lilith, the bride of the desert, whom Blake elsewhere calls the Shadowy Female. The Boy as an old man is in an 'alastor' relation to her: he ought to be still making the kind of creative effort that produced the Female Babe, but instead he keeps seeking his 'emanation' or created form outside himself, until eventually the desert is partially renewed by his efforts, he comes again into the place of seed, and the cycle starts once more.

A greatly abbreviated account of the same cycle, in a more purely historical context, is in the 'Argument' of *The Marriage of Heaven and Hell*. Here we start with Rintrah, the prophet in the desert, the Moses or Elijah or John the Baptist who announces a new era of history; then we follow the historical cycle as it makes the desert blossom and produces the honey of the Promised Land. We notice how, as in the time of Moses, water springs up in the desert and how Orc's 'red clay' puts life on the white bones of Urizen. Eventually the new society becomes decadent and tyrannical, forcing the prophet out into the desert once more to begin another cycle.

The poem called *The Gates of Paradise*, based on a series of illustrations reproduced in the standard editions of Blake, describes the same cycle in slightly different and more individualized terms. Here conception in the womb, the mutilation of birth which produces the 'mother's grief', is symbolized by the caterpillar and by the mandrake. The mandrake is traditionally an aphrodisiac, a plant with male and female forms, an opiate, the seed of hanged men, a 'man-dragon' that shrieks when uprooted (i.e. born), and recalls the frustrated sunflower of the *Songs of Experience*. The association of the mandrake with the mother in Genesis 30:14 is the main reason why Blake uses 'Reuben' instead of 'Adam' as the symbol of ordinary man in *Jerusalem*. The embryo then takes on the substance of the four elements and the four humours that traditionally correspond to them, of which 'Earth's Melancholy' is the dominant one. Then the infant is born and grows into an aggressive adolescent, like the Boy in *The Mental Traveller* binding nature down for his delight. This attitude divides nature into a part that is possessed and a part that eludes, and the separation indicates that the boy in this poem also is bound to the cyclical movement. The youth then collides with Urizen, the spear in the revolutionary left hand being opposed to the sword of established order in the right. The caption of this emblem, 'My Son! My Son!' refers to Absalom's revolt against David. Orc is not the son of Urizen, but Absalom, hung on a tree (traditionally by his golden hair, like the mistletoe: cf. *The Book of Ahania*, II, 9), is another dying god or Druid victim.

The other plates are not difficult to interpret: they represent the frustration of desire, the reaction into despair, and the growing of the youthful rebellious Orc into a wing-clipping Urizen again. Finally the hero, like the early Tiriel and like the Boy of *The Mental Traveller* in his old age, becomes a wandering pilgrim making his way, like the old man in the *Pardoner's Tale*, toward his own death. He enters 'Death's Door', the lower half of a design from Blair's *Grave* omitting the resurrection theme in the upper half, and is once more identified with Mother Nature, with a caption quoted from Job 17:14. The Prologue asks us why we worship this dreary womb-to-tomb treadmill as God – that is, why we think of God as a sky-god of automatic order, when this sky-god is really Satan, the corpse of God. The Epilogue returns to the same attack, and concludes by calling Satan 'The lost traveller's Dream under the Hill'. Apart from the general theme of the dreaming traveller which is common to this poem and to *The Mental Traveller* (where the 'mental' travelling is done by the poet and reader, not the hero), there is a more specific allusion to the passage in *The Pilgrim's Progress* where Christian, after falling asleep under Hill Difficulty and losing his roll, is forced to retrace his steps like the Israelites in the desert, to whom Bunyan explicitly refers.

The passage from death to rebirth is represented in Blake's symbolism by Tharmas, the power of renewing life. The ability of the individual to renew his life is resurrection, and the resurrection is a break with the cycle, but in ordinary life such a renewal takes place only in the group or species, and within the cycle. Tharmas is symbolized by the sea, the end and the beginning of life. As the original fall of man was also the deluge, we are in this world symbolically under water, our true home being Atlantis, or the Red Sea, which the Israelites found to be dry land. Tharmas and Orc are the strength and beauty, the sublime and the pathetic, the uprights of the Druid trilithon already mentioned, with Urizen, the anti-intellectual 'reason', connecting them. Thus:

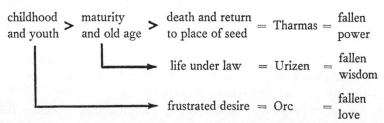

WESTERN GATE: FOURFOLD VISION

In *The Marriage of Heaven and Hell*, Blake presents the revolutionary vision of man as a self-centred anxious ego sitting on top of a rebellious desire, and he associates the emancipating of desire with the end of the world as we know it. The Proverbs of Hell say: 'He who desires but acts not, breeds pestilence.' Putting desire into action does not lead to anarchy, for the fires of Orc are 'thought-creating': what it does lead to is an apocalypse in which 'the whole creation will be consumed and appear infinite and holy, whereas it now appears finite & corrupt'. But when we read other works of Blake, we begin to wonder if this 'Voice of the Devil' tells the whole story. Blake certainly means what he says in *The Marriage of Heaven and Hell*, but that work is a satire, deriving its norms from other conceptions. As we read further in Blake, it becomes clear that the emancipating of desire, for him, is not the cause but the effect of the purging of reality. There was some political dis-illusionment as Blake proceeded – the perversion of the French Revo-lution into Napoleonic imperialism, the strength of the reactionary power in Britain, the continued ascendancy of the slave-owners in America, and a growing feeling that Voltaire and Rousseau were reactionaries and not revolutionaries were the main elements in it – but although this leads to some changes in emphasis in later poems, there is no evidence that he was ever really confused about the difference between the apocalyptic and the historical versions of reality.

Blake dislikes any terminology which implies that there are two perceivers in man, such as a soul and a body, which perceive different worlds. There is only one world, but there are two kinds of things to be done with it. There is, first, what Blake calls the natural vision, which assumes that the objective world is essentially independent of man. This vision becomes increasingly hypnotized by the automatic order and tantalizing remoteness of nature, creates gods in the image of its mindless mechanism, and rationalizes all evils and injustices of exis-tence under some such formula as 'Whatever is, is right'. In extreme forms, this alienating vision becomes the reflection of the death wish in the soul, and develops annihilation wars like those of Blake's own time. Then there is the human vision, which takes the objective world to be the 'starry floor', the bottom of reality, its permanence being important only as a stable basis for human creation. The goal of the human vision is 'Religion, or Civilized Life such as it is in the Christian Church'. This is a life of pure creation, such as is ascribed in Christianity to God, and which for Blake would participate in the infinite and eternal perspective of God. We note that Blake, like Kierkegaard, leads us toward an 'either/or' dilemma, but that his terms are the reverse of Kierkegaard's. It is the aesthetic element for Blake which moves in the sphere of existential freedom; it is the ethical element which is the spectator, under the bondage of the law and the knowledge of good and evil.

We begin, then, with the view of an orthodox or moral 'good', founded on an acceptance of the world out there, contrasted with the submerged 'evil' desires of man to live in a world that makes more human sense. This vision of life turns out to be, when examined, a cyclical vision, completed by the more elaborate cycles just examined. But in addition to the cyclical vision there is also a dialectic, a separating-out of the two opposing human and natural visions. The categories of these visions are not moral good and evil, but life and death, one producing the real heaven of creation and the other the real hell of torture and tyranny. We have met one pole of this dialectic already in the conception of Satan, or death, as the only possible goal of all human effort from one point of view. The other pole is the impulse to transform the world into a human and imaginative form, the impulse that creates all art, all genuine religion, all culture and civilization. This impulse is personified by Blake as Los, the spirit of prophecy and creativity, and it is Los, not Orc, who is the hero of Blake's prophecies. Los derives, not from the suppressed desires of the individual child, but from a deeper creative impulse alluded to in Biblical myths about the unfallen state. These myths tell us that man's original state was not primitive, or derived from nature at all, but civilized, in the environment of a garden and a city. This unfallen state is, so to speak, the previous tree of which contemporary man is the seed, and the form he is attempting to re-create. Thus:

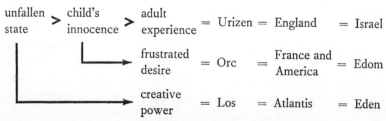

It seems curious that, especially in the earlier prophecies, Los appears to play a more reactionary and sinister role than Urizen himself. We discover that it is Los, not Urizen, who is the father of Orc; Los, not Urizen, who actively restrains Orc, tying him down under Mount Atlas with the 'Chain of Jealousy'; and Los who is the object of Orc's bitter Oedipal resentments. In the Preludium to *America*, he is referred to by his alternative name of Urthona, and there it is he and not Urizen who rivets Orc's 'tenfold chains'. These chains evidently include an incest taboo, for Orc is copulating with his sister in this Preludium. Evidently, as Blake conceives it, there is a deeply conservative element in the creative spirit that seems to help perpetuate the reign of Urizen. In fact, certain functions given to Urizen in earlier prophecies are transferred to Los in later ones. According to William Morris, the joy that the medieval craftsman took in his work was so complete that he was able to accept the tyranny of medieval society: similarly, Blake is able to live in the age of Pitt and Nelson and yet be absorbed in building his palace of art on the 'Great Atlantic Mountains', which will be here after the 'Sea of Time and Space' above it is no more.

This principle that effective social action is to be found in the creation of art and not in revolution is, of course, common to many Romantics in Blake's period. It should not, however – certainly not in Blake – be regarded as a mere neurotic or wish-fulfilment substitute for the failure of revolution. Apart from the fact that the creation of art is a highly social act, Blake's conception of art is very different from the dictionary's. It is based on what we call the arts, because of his doctrine that human reality is created and not observed. But it includes much that we do not think of as art, and excludes much that we do, such as the paintings of Reynolds.

We notice that in *The Gates of Paradise* cycle there is one point at which there is a break from the cycle, the plate captioned 'Fear & Hope are – Vision', and described in the commentary as a glimpse of 'The Immortal Man that cannot Die'. The corresponding point in *The Mental Traveller* comes in describing the form ('emanation') of the life that the Boy has been constructing, just before it takes shape as the elusive 'Female Babe':

> And these are the gems of the Human Soul,
> The rubies & pearls of a lovesick eye,

> The countless gold of the akeing heart,
> The martyr's groan & the lover's sigh.

The curiously wooden allegory is not characteristic of Blake, but it recurs in *Jerusalem* 12, where the same theme is under discussion. Evidently, Blake means by 'art' a creative life rooted in the arts, but including what more traditional language calls charity. Every act man performs is either creative or destructive. Both kinds seem to disappear in time, but in fact it is only the destructive act, the act of war or slavery or parasitism or hatred, that is really lost.

Los is not simply creative power, but the spirit of time: more accurately, he is the power that constructs in time the palace of art (Golgonooza), which is timeless. As Blake says in a grammatically violent aphorism, the ruins of time build mansions in eternity. The products of self-sacrifice and martyrdom and endurance of injustice still exist, in an invisible but permanent world created out of time by the imagination. This world is the genuine Atlantis or Eden that we actually live in. As soon as we realize that we do live in it, we enter into what Blake means by the Last Judgement. Most people do not make this act of realization, and those who do make it have the responsibility of being evangelists for it. According to Blake, most of what the enlightened can do for the unenlightened is negative: their task is to sharpen the dialectic of the human and natural visions by showing that there are only the alternatives of apocalypse and annihilation.

Blake obviously hopes for a very considerable social response to vision in or soon after his lifetime. But even if everybody responded completely and at once, the City of God would not become immediately visible: if it did, it would simply be one more objective environment. The real 'heaven' is not a glittering city, but the power of bringing such cities into existence. In the poem 'My Spectre around me', Blake depicts a figure like the Boy of *The Mental Traveller* in old age, searching vainly for his 'emanation', the total body of what he can love and create, outside himself instead of inside. The natural tendency of desire (Orc) in itself is to find its object. Hence the effect of the creative impulse on desire is bound to be restrictive until the release of desire becomes the inevitable by-product of creation.

The real world, being the source of a human vision, is human and not natural (which means indefinite) in shape. It does not stretch away for ever into the stars, but has the form of a single giant man's body, the parts of which are arranged thus:

Urizen   = head = city
Tharmas = body = garden
Orc   = loins = soil or bed of love
Urthona = legs = underworld of dream and repose
(Los)

Except that it is unfallen, the four levels of this world correspond very closely to the four traditional levels that we find in medieval and Renaissance poetry. The present physical world, by the 'improvement of sensual enjoyment', would become an integral part of nature, and so Comus's attempt to seduce the Lady by an appeal to 'nature' would no longer be a seduction or a specious argument. But the really important distinction is that for earlier poets the two upper levels, the city and the garden, were divine and not human in origin, whereas for Blake they are both divine and human, and their recovery depends on the creative power in man as well as in God.

The difference between the traditional and the Blakean versions of reality corresponds to the difference between the first and the last plates of the Job illustrations. In the first plate, Job and his family are in the state of innocence (Beulah), in a peaceful pastoral repose like that of the twenty-third Psalm. They preserve this state in the traditional way, by obeying a divine Providence that has arranged it, and hence are imaginatively children. There is nothing in the picture that suggests anything inadequate except that, in a recall of a very different Psalm (137), there are musical instruments hung on the tree above. In the last plate, things are much as they were before, but Job's family have taken the instruments down from the tree and are playing them. In Blake, we recover our original state, not by returning to it, but by re-creating it. The act of creation, in its turn, is not producing something out of nothing, but the act of setting free what we already possess.

12 THE DRUNKEN BOAT: THE REVOLUTIONARY ELEMENT IN ROMANTICISM

Any such conception as 'Romanticism' is at one or more removes from actual literary experience, in an inner world where ten thousand different things flash upon the inward eye with all the bliss of oversimplification. Some things about it, however, are generally accepted, and we may start with them. First, Romanticism has a historical centre of gravity, which falls somewhere around the 1790–1830 period. This gets us at once out of the fallacy of timeless characterization, where we say that Romanticism has certain qualities, not found in the age of Pope, of sympathy with nature or what not, only to have someone produce a poem of Propertius or Kalidasa, or, eventually, Pope himself, and demand to know if the same qualities are not there. Second, Romanticism is not a general historical term like 'medieval': it appears to have another centre of gravity in the creative arts. We speak most naturally of Romantic literature, painting, and music. We do, it is true, speak of Romantic philosophy, but what seems to us most clearly Romantic in that are such things as the existential ethic of Fichte or the analogical constructs of Schelling; both of them, in different ways, examples of philosophy produced by an essentially literary mind, like the philosophies of Sartre or Maritain in our day. So at least they seemed to Kant, if one may judge from Kant's letter to Fichte suggesting that Fichte abandon philosophy, as a subject too difficult for him, and confine himself to lively popularizations.

Third, even in its application to the creative arts Romanticism is a selective term, more selective even than 'Baroque' appears to be becoming. We think of it as including Keats, but not, on the whole, Crabbe; Scott, but not, in general, Jane Austen; Wordsworth, but not, on any account, James Mill. As generally used, 'Romantic' is contrasted with two other terms, 'classical' and 'realistic'. Neither contrast seems satisfactory. We could hardly call Wordsworth's preface to the *Lyrical Ballads* anti-realistic, or ignore the fact that Shelley was a better classical scholar than, say, Dryden, who, according to Samuel Johnson, translated the first book of the *Iliad* without knowing what was in the second. Still, the pairings exist, and we shall have to examine them. And yet, fourth, though selective, Romanticism is not a voluntary category. It does not see Byron as the successor to Pope or Wordsworth as the successor to Milton, which would have been acceptable enough to both poets: it associates Byron and Wordsworth, to their mutual disgust, with each other.

Accepting all this, we must also avoid the two traps in the phrase 'history of ideas'. First, an idea, as such, is independent of time and can be argued about; an historical event is not and cannot be. If Romanticism is in part an historical event, as it clearly is, then to say with T. E. Hulme: 'I object to even the best of the Romantics' is much like saying: 'I object to even the best battles of the Napoleonic War.' Most general value-judgements on Romanticism as a whole are rationalizations of an agreement or disagreement with some belief of which Romantic poetry is supposed to form the objective correlative.

This latter is the second or Hegelian trap in the history of ideas, which we fall into when we assume that around 1790 or earlier some kind of thesis arose in history and embodied itself in the Romantic movement. Such an assumption leads us to examining all the cultural products we call Romantic as allegories of that thesis. Theses have a way of disagreeing with each other, and if we try to think of Romanticism as some kind of single 'idea', all we can do with it is what Lovejoy[1] did: break it down into a number of contradictory ideas with nothing significant in common. In literature, and more particularly poetry, ideas are subordinated to imagery, to a language more 'simple, sensuous, and passionate' than the language of philosophy. Hence it may be possible for two poets to be related by common qualities of imagery even when they do not agree on a single thesis in religion, politics, or the theory of art itself.

The history of imagery, unlike the history of ideas, appears to be for the most part a domain where, in the words of a fictional Canadian poetess[2], 'the hand of man hath never trod'. Yet we seem inexorably led to it by our own argument, and perhaps the defects in what follows may be in part excused by the novelty of the subject, to me at least. After making every allowance for a prodigious variety of technique and approach, it is still possible to see a consistent framework (I wish the English language had a better equivalent for the French word *cadre*) in the imagery of both medieval and Renaissance poetry. The most remarkable and obvious feature of this framework is the division of being into four levels. The highest level is heaven, the place of the presence of God. Next come the two levels of the order of nature, the human level and the physical level. The order of human nature, or man's proper home, is represented by the story of the Garden of Eden in the Bible and the myth of the Golden Age in Boethius and elsewhere. Man is no longer in it, but the end of all his religious, moral, and social cultivation is to raise him into something resembling it. Physical nature, the world of animals and plants, is the world man is now in, but unlike the animals and plants he is not adjusted to it. He is confronted from birth with a moral dialectic, and must either rise above it to his proper human home or sink below it into the fourth level of sin, death, and hell. This last level is not part of the order of nature, but its existence is what at present corrupts nature. A very similar framework can be found in classical poetry, and the alliance of the two, in what is so often called Christian humanism, accounts for the sense of an antagonism between the Romantic movement and the classical tradition, in spite of its many and remarkable affinities with that tradition.

Such a framework of images, however closely related in practice to belief, is not in itself a belief or an expression of belief: it is in itself simply a way of arranging images and providing for metaphors. At the same time the word 'framework' itself is a spatial metaphor, and any framework is likely to be projected in space, even confused or identified with its spatial projection. In Dante Eden is a long way up, on the top of a mountain of purgatory; heaven is much further up, and hell is down, at the centre of the earth. We may know that such conceptions as heaven and hell do not depend on spatial metaphors of up and down, but a cosmological poet, dealing with them as images, has to put them somewhere. To Dante it was simple enough to put them at the top and bottom of the natural order, because he knew of no alternative to the

Ptolemaic picture of the world. To Milton, who did know of an alternative, the problem was more complex, and Milton's heaven and hell are outside the cosmos, in a kind of absolute up and down. After Milton comes Newton, and after Newton ups and downs become hopelessly confused.

What I see first of all in Romanticism is the effect of a profound change, not primarily in belief, but in the spatial projection of reality. This in turn leads to a different localizing of the various levels of that reality. Such a change in the localizing of images is bound to be accompanied by, or even cause, changes in belief and attitude, and changes of this latter sort are exhibited by the Romantic poets. But the change itself is not in belief or attitude, and may be found in, or at least affecting, poets of a great variety of beliefs.

In the earlier framework, the disorder of sin, death, and corruption was restricted to the sublunary world of four elements. Above the moon was all that was left of nature as God had originally planned it before the fall. The planets, with their angel-guided spheres, are images of a divinely sanctioned order of nature which is also the true home of man. Hence there was no poetic incongruity in Dante's locating his Paradiso in the planetary spheres, nor in Milton's associating the music of the spheres with the song of the angels in the *Nativity Ode*, nor in using the same word 'heaven' for both the kingdom of God and the sky. A post-Newtonian poet has to think of gravitation and the solar system. Newton, Miss Nicolson[3] has reminded us, demanded the muse, but the appropriate muse was Urania, and Urania had already been requested by Milton to descend to a safer position on earth for the second half of *Paradise Lost*.

Let us turn to Blake's poem *Europe*, engraved in 1794. *Europe* surveys the history of the Western world from the birth of Christ to the beginning of the French Revolution, and in its opening lines parodies the *Nativity Ode*. For Blake all the deities associated with the planets and the starry skies, of whom the chief is Enitharmon, the Queen of Heaven, are projections of a human will to tyranny, rationalized as eternal necessity and order. Christianity, according to this poem, had not abolished but confirmed the natural religion in the classical culture which had deified the star-gods. The doom of tyranny is sealed by the French Revolution, and the angel who blows the last trumpet as the sign of the final awakening of liberty is Isaac Newton. The frontispiece of *Europe* is the famous vision of the sky-god Urizen generally called the Ancient of Days, holding a compass in his left hand, and this picture is closely related to Blake's portrait of Newton, similarly preoccupied with a compass and oblivious of the heavens he is supposed to be studying.

Blake's view, in short, is that the universe of modern astronomy, as revealed in Newton, exhibits only a blind, mechanical, subhuman order, not the personal presence of a deity. Newton himself tended to think of God still as 'up there'; but *what* was up there, according to Blake, is only a set of interlocking geometrical diagrams, and God, Blake says, is not a mathematical diagram. Newtonism leads to what for Blake are intellectual errors, such as a sense of the superiority of abstractions to actual things and the notion that the real world is a measurable but invisible world of primary qualities. But Blake's main point is that admiring the mechanisms of the sky leads to establishing human life in mechanical patterns too. In other words, Blake's myth of Urizen is a fuller and more sophisticated version of the myth of Frankenstein.

Blake's evil, sinister, or merely complacent sky-gods, Urizen, Nobodaddy, Enitharmon, Satan, remind us of similar beings in other Romantics: Shelley's Jupiter, Byron's Arimanes, the Lord in the Prologue to *Faust*. They in their turn beget later Romantic gods and goddesses, such as Baudelaire's female 'froide majesté', Hardy's Immanent Will, or the God of Housman's 'The chestnut casts his flambeaux', who is a brute and blackguard because he is a sky-god in control of the weather, and sends his rain on the just and on the unjust. The association of sinister or unconscious mechanism with what we now call outer space is a commonplace of popular literature today which is a Romantic inheritance. Perhaps Orwell's *1984*, a vision of a mechanical tyranny informed by the shadow of a Big Brother who can never die, is the terminal point of a development of imagery that began with Blake's Ancient of Days. Not every poet, naturally, associates mechanism with the movements of the stars as Blake does, or sees it as a human imitation of the wrong kind of divine creativity. But the contrast between the mechanical and the organic is deeply rooted in Romantic thinking, and the tendency is to associate the mechanical with ordinary consciousness, as we see in the account of the associative fancy in Coleridge's *Biographia* or of discursive thought in Shelley's *Defence of Poetry*. This is in striking contrast to the Cartesian tradition, where the mechanical is, of course, associated with the subconscious. The mechanical being characteristic of ordinary experience, it is found particularly in the world 'outside'; the superior or organic world is consequently 'inside', and although it is still called superior or higher, the natural metaphorical direction of the inside world is downward, into the profounder depths of consciousness.

If a Romantic poet, therefore, wishes to write of God, he has more difficulty in finding a place to put him than Dante or even Milton had, and on the whole he prefers to do without a place, or finds 'within' metaphors more reassuring than 'up there' metaphors. When Wordsworth speaks, in *The Prelude* and elsewhere, of feeling the presence of deity through a sense of interpenetration of the human mind and natural powers, one feels that his huge and mighty forms, like the spirits of Yeats, have come to bring him the right metaphors for his poetry. In the second book of *The Excursion* we have a remarkable vision of what has been called the heavenly city[4] of the eighteenth-century philosophers, cast in the form of an ascent up a mountain, where the city is seen at the top. The symbolism, I think, is modelled on the vision of Cleopolis in the first book of *The Faerie Queene*, and its technique is admirably controlled and precise. Yet surely this is not the real Wordsworth. The spirits have brought him the wrong metaphors; metaphors that Spenser used with full imaginative conviction, but which affect only the surface of Wordsworth's mind.

The second level of the older construct was the world of original human nature, now a lost paradise or golden age. It is conceived as a better and more appropriate home for man than his present environment, whether man can regain it or not. But in the older construct this world was ordinarily not thought of as human in origin or conception. Adam awoke in a garden not of his planting, in a fresh-air suburb of the City of God, and when the descendants of Cain began to build cities on earth, they were building to models already existing in both heaven and hell. In the Middle Ages and the Renaissance the agencies which helped to raise man from the physical to the human world were such things as the sacraments of religion, the moral law, and the habit of virtue, none of them strictly human inventions. These were the safe and unquestioned agencies, the genuinely educational media. Whether the human arts of poetry and painting and music were genuinely educational in this sense could be and was disputed or denied; and the poets themselves, when they wrote apologies for poetry, seldom claimed equality with religion or law, beyond pointing out that the earliest major poets were prophets and lawgivers.

For the modern mind there are two poles of mental activity. One may be described as sense, by which I mean the recognition of what is presented by experience: the empirical, observant habit of mind in which, among other things, the inductive sciences begin. In this attitude reality is, first of all, 'out there', whatever happens to it afterwards. The other pole is the purely formalizing or constructive aspect of the mind, where reality is something brought into being by the act of construction. It is obvious that in pre-Romantic poetry there is a strong affinity with the attitude that we have called sense. The poet, in all ages and cultures, prefers images to abstractions, the sensational to the conceptual. But the pre-Romantic structure of imagery belonged to a nature which was the work of God; the design in nature was, as Sir Thomas Browne calls it, the art of God; nature is thus an objective structure or system for the poet to follow. The appropriate metaphors of imitation are visual and physical ones, and the creative powers of the poet have models outside him.

It is generally recognized that Rousseau represents, and to some extent made, a revolutionary change in the modern attitude. The primary reason for his impact was, I think, not in his political or educational views as such, but in his assumption that civilization was a purely human artefact, something that man had made, could unmake, could subject to his own criticism, and was at all times entirely responsible for[5]. Above all, it was something for which the only known model was in the human mind. This kind of assumption is so penetrating that it affects those who detest Rousseau, or have never heard of him, equally with the small minority of his admirers. Also, it gets into the mind at once, whereas the fading out of such counter-assumptions as the literal and historical nature of the Garden of Eden story is very gradual. The effect of such an assumption is twofold. First, it puts the arts in the centre of civilization. The basis of civilization is now the creative power of man; its model is the human vision revealed in the arts. Second, this model, as well as the sources of creative power, are now located in the mind's internal heaven, the external world being seen as a mirror reflecting and making visible what is within. Thus the 'outside' world, most of which is 'up there', yields importance and priority to the inner world, in fact derives its poetic significance at least from it. 'In looking at objects of Nature,' says Coleridge in the Notebooks, 'I seem rather to be seeking, as it were *asking* for, a symbolical language for something within me that already and forever exists, than observing anything new.' This principle extends both to the immediate surrounding world which is the emblem of the music of humanity in Wordsworth and to the starry heavens on which Keats read 'Huge cloudy symbols of a high romance'.

Hence in Romantic poetry the emphasis is not on what we have called sense, but on the constructive power of the mind, where reality is brought into being by experience. There is a contrast in popular speech between the romantic and the realist, where the word 'romantic' implies a sentimentalized or rose-coloured view of reality. This vulgar sense of the word may throw some light on the intensity with which the Romantic poets sought to defy external reality by creating a uniformity of tone and mood. The establishing of this uniformity, and the careful excluding of anything that would dispel it, is one of the constant and typical features of the best Romantic poetry, though we may call it a dissociation of sensibility if we happen not to like it. Such a poetic technique is, psychologically, akin to magic, which also aims at bringing spiritual forces into reality through concentration on a certain type of experience. Such words as 'charm' or 'spell' suggest uniformity of mood as well as a magician's repertoire. Historically and generically, it is akin to romance, with its effort to maintain a self-consistent idealized world without the intrusions of realism or irony.

For these reasons Romanticism is difficult to adapt to the novel, which demands an empirical and observant attitude; its contribution to prose fiction is rather, appropriately enough, a form of romance. In the romance the characters tend to become psychological projections, and the setting a period in a past just remote enough to be re-created rather than empirically studied. We think of Scott as within the Romantic movement; Jane Austen as related to it chiefly by her parodies of the kind of sensibility that tries to live in a self-created world instead of adapting to the one that is there. Marianne in *Sense and Sensibility*, Catherine in *Northanger Abbey*, and, of course, everybody in *Love and Freindship*, are examples. Crabbe's naturalistic manifesto in the opening of *The Village* expresses an attitude which in itself is not far from Wordsworth's. But Crabbe is a metrical novelist in a way that Wordsworth is not. The soldier in *The Prelude* and the leech-gatherer in *Resolution and Independence* are purely romantic characters in the sense just given of psychological projections: that is, they become temporary or epiphanic myths. We should also notice that the internalizing of reality in Romanticism proper develops a contrast between it and a contemporary realism which descends from the pre-Romantic tradition, but acquires a more purely empirical attitude to the external world.

The third level of the older construct was the physical world, theologically fallen, which man is born into, but which is not the real world of human nature. Man's primary attitude to external physical nature is thus one of detachment. The kind of temptation represented by Spenser's Bower of Bliss or Milton's Comus is based on the false suggestion that physical nature, with its relatively innocent moral freedom, can be the model for human nature. The resemblances between the poetic techniques used in the Bower of Bliss episode and some of the techniques of the Romantics are superficial: Spenser, unlike the Romantics, is consciously producing a rhetorical set piece, designed to show that the Bower of Bliss is not natural but artificial in the modern sense. Man for pre-Romantic poets is not a child of Nature in the sense that he was originally a primitive. Milton's Adam becomes a noble savage immediately after his fall; but that is not his original nature. In Romanticism the cult of the primitive is a by-product of the internalizing of the creative impulse. The poet has always been supposed to be imitating nature, but if the model of his creative power is in his mind, the nature that he is to imitate is now inside him, even if it is also outside.

The original form of human society also is hidden 'within'. Keats refers to this hidden society when he says in a letter to Reynolds: 'Man should not dispute or assert but whisper results to his neighbour . . . and Humanity . . . would become a grand democracy of Forest Trees!' Coleridge refers to it in the *Biographia* when he says: 'The medium, by which spirits understand each other, is not the surrounding air; but the *freedom* which they possess in common.' Whether the

Romantic poet is revolutionary or conservative depends on whether he regards this original society as concealed by or as manifested in existing society. If the former, he will think of true society as a primitive structure of nature and reason, and will admire the popular, simple, or even the barbaric more than the sophisticated. If the latter, he will find his true inner society manifested by a sacramental church or by the instinctive manners of an aristocracy. The search for a visible ideal society in history leads to a good deal of admiration for the Middle Ages, which on the Continent was sometimes regarded as the essential feature of Romanticism. The affinity between the more extreme Romantic conservatism and the subversive revolutionary movements of fascism and nazism in our day has been often pointed out. The present significance for us of this fact is that the notion of the inwardness of creative power is inherently revolutionary, just as the pre-Romantic construct was inherently conservative, even for poets as revolutionary as Milton. The self-identifying admiration which so many Romantics expressed for Napoleon has much to do with the association of natural force, creative power, and revolutionary outbreak. As Carlyle says, in an uncharacteristically cautious assessment of Napoleon: 'What Napoleon *did* will in the long-run amount to what he did *justly*; what Nature with her laws will sanction.'

Further, the Romantic poet is a part of a total process, engaged with and united to a creative power greater than his own because it includes his own. This greater creative power has a relation to him which we may call, adapting a term of Blake's, his vehicular form. The sense of identity with a larger power of creative energy meets us everywhere in Romantic culture, I think even in the crowded excited canvases of Delacroix and the tremendous will-to-power finales of Beethoven. The symbolism of it in literature has been too thoroughly studied in Professor Abrams's *The Mirror and the Lamp* and in Professor Wasserman's *The Subtler Language* for me to add more than a footnote or two at this point. Sometimes the greater power of this vehicular form is a rushing wind, as in Shelley's Ode and in the figure of the 'correspondent breeze'[6] studied by Professor Abrams. The image of the Aeolian harp, or lyre – Romantic poets are apt to be sketchy in their orchestration – belongs here. Sometimes it is a boat driven by a breeze or current, or by more efficient magical forces in the *Ancient Mariner*. This image occurs so often in Shelley that it has helped to suggest my title; the introduction to Wordsworth's *Peter Bell* has a flying-boat closely associated with the moon. Those poems of Wordsworth in which we feel driven along by a propelling metrical energy, *Peter Bell, The Idiot Boy, The Waggoner,* and others, seem to me to be among Wordsworth's most central poems. Sometimes the vehicular form is a heightened state of consciousness in which we feel that we are greater than we know, or an intense feeling of communion, as in the sacramental corn-and-wine images of the great Keats odes.

The sense of unity with a greater power is surely one of the reasons why so much of the best Romantic poetry is mythopoeic. The myth is typically the story of the god, whose form and character are human, but who is also a sun-god or tree-god or ocean-god. It identifies the human with the non-human world, an identification which is also one of the major functions of poetry itself. Coleridge makes it a part of the primary as well as the secondary imagination. 'This I call *I*,' he says in the Notebooks, 'identifying the percipient and the perceived.' The 'Giant Forms' of Blake's prophecies are states of being and feeling in which we have our own being and feeling; the huge and mighty forms of Wordsworth's *Prelude* have similar affinities; even the dreams of De Quincey seem vehicular in the same sense. It is curious that there seems to be so little mythopoeic theory in Romantic poets, considering that the more expendable critics of the time complained as much about the obscurity of myth as their counterparts of today do now.

One striking feature of the Romantic poets is their resistance to fragmentation: their compulsion, almost, to express themselves in long continuous poems is quite as remarkable as their lyrical gifts. I have remarked elsewhere that the romance, in its most naïve and primitive form, is an endless sequence of adventures, terminated only by the author's death or disgust. In Romanticism something of this inherently endless romance form recurs. Childe Harold and Don Juan are Byron to such an extent that the poems about them can be finished only by Byron's death or boredom with the *persona. The Prelude,* and still more the gigantic scheme of which it formed part, has a similar relation to Wordsworth, and something parallel is beginning to show its head at once in Keats's *Sleep and Poetry* and Shelley's *Queen Mab.* We touch here on the problem of the Romantic unfinished poem, which has been studied by Professor Bostetter.[7] My present interest, however, is rather in the feature of unlimited continuity, which seems to be connected with the sense of vehicular energy, of being carried along by a greater force, the quality which outside literature, according to Keats, makes a man's life a continual allegory.

We have found, then, that the metaphorical structure of Romantic poetry tends to move inside and downward instead of outside and upward; hence the creative world is deep within, and so is heaven or the place of the presence of God. Blake's Orc and Shelley's Prometheus are Titans imprisoned underneath experience; the Gardens of Adonis are down in *Endymion*, whereas they are up in *The Faerie Queene* and *Comus*; in *Prometheus Unbound* everything that aids mankind comes from below, associated with volcanoes and fountains. In *The Revolt of Islam* there is a curious collision with an older habit of metaphor when Shelley speaks of

A power, a thirst, a knowledge . . . below
All thoughts, like light beyond the atmosphere.

The *Kubla Khan* geography of caves and underground streams haunts all Shelley's language about creative processes: in *Speculations on Metaphysics*, for instance, he says: 'But thought can with difficulty visit the intricate and winding chambers which it inhabits. It is like a river whose rapid and perpetual stream flows outwards. . . . The caverns of the mind are obscure, and shadowy, or pervaded with a lustre, beautifully bright indeed, but shining not beyond their portals.'

In pre-Romantic poetry heaven is the order of grace, and grace is normally thought of as descending from above into the soul. In the Romantic construct there is a centre where inward and outward manifestations of a common motion and spirit are unified, where the ego is identified as itself because it is also identified with something which is not itself. In Blake[8] this world at the deep centre is Jerusalem, the City of God that mankind, or Albion, has sought all through history without success because he has been looking in the wrong direction, outside. Jerusalem is also the garden of Eden where the Holy Word walked among the ancient trees; Eden in the unfallen world would be the same place as England's green and pleasant land where Christ also walked; and England's green and pleasant land is also Atlantis, the sunken island kingdom which we can rediscover by draining the 'Sea of Time and Space' off the top of the mind. In *Prometheus Unbound* Atlantis reappears when Prometheus is liberated, and the one great flash of vision which is all that is left to us of Wordsworth's *Recluse* uses the same imagery:

> Paradise, and groves
> Elysian, Fortunate Fields – like those of old
> Sought in the Atlantic Main – why should they be
> A history only of departed things,
> Or a mere fiction of what never was? . . .
> – I, long before the blissful hour arrives,
> Would chant, in lonely peace, the spousal verse
> Of this great consummation.

The Atlantis theme is in many other Romantic myths: in the Glaucus episode of *Endymion* and in De Quincey's *Savannah-la-Mar*, which speaks of 'human life still subsisting in submarine asylums sacred from the storms that torment our upper air'. The theme of land reclaimed from the ocean plays also a somewhat curious role in Goethe's *Faust*. We find the same imagery in later writers who continue the Romantic tradition, such as D. H. Lawrence in the 'Song of a Man Who Has Come Through':

> If only I am keen and hard like the sheer tip of a wedge
> Driven by invisible blows,
> The rock will split, we shall come at the wonder, we
>   shall find the Hesperides.

In *The Pilgrim's Progress*, Ignorance is sent to hell from the very gates of heaven. The inference seems to be that only Ignorance knows the precise location of both kingdoms. For knowledge, and still more for imagination, the journey within to the happy island garden or the city of light is a perilous quest, equally likely to terminate in the blasted ruin of Byron's *Darkness*. In many Romantic poems, including Keats's nightingale ode, it is suggested that the final identification of and with reality may be or at least include death. The suggestion that death may lead to the highest knowledge, dropped by Lucifer in Byron's *Cain*, haunts Shelley continually. A famous passage in *Prometheus Unbound* associates the worlds of creation and death in some inner area, where

Zoroaster meets his image in a garden. Just as the sun is the means but not a tolerable object of sight, so the attempt to turn around and see the source of one's vision may be destructive, as the Lady of Shalott found when she turned away from the mirror. Thus the world of the deep interior in Romantic poetry is morally ambivalent, retaining some of the demonic qualities that the corresponding pre-Romantic lowest level had.

This sense that the source of genius is beyond good and evil, that the possession of genius may be a curse, that the only real knowledge given to Adam in Paradise, however disastrous, came to him from the devil – all this is part of the contribution of Byron to modern sensibility, and part of the irrevocable change that he made in it. Of his Lara[9] Byron says:

> He stood a stranger in this breathing world,
> An erring spirit from another hurl'd;
> A thing of dark imaginings, that shaped
> By choice the perils he by chance escaped;
> But 'scaped in vain, for in their memory yet
> His mind would half exult and half regret . . .
> But haughty still and loth himself to blame,
> He call'd on Nature's self to share the shame,
> And charged all faults upon the fleshly form
> She gave to clog the soul, and feast the worm;
> Till he at last confounded good and ill,
> And half mistook for fate the acts of will.

It would be wrong to regard this as Byronic hokum, for the wording is very precise. Lara looks demonic to a nervous and conforming society, as the dragon does to the tame villatic fowl in Milton. But there is a genuinely demonic quality in him which arises from his being nearer than other men to the unity of subjective and objective worlds. To be in such a place might make a poet more creative; it makes other types of superior beings, including Lara, more destructive.

We said earlier that a Romantic poet's political views would depend partly on whether he saw his inner society as concealed by or as manifested in actual society. A Romantic poet's moral attitude depends on a similar ambivalence in the conception of nature. Nature to Wordsworth is a mother-goddess who teaches the soul serenity and joy, and never betrays the heart that loves her; to the Marquis de Sade nature is the source of all the perverse pleasures that an earlier age had classified as 'unnatural'. For Wordsworth the reality of Nature is manifested by its reflection of moral values; for de Sade the reality is concealed by that reflection. It is this ambivalent sense (for it is ambivalent, and not simply ambiguous) of appearance as at the same time revealing and concealing reality, as clothes simultaneously reveal and conceal the naked body, that makes *Sartor Resartus* so central a document of the Romantic movement. We spoke of Wordsworth's Nature as a mother-goddess, and her psychological descent from mother-figures is clearly traced in *The Prelude*. The corn-goddess in Keats's *To Autumn*, the parallel figure identified with Ruth in the *Ode to a Nightingale*, the still unravished bride of the Grecian urn, Psyche, even the veiled Melancholy, are all emblems of a revealed Nature. Elusive nymphs or teasing and mocking female figures who refuse to take definite form, like the figure in *Alastor* or Blake's 'female will' types; terrible and sinister white goddesses like La Belle Dame sans Merci, or females associated with something forbidden or demonic, like the sister-lovers of Byron and Shelley, belong to the concealed aspect.

For Wordsworth, who still has a good deal of the pre-Romantic sense of nature as an objective order, nature is a landscape nature, and from it, as in Baudelaire's *Correspondances*, mysterious oracles seep into the mind through eye or ear, even a bird with so predictable a song as the cuckoo being an oracular wandering voice. This landscape is a veil dropped over the naked nature red in tooth and claw which haunted a later generation. Even the episode of the dog and the hedgehog. In the *Prelude* is told from the point of view of the dog. But the more pessimistic, and perhaps more realistic, conception of nature in which it can be a source of evil or suffering as well as good is the one that gains ascendancy in the later period of Romanticism, which extends to our own day.

The major constructs which our own culture has inherited from its Romantic ancestry are also of the 'drunken boat' shape, but represent a later and a different conception of it from the 'vehicular form' described above. Here the boat is usually in the position of Noah's ark, a fragile container of sensitive and imaginative values threatened by a chaotic and unconscious power below it. In Schopenhauer, the world as idea rides precariously on top of a 'world as will' which engulfs practically the whole of existence in its moral indifference. In Darwin, who readily combines with Schopenhauer, as the later work of Hardy illustrates, consciousness and morality are accidental sports from a ruthlessly competitive evolutionary force. In Freud, who has noted the resemblance of his mythical structure to Schopenhauer's, the conscious ego struggles to keep afloat on a sea of libidinous impulse. In Kierkegaard, all the 'higher' impulses of fallen man pitch and roll on the surface of a huge and shapeless 'dread'. In some versions of this construct the antithesis of the symbol of consciousness and the destructive element in which it is immersed can be overcome or transcended: there is an Atlantis under the sea which becomes an Ararat for the beleaguered boat to rest on.

I give an example from Auden, partly to show that the Romantic structures of symbolism are still ours. In Freud, when the conscious mind feels threatened by the subconscious, it tries to repress it, and so develops a neurosis. In Marxism, the liberal elements in an ascendant class, when they feel threatened by a revolutionary situation, develop a police state. In both cases the effort is to intensify the antithesis between the two, but this effort is mistaken, and when the barriers are broken down we reach the balanced mind and the classless society respectively. *For the Time Being* develops a religious construct out of Kierkegaard on the analogy of those of Marx and Freud. The liberal or rational elements represented by Herod feel threatened by the revival of superstition in the Incarnation, and try to repress it. Their failure means that the effort to come to terms with a nature outside the mind, the primary effort of reason, has to be abandoned, and this enables the Paradise or divine presence which is locked up inside the human mind to manifest itself after the reason has searched the whole of objective nature in vain to find it. The attitude is that of a relatively orthodox Christianity; the imagery and the structure of symbolism is that of *Prometheus Unbound* and *The Marriage of Heaven and Hell*.

In Romanticism proper a prominent place in sense experience is given to the ear, an excellent receiver of oracles but poor in locating things accurately in space. This latter power, which is primarily visual, is associated with the fancy in Wordsworth's 1815 preface, and given the subordinate position appropriate to fancy. In later poetry, beginning with *symbolisme* in France, when there is a good deal of reaction against earlier Romanticism, more emphasis is thrown on vision. In Rimbaud, though his *Bateau Ivre* has given me my title, the poet is to *se faire voyant*, the *illuminations* are thought of pictorially; even the vowels must be visually coloured. Such an emphasis has nothing to do with the pre-Romantic sense of an objective structure in nature: on the contrary, the purpose of it is to intensify the Romantic sense of oracular significance into a kind of autohypnosis. The association of autohypnosis and the visual sense is discussed in Marshall McLuhan's book, *The Gutenberg Galaxy*[10]. Such an emphasis leads to a technique of fragmentation. Poe's attack on the long poem is not a Romantic but an anti-Romantic manifesto, as the direction of its influence indicates. The tradition of *symbolisme* is present in imagism, where the primacy of visual values is so strongly stated in theory and so cheerfully ignored in practice, in Pound's emphasis on the spatial juxtaposing of metaphor, in Eliot's insistence on the superiority of poets who present the 'clear visual images' of Dante. T. E. Hulme's attack on the Romantic tradition is consistent in preferring fancy to imagination and in stressing the objectivity of the nature to be imitated; less so in his primitivism and his use of Bergson. The technique of fragmentation is perhaps intended to reach its limit in Pound's publication of the complete poetical works of Hulme on a single page.

As I have tried to indicate by my reference to Auden, what this anti-Romantic movement did not do was to create a third framework of imagery. Nor did it return to the older construct, though Eliot, by sticking closely to Dante and by deprecating the importance of the prophetic element in art, gives some illusion of doing so. The charge of subjectivity, brought against the Romantics by Arnold and often repeated later, assumes that objectivity is a higher attribute of poetry, but this is itself a Romantic conception, and came into English criticism with Coleridge. Anti-Romanticism, in short, had no resources for becoming anything more than a post-Romantic movement. The first phase of the reconsideration of Romanticism is to understand its continuity with modern literature. All we need do to complete it is to examine Romanticism by its own standards and canons. We should not look for precision where vagueness is wanted; not extol the virtues of constipation when the Romantics were exuberant; not insist on visual values when the poet listens darkling to a nightingale. Then, perhaps, we may see in Romanticism also the quality that Melville found in Greek architecture:

> Not innovating wilfulness,
> But reverence for the Archetype.

13 DICKENS AND THE COMEDY OF HUMOURS

Dickens presents special problems to any critic who approaches him in the context of a 'Victorian novelist'. In general, the serious Victorian fiction writers are realistic and the less serious ones are romancers. We expect George Eliot or Trollope to give us a solid and well-rounded realization of the social life, attitudes, and intellectual issues of their time: we expect Disraeli and Bulwer-Lytton, because they are more 'romantic', to give us the same kind of thing in a more flighty and dilettantish way; from the cheaper brands, Marie Corelli or Ouida, we expect nothing but the standard romance formulas. This alignment of the serious and the realistic, the commercial and the romantic, where realism has a moral dignity that romance lacks, intensified after Dickens's death, survived through the first half of the twentieth century, and still lingers vestigially. But in such an alignment Dickens is hard to place. What he writes, if I may use my own terminology for once, are not realistic novels but fairy tales in the low mimetic displacement. Hence there has grown up an assumption that, if we are to take Dickens seriously, we must emphasize the lifelikeness of his characters or the shrewdness of his social observation; if we emphasize his violently unplausible plots and his playing up of popular sentiment, we are emphasizing only his concessions to an undeveloped public taste. This was a contemporary view of him, expressed very lucidly by Trollope in *The Warden*, and it is still a natural one to take.

A refinement of the same view sees the real story in Dickens's novels as a rather simple set of movements within a large group of characters. To this a mechanical plot seems to have been attached like an outboard motor to a rowboat, just to get things moving faster and more noisily. Thus our main interest, in reading *Little Dorrit*, is in the straightforward and quite touching story of Clennam's love for the heroine, of their separation through her suddenly acquired wealth, and of their eventual reunion through her loss of it. Along with this goes a preposterous melodrama about forged wills, identical twins, a mother who is not a mother, skulking foreigners, and dark mysteries of death and birth which seems almost detachable from the central story. Similarly, we finish *Our Mutual Friend* with a clear memory of a vast panoramic pageant of Victorian society, from the nouveau-riche Veneerings to Hexham living on the refuse of the Thames. But the creaky Griselda plot, in which John Harmon pretends to be dead in order to test the stability of his future wife, is something that we can hardly take in even when reading the book, much less remember afterwards.

Some works of fiction present a clearly designed or projected plot, where each episode seems to us to be logically the sequel to the previous episode. In others we feel that the episode that comes next does so only because the author has decided that it will come next. In stories with a projected plot we explain the episode from its context in the plot; in stories lacking such a plot, we are often thrown back on some other explanation, often one that originates in the author's wish to tell us something besides the story. This last is particularly true of thematic sequences like the 'Dream Play' of Strindberg, where the succession of episodes is not like that of a projected plot, nor particularly like a dream either, but has to be accounted for in different terms. In Dickens we often notice that when he is most actively pursuing his plot he is careless, to the verge of being contemptuous, of the inner logic of the story. In *Little Dorrit*, the mysterious rumblings and creakings in the Clennam house, referred to at intervals throughout, mean that it is about to fall down. What this in turn means is that Dickens is going to push it over at a moment when the villain is inside and the hero outside. Similarly, Clennam, after a good deal of detective work, manages to discover where Miss Wade is living on the Continent. She did not expect him to ferret out her address, nor had she anything to say to him when he arrived; but, just in case he did come, she had written out the story of her life and had kept it in a drawer ready to hand to him. The outrage on probability seems almost deliberate, as does the burning up of Krook in *Bleak House* by spontaneous combustion as soon as the author is through with him, despite Dickens's protests about the authenticity of his device.

Dickens's daughter, Mrs Pellegrini, remarked shrewdly that there was no reason to suppose that *The Mystery of Edwin Drood* would have been any more of an impeccable plot-structure than the novels that Dickens had already completed. But, because it is unfinished, the plot has been the main focus of critical attention in that story, usually on the assumption that this once Dickens was working with a plot which was not, like a fictional Briareus, equipped with a hundred arms of coincidence.

T. S. Eliot, in his essay on Dickens and Wilkie Collins, remarks on the 'spurious fatality' of Collins's detective-story plots. This is no place to raise the question of why the sense of fatality in *The Moonstone* should be more spurious than in *The Family Reunion*, but we notice in Dickens how strong the impulse is to reject a logicality inherent in the story in favour of impressing on the reader an impatient sense of absolutism: of saying, in short, *la fatalité, c'est moi*. This disregard of plausibility is worth noticing, because everyone realizes that Dickens is a great genius of the absurd in his characterization, and it is possible that his plots are also absurd in the same sense, not from incompetence or bad taste, but from a genuinely creative instinct. If so, they are likely to be more relevant to the entire conception of the novel than is generally thought. I proceed to explore a little the sources of absurdity in Dickens, to see if that will lead us to a clearer idea of his total structure.

The structure that Dickens uses for his novels is the New Comedy structure, which has come down to us from Plautus and Terence through Ben Jonson, an author we know Dickens admired, and Molière. The main action is a collision of two societies which we may call for convenience the obstructing and the congenial society. The congenial society is usually centred on the love of hero and heroine, the obstructing society on the characters, often parental, who try to thwart this love. For most of the action the thwarting characters are in the ascendant, but towards the end a twist in the plot reverses the situation and the congenial society dominates the happy ending. A frequent form of plot-reversal was the discovery that one of the central characters, usually the heroine, was of better social origin than previously thought. This theme of mysterious parentage is greatly expanded in the late Greek romances, which closely resemble some of the plots of Menander. Here an infant of noble birth may be stolen or exposed and brought up by humble foster-parents, being restored to his original status at the end.

In drama such a theme involves expounding a complicated antecedent action, and however skilfully done not all audiences have the patience to follow the unravelling, as Ben Jonson discovered to his cost at the opening of his *New Inn*. But in narrative forms, of course, it can have room to expand. Shakespeare gets away with it in *The Winter's Tale* by adopting a narrative-paced form of drama, where sixteen years are encompassed by the action.

Dickens is, throughout his career, very conventional in his handling of the New Comedy plot structure. All the stock devices, listed in Greek times[1] as laws, oaths, compacts, witnesses, and ordeals, can be found in him. *Oliver Twist* and *Edwin Drood* are full of oaths, vows, councils of war, and conspiracies, on both benevolent and sinister sides. Witnesses include eavesdroppers like the Newman Noggs of *Nicholas Nickleby* or Morfin the cello-player in *Dombey and Son*. Ordeals are of various kinds: near-fatal illnesses are common, and we may compare the way that information is extracted from Rob the Grinder by Mrs Brown in *Dombey and Son* with the maltreating of the tricky slave in Menander and Plautus. Many thrillers (perhaps a majority) use a stock episode of having the hero entrapped by the villain, who instead of killing him at once imparts an essential piece of information about the plot to him, after which the hero escapes, gaining his wisdom at the price of an ordeal of facing death. This type of episode occurs in *Great Expectations* in the encounter with Orlick.

Every novel of Dickens is a comedy (*N.B.*: such words as 'comedy' are not essence words but context words; hence this means: 'for every novel of Dickens the obvious context is comedy'). The death of a central character does not make a story tragic, any more than a similar device does in *The King and I* or *The Yeomen of the Guard*. Sydney Carton is a man without a social function who achieves that function by sacrificing himself for the congenial society; Little Nell's death is so emotionally luxurious that it provides a kind of muted festivity for the conclusion, or what *Finnegans Wake* calls a 'funferall'. The emphasis at the end of a comedy is sometimes thrown, not on the forming of a new society around the marriage of hero and heroine, but on the maturing or enlightening of the hero, a process which may detach him from marriage or full participation in the congenial group. We find this type of conclusion in Shaw's *Candida*: Dickens's contribution to it is *Great*

Expectations. Again, there is usually a mystery in Dickens's stories, and this mystery is nearly always the traditional mystery of birth, in sharp contrast to the mystery of death on which the modern whodunit is based. In Dickens, when a character is murdered, we usually see it done, and if not the suspense is still perfunctory. A detective appears in *Bleak House* to investigate the murder of Tulkinghorn, but his task is easy: Lady Dedlock keeps a French maid, and French maids, being foreign, are emotionally unpredictable and morally insensitive. The problem is much less interesting than the problem of Lady Dedlock's guilty secret, which involves a birth. Unless Edwin Drood was very unlike Dickens's other heroes, the mystery about him is much more likely to have been a mystery of how he got into the world than of how he disappeared from it.

The emergence of the congenial society at the conclusion of the story is presented in the traditional New Comedy terms of festivity. It usually holds several marriages; it dispenses money if it has money, and it dispenses a good deal of food. Such features have remained unchanged in the New Comedy tradition since Greek times. Dickens's predilection for feasting scenes needs no labouring: it may be significant that his last written words are 'falls to with an appetite'. This feature accounts for his relentless plugging of Christmas, always for him the central symbol of the congenial family feast. The famous sentimentality of Dickens is largely confined to demonstrations of family affection, and is particularly evident in certain set scenes that immediately precede the dénouement, where the affection of brother and sister, of father and daughter, or more rarely of mother and son, is the main theme. Examples are the housekeeping of Tom and Ruth Pinch in *Martin Chuzzlewit*, the dinner of Kit and his mother in *The Old Curiosity Shop*, the meetings of Bella Wilfer with her father in *Our Mutual Friend*. Such relationships, though occasionally described as marriages, are 'innocent' in the technical Victorian sense of not involving sexual intercourse, and if they seem to post-Freudian readers to be emotionally somewhat overcharged, it is because they contribute to, and anticipate, the final triumph of Eros at the end of the story. The disregard of plausibility, already mentioned, is another traditional feature, being part of the violent manipulation of the story in the direction of a happy ending. Those who object to such endings on the grounds of probability are often put in the position of questioning the ways of divine providence, which uses the author as its agent for vindicating virtue and baffling vice.

Most of the people who move across the pages of Dickens are neither realistic portraits, like the characters of Trollope, nor 'caricatures', so far as that term implies only a slightly different approach to realistic portraiture. They are humours, like the characters in Ben Jonson, who formulated the principle that humours were the appropriate characters for a New Comedy plot. The humour is a character identified with a characteristic, like the miser, the hypochondriac, the braggart, the parasite, or the pedant. He is obsessed by whatever it is that makes him a humour, and the sense of our superiority to an obsessed person, someone bound to an invariable ritual habit, is, according to Bergson, one of the chief sources of laughter. But it is not because he is incidentally funny that the humour is important in New Comedy: he is important because his obsession is the feature that creates the conditions of the action, and the opposition of the two societies. In *The Silent Woman*, everything depends on Morose's hatred of noise; covetousness and gullibility set everything going in *Volpone* and *The Alchemist* respectively. Thus it is only the obstructing society which is 'humorous', in the Jonsonian sense, as a society. In Dickens we find humours on both sides of the social conflict, genial, generous, and lovable humours as well as absurd or sinister ones. But the humours in the congenial society merely diversify it with amiable and harmless eccentricities; the humours of the obstructing society help to build up that society, with all its false standards and values.

Most of the standard types of humour are conspicuous in Dickens, and could be illustrated from *Bleak House* alone: the miser in Smallweed; the hypocrite in Chadband; the parasite in Skimpole and Turveydrop; the pedant in Mrs Jellyby. The braggart soldier is not much favoured: Major Bagstock in *Dombey and Son* is more of a parasite. Agreeably to the conditions of Victorian life, the braggart soldier is replaced by a braggart merchant or politician. An example, treated in a thoroughly traditional manner, is Bounderby in *Hard Times*. Another Victorian commonplace of the braggart-soldier family, the duffer sportsman, whose pretensions are far beyond his performance, is represented by Winkle in *The Pickwick Papers*. There are, however, two

Winkles in *The Pickwick Papers*, the duffer sportsman and the pleasant young man who breaks down family opposition on both sides to acquire a pleasant young woman. The duality reflects the curious and instructive way that *The Pickwick Papers* came into being. The original scheme proposed to Dickens was a comedy of humours in its most primitive and superficial form: a situation comedy in which various stock types, including an incautious amorist (Tupman), a melancholy poet (Snodgrass), and a pedant (Pickwick), as well as Winkle, get into one farcical predicament after another. This form is frequent in stories for children, and was represented in my childhood by now obsolete types of comic strip and silent movie comedies. It must have left some descendants in television, but my impression is that contemporary children are deficient in this vitamin. But although traces of the original scheme persist throughout *The Pickwick Papers*, it quickly turns inside out into a regular New Comedy story, which leads up in the regular way to a recognition scene and a reversal of direction in the plot at its most serious point, in the debtors' prison. The pedant becomes a man of principle, and the humour of pedantry is transferred to the law which entraps him. Thus the comedy of humours takes root in society, as Dickens sees society, instead of merely extending from one incident to another.

The simplest form of humour is the tagged humour, who is associated with the repetition of a set phrase. Thus we have Mrs Micawber, whose tag is that she will never desert Mr Micawber, and Major Bagnet in *Bleak House*, who admires his wife but asserts that he never tells her so because 'discipline must be maintained'. We notice that our sense of superiority to such characters is edged with antagonism: when the repeated trait is intended to be endearing we are more likely to find it irritating, as E. M. Forster[2] does Mrs Micawber's. Jarndyce with his 'east wind' tag and Esther Summerson's constant bewilderment that other people should find her charming do not stick in our minds in the way that Chadband and Mrs Jellyby do. The humour is, almost by definition, a bore, and the technical skill in handling him consists in seeing that we get just enough but not too much of him. The more unpleasant he is, the easier this problem is to solve. Repetition which is excessive even by Dickensian standards, like the emphasis on Carker's teeth in *Dombey and Son*, is appropriate for a villain, as its effect is to dehumanize and cut off sympathy. We cannot feel much concern over the fate of a character who is presented to us mainly as a set of teeth, like Berenice in Poe. The 'lifelikeness' of a humour depends on two things: on the fact that we are all very largely creatures of ritual habit, and on the strength of a perverse tendency in most of us to live up to our own caricatures. Pecksniff may be a humbug, but that can hardly be the whole of our feeling about him when he begins to sound like a member of my own profession attempting to extract a discussion from a group of clammed-up freshmen:

> 'The name of those fabulous animals (pagan, I regret to say) who used to sing in the water, has quite escaped me.'
>
> Mr. George Chuzzlewit suggested 'Swans.'
>
> 'No,' said Mr. Pecksniff. 'Not swans. Very like swans, too. Thank you.'
>
> The nephew with the outline of a countenance, speaking for the first and last time on that occasion, propounded 'Oysters.'
>
> 'No,' said Mr. Pecksniff, with his own peculiar urbanity, 'nor oysters. But by no means unlike oysters: a very excellent idea; thank you, my dear sir, very much. Wait! Sirens. Dear me! sirens, of course.'

Humours are, at least dramatically, 'good' if they are on the side of the congenial society, 'bad' or ridiculous if on the side of the obstructing one. Thus the humour comedy has an easy and natural connection with the morality play. We notice this in the allegorical names that Dickens often gives some of his minor characters, like the 'Pyke' and 'Pluck' who are the satellites of Sir Mulberry Hawk in *Nicholas Nickleby*, or the 'Bar', 'Bishop', and 'Physician' who turn up at Merdle's dinners in *Little Dorrit*. We notice it also in Dickens's tendency to arrange his humours in moral pairs, whether both are in the same novel or not. As just indicated, we have a 'good' major in *Bleak House* and a 'bad' one with a very similar name in *Dombey and Son*; we have a villainous Jew in *Oliver Twist* and a saintly Jew in *Our Mutual Friend*, and so on. Within *Dombey and Son* itself the 'bad' major is paired against a 'good' navy man, Captain Cuttle. If characters change sides, there may be a metamorphosis of character, which is not difficult in the humour technique, because it simply means putting on a different mask. Thus the generous Boffin pretends to be a miser for a while; Scrooge goes through the reverse process; Mercy Pecksniff changes roles from the feather-head to the faithful ill-used wife, and so on. Many humours are really chorus characters, who cannot do anything in the plot unless they step out of their roles: an example is Lord Frederick Verisopht in *Nicholas Nickleby*, who has to harden up a good deal to make his tragic end appropriate. The commonest form of this metamorphosis, and the most traditional one, is the release of the humour from his obsession at the end of the story: through the experience gained in the story, he is able to break through his besetting fault. At the end of *Martin Chuzzle-wit* there is a whole series of these changes: the hero escapes from his selfishness, Mark Tapley from his compulsion to search for difficult situations in order to 'come out strong', and Tom Pinch from an innocence that Dickens recognizes to be more obsessive than genuine innocence, and which we should now think of as a streak of masochism.

The rhetoric of the tagged humour consists mainly of variations of the stock identifying phrase or phrases. Some humours acquire a personal rhetorical rhythm of a strongly associative kind, which because it is associative gives the effect of being obsessive. The disjointed phrases of Jingle and the asyntactic babble of Mrs Nickelby and Flora Finching are perhaps the most consistently successful examples. Closer to the single identifying phrase are Uriah Heep's insistence on his ''umble' qualities, which reminds us a little of Iago's 'honest' tag, and the repetitions that betray the hypocrisy of Casby, the squeezing landlord in *Little Dorrit*. Others develop parodies of standard types of oratory, like Chadband with his parsonical beggar's whine or Micawber with his Parliamentary flourishes.

More significant, for a reason that will meet us in a moment, is the humour of stock response, that is, the humour whose obsession it is to insist that what he or she has been conditioned to think proper and acceptable is in fact reality. This attitude gives us the Bouvard-et-Pécuchet type of humour, whose mind is confined within a dictionary of accepted ideas. Such humours, it is obvious, readily expand into cultural allegories, representatives of the kind of anxiety that caricatures an age. Thus our stereotypes about 'Victorian prudery' are represented by Podsnap in *Our Mutual Friend* and Mrs General (the prunes-and-prisms woman) in *Little Dorrit*. Martin Chuzzlewit finds that America is full of such humours: American shysters are no better and no worse than their British counterparts, but there is a more theoretical element in their lying, and bluster about their enlightened political institutions is much more used as a cover for swindling. In America, in other words, the complacent Podsnap and the rascally Lammle are more likely to be associated in the same person. The implication, which Dickens is not slow to press, is that American life is more vulnerable than British life to character assassination, personal attacks, charges of being un-American, and mob violence. A humour of this stock-response type is comic on Freudian principles: he often says what more cautious people would not say, but show by their actions that they believe. Thus Bumble's remarks about 'them wicious paupers' are funny, not as typical of a Victorian beadle, but as revealing the hatred and contempt for the poor that official charity attempts to disguise.

Sometimes a humour's obsessed behaviour and repetitive speech suggest a puppet or mechanical doll, whose response is invariable whatever the stimulus. We may feel with some of these characters that the mechanical quality is simply the result of Dickens's not having worked hard enough on them, but occasionally we realize that Dickens himself is encouraging us to see them as inanimate objects. Wemmick the postbox in *Great Expectations*, Pancks the 'tug' in *Little Dorrit*, and several characters who are figuratively and to some extent literally wooden, like Silas Wegg, are examples. The Captain Cuttle of *Dombey and Son*, in particular, impresses us as an animated version of the Wooden Midshipman over the shop he so often inhabits. In *The Old Curiosity Shop*, after we have been introduced to Quilp, Little Nell and her grandfather set out on their travels and see a Punch and Judy show. It occurs to us that Quilp, who is described as a 'grotesque puppet', who lies, cheats, beats his wife, gets into fistfights, drinks like a salamander, and comes to a sticky end in a bog, *is* Punch, brought to life as a character. Wyndham Lewis, in an essay on Joyce (another admirer of Ben Jonson), notes the Dickensian ancestry of Bloom's interior monologue in the speech of Jingle. He might have noted a similar connection between Flora Finching's unpunctuated harangues in *Little Dorrit* and the reverie of Molly Bloom. Lewis in his turn developed, mainly out of Bergson, a theory of satire as a vision of human behaviour in mechanical terms, where his main predecessor, if not one he recognized, was Dickens. We notice also the reappearance of the Punch figure in the centre of *The Human Age*.

We noted that, while there are humours on both sides of the social conflict in Dickens, it is only the obstructing society which is humorous as a society. This takes us back to the feature I mentioned at the beginning which distinguishes Dickens from his major contemporaries in fiction. In most of the best Victorian novels, apart from Dickens, the society described is organized by its institutions: the church, the government, the professions, the rural squirearchy, business, and the trade unions. It is a highly structured society, and the characters function from within those structures. But in Dickens we get a much more free-wheeling and anarchistic social outlook. For him the structures of society, as structures, belong almost entirely to the absurd, obsessed, sinister aspect of it, the aspect that is overcome or evaded by the comic action. The comic action itself moves toward the regrouping of society around the only social unit that Dickens really regards as genuine, the family. In other Victorian novelists characters are regrouped within their social structures; in Dickens the comic action leads to a sense of having broken down or through those structures. Naturally there are limits to this: the same social functions have to continue; but the sense that social institutions have to reverse their relationship to human beings before society really becomes congenial is very strong.

The law, for instance, as represented by the Chancery suit in *Bleak House* and the Circumlocution Office in *Little Dorrit*, is a kind of social vampire, sucking out family secrets or draining off money through endless shifts and evasions. It is explicitly said in both novels that the legal establishment is not designed to be an instrument of society, but to be a self-perpetuating social parasite. Education, again, is usually presented in Dickens as a racket, a brutal and malignant racket with Squeers and Creakle, a force-feeding racket in the 'fact' school of *Hard Times* and the Classical cram school of Dr Blimber in *Dombey and Son*. Dickens's view of the liberalizing quality of the Victorian Classical training is perhaps symbolized in the grotesque scenes of Silas Wegg stumbling through Gibbon's *Decline and Fall* to the admiration of the illiterate Boffins: an unskilful performance which nobody understands. As for religion, even the respectable churches have little to do except marry the hero and heroine, and the spokesmen of the chapel, Chadband and Stiggins, are the same type of greasy lout as their ancestor in Ben Jonson, Zeal-of-the-Land Busy. Politics, from the Eatanswill election in *Pickwick* to the Parliamentary career of Veneering in *Our Mutual*

Friend, is a farce, only tolerable when an amusing one. Industry is equally repulsive whether its spokesman is Bounderby or the labour organizer Slackbridge. The amassing of a fortune in the City, by Dombey, Ralph Nickleby, or Merdle in *Little Dorrit*, is an extension of miserliness: it is closely associated with usury; the debtors' prison is clearly the inseparable other side of it, and it usually blows up a bubble of credit speculation with no secured assets, ending in an appalling financial crash and endless misery. *Martin Chuzzlewit* carefully balances the swindling of American real-estate speculators with the precisely similar activities of Montague's Anglo-Bengalee Company in London. In several of the novels there are two obstructing societies, one a social establishment and the other a criminal anti-establishment. When this occurs there is little if anything morally to choose between them. We find the Artful Dodger no worse than the respectable Bumble in his beadle's uniform, and Pip discovers a human companionship with the hunted convict on the marshes that the Wopsles and Pumblechooks of his Christmas dinner exclude him from.

It is perhaps in *Little Dorrit* that we get the most complete view of the obstructing society, a society which is shown to be a self-imprisoning society, locking itself in to the invariable responses of its own compulsions. At the beginning we are introduced to various types of prison: the Marseilles prison with Blandois, the quarantine prison with the discontented Tattycoram and her Lesbian familiar Miss Wade, the prison-house of the paralysed Mrs Clennam, and finally the Marshalsea. As the story goes on these external prisons give place to internal ones. With the Circumlocution Office the prison image modulates to a maze or labyrinth, a very frequent sinister image in Dickens, and gradually a unified vision of the obstructing society takes shape. This society is symbolized by the Barnacles, who, as their name indicates, represent a social parasitism inherent in the aristocracy, and operating through the political and legal establishment. They are a family, but not a genuine family: their loyalties are class or tribal loyalties cutting across the real structure of society. One of their members, Mrs Gowan, even goes so far as to speak of marriage as 'accidental', and stresses the primary necessity of defending the position of her class, or rather of her private myth about her class. The fact that her son becomes the husband of the only child of the Meagles family gives a most ambiguous twist to the happy ending of the novel. We may compare the disaster wrought by Steerforth in *David Copperfield*, whose mother is similarly obsessed with making her son into a symbol of class arrogance. We begin to understand how consistent the pitiful pretence of aristocracy that old Dorrit tries to maintain, first in the prison, then in prosperity, is with the general scheme of the story. Miss Wade's autobiography, headed 'The History of a Self-Tormentor', however arbitrarily introduced into the story, has a genuine symbolic relevance to it, and one of the most sharply observed passages in the novel is the moment of self-awareness when Fanny Dorrit realizes that her own selfishness is implacably driving her into an endless, pointless, pleasureless game of one-upmanship with Mrs Merdle. Similarly in *Great Expectations* the 'gentleman's' world which entraps Pip is symbolized by the decaying prison-house where all the clocks have been stopped at the moment of Miss Havisham's humiliation, the rest of her life consisting only of brooding on that moment.

The obstructing society in Dickens has two main characteristics: it is parasitic and it is pedantic. It is parasitic in the sense of setting up false values and loyalties which destroy the freedom of all those who accept them, as well as tyrannizing over many of those who do not. Dickens's implicit social vision is also radical, to an extent he hardly realized himself, in dividing society between workers and idlers, and in seeing in much of the leisure class a social sanctioning of parasitism. As for its pedantry, it is traditional in New Comedy to set up a pragmatic standard, based on experience, as a norm, and contrast it with the theoretical approaches to life typical of humours who cannot escape from their reflex responses. Like Blake, like every writer with any genuine radicalism in him, Dickens finds the really dangerous social evils in those which have achieved some acceptance by being rationalized. Already in *Oliver Twist* the word 'experience' stands as a contrast to the words 'experimental' and 'philosophical', which are invariably pejorative. This contrast comes into Bumble's famous 'the law is a ass' speech. In *Hard Times* the pedantry of the obstructing society is associated with a utilitarian philosophy and an infantile trust in facts, statistics, and all impersonal and generalized forms of knowledge. We may wonder why Dickens denounces this philosophy so earnestly and caricatures it so crudely, instead of letting its absurdities speak for themselves. But it is clear that *Hard Times*, of all Dickens's stories, comes nearest to being what in our day is sometimes called the dystopia, the book which, like *Brave New World* or *1984*, shows us the nightmare world that results from certain perverse tendencies inherent in society getting free play. The most effective dystopias are likely to be those in which the author isolates certain features in his society that most directly threaten his own social function as a writer. Dickens sees in the cult of facts and statistics a threat, not to the realistic novelist, and not only to a life based on concrete and personal relations, but to the un-fettered imagination, the mind that can respond to fairy tales and fan-tasy and understand their relevance to reality. The insistence on the importance of fairy tales, nursery rhymes, and similar genres in educa-tion often meets us in Dickens, and implies that Dickens's fairy-tale plots are regarded by Dickens himself as an essential part of his novels.

The action of a comedy moves toward an identity which is usually a social identity. In Dickens the family, or a group analogous to a family, is the key to social identity. Hence his recognition scenes are usually genealogical, concerned with discovering unknown fathers and mothers or articulating the correct family relationships. There are often three sets of parental figures attached to a central character, with several doubles of each. First are the actual parents. These are often dead before the story begins, like the fathers of Nicholas Nickleby and David Copperfield, or stagger on weakly for a few pages, like David Copper-field's mother, or are mysterious and emerge at the end, sometimes as bare names unrelated to the story, like Oliver Twist's father or the parents of Little Nell. The father of Sissy Jupe in *Hard Times* deserts her without ever appearing in the novel; the first things we see in *Great Expectations* are the tombstones of Pip's parents. Pip himself is brought up by a sister who is twenty years older and (as we learn on practically the last page of the book) has the same name as his mother. Next come the parental figures of the obstructing society, generally cruel or foolish, and often descended from the harsh step-parents of folk-tale. Murd-stone and his sister, Pip's sister, the pseudo-mothers of Esther Summer-son and Clennam, belong to this group. One very frequent device which combines these two types of relationship is that of the preternaturally loving and hard-working daughter who is the sole support of a weak or foolish father. We have, among others, Little Dorrit, Little Nell, whose grandfather is a compulsive gambler, Jenny Wren in *Our Mutual Friend* with her drunken 'child', Madeline Bray in *Nicholas Nickleby*, and, in a different way, Florence Dombey. Naturally the marriage of such a heroine, following on the death of the parent, transfers her to the more congenial society. Finally we have the parental or avuncular figures of the congenial society itself, those who take on a protective relation to the central characters as the story approaches its conclusion. Brownlow in *Oliver Twist*, who adopts the hero, Jarndyce in *Bleak House*, Abel Magwitch in *Great Expectations*, the Cheeryble brothers in *Nicholas Nickleby*, the Boffins in *Our Mutual Friend*, are examples. Abel Magwitch, besides being the ultimate father of Pip, is also the actual father of Estella, which makes Estella in a sense Pip's sister: this was doubtless one reason why Dickens so resisted the conventional ending of marriage for these two. The more realistic developments of New Comedy tend to eliminate this genealogical apparatus. When one of the girls in *Les Précieuses Ridicules* announces that being so interesting a girl she is quite sure that her real parents are much more interesting people than the ones she appears to have, we do not take her very seriously. But Dickens is always ready to co-operate with the lonely child's fantasies about lost congenial parents, and this marks his affinity with the romantic side of the tradition, the side related to Classical romance.

I have used the word 'anarchistic' in connection with Dickens's view of society, but it is clear that, so far as his comic structure leads to any sort of vision of a social ideal, that ideal would have to be an intensely paternalistic society, an expanded family. We get a somewhat naïve glimpse of this with the Cheeryble brothers in *Nicholas Nickleby*, giving a party where the faithful servitors are brought in at the end for a drink of champagne, expressing undying loyalty and enthusiasm for the patronizing social arrangements. The reader gets the uneasy feeling that he is listening to the commercial. When in *Little Dorrit* Tattycoram runs away from the suffocating geniality of the Meagles family she has to be brought back repentant, though she may well have had much more of the reader's sympathy than Dickens intended her to have. Even the Dedlock ménage in *Bleak House*, hopeless social anachronism as Dickens clearly recognizes it to be, is still close enough to a family to gather a fair amount of the society of the novel around it at the end. In contrast, social parasites often assume the role of a false father. Examples include the Marquis in *A Tale of Two Cities* whose assassin is technically guilty of parricide, Sir Joseph Bowley, the Urizenic friend and father of the poor in *The Chimes*, and the elder Chester in *Barnaby Rudge*.

In New Comedy the obstructing humours absorb most of the character interest: the heroes and heroines are seldom individualized. Such characters as Bonario in *Volpone* or Valère in *Tartuffe* are only pleasant young men. In Dickens, too, the heroes and heroines resemble humours only in the fact that their responses are predictable, but they are predictable in terms of a norm, and they seldom if ever appear in the ridiculous or self-binding role of the humour. Such characters, who encourage the reader to identify with them, and who might be called norm-figures, could not exist in serious twentieth-century fiction, which belongs to the ironic mode, and sees all its characters as affected in some degree by hampering social forces. But they have some validity in nineteenth-century low mimetic conventions, which present only what is conventionally presentable, and whose heroes and heroines may therefore logically be models of presentability.

Comedy usually depicts the triumph of the young over the old, but Dickens is unusual among comic writers in that so many of his heroes and heroines are children, or are described in ways that associate them with childhood. Nobody has described more vividly than Dickens the reactions of a sensitive child in a Brobdingnagian world dominated by noisome and blundering adults. And because nearly all these children are predestined to belong to the congenial society, they can only be hurt, not corrupted, by the obstructing society. The one striking exception is Pip, whose detachment from the false standards of the obstructing group forms the main theme of *Great Expectations*. But David Copperfield is only superficially affected by his environment, and Oliver Twist escapes from the activities of the Fagin gang as miraculously as Marina does from the brothel in Shakespeare's *Pericles*. Usually this predestined child-figure is a girl. Many of the heroines, even when grown women, are described as 'little' or are compared to fairies. A frequent central theme in Dickens is the theme of *Alice in Wonderland*: the descent of the invulnerable girl-child into a grotesque world. In the preface to *The Old Curiosity Shop* Dickens speaks of his interest in the beauty-and-beast archetype, of the girl-child surrounded by monsters, some of them amiable like Kit, others sinister like Quilp. Little Nell descends to this grotesque world and then rejoins the angels; the other heroines marry into the congenial society. The girl-child among grotesques recurs in Florence Dombey's protection by Captain Cuttle, in Little Dorrit's mothering of Maggie, and in many similar scenes. Sometimes an amiable grotesque, Toots or Kit or Smike or Chivery, will attach himself to such a girl-figure, not good enough to marry her but protesting eternal devotion none the less, a kind of late farcical vestige of the Courtly Love convention. Nobody turns up in *The Old Curiosity Shop* good enough to marry Little Nell, which is doubtless one reason why she dies. We may also notice the role of the old curiosity shop itself: it plays little part in the story, but is a kind of threshold symbol of the entrance into the grotesque world, like the rabbit-hole and mirror in the Alice books. Its counterparts appear in the Wooden Midshipman shop in *Dombey and Son*, the Peggotty cottage in *David Copperfield*, the bone-shop of Venus in *Our Mutual Friend*, and elsewhere.

Many of the traditional features of romantic New Comedy reached their highest point of development in nineteenth-century Britain, making it the obvious time and place for a great genius in that form to emerge. One of these, already glanced at, is the domination of narrative genres, along with a moribund drama. Dickens had many dramatic interests, but his genius was for serial romance and not for the stage. Another is the Victorian assumption of moral standards shared between author and reader. This feature makes for melodrama, where the reader emotionally participates in the moral conflict of hero and villain, or of virtue and temptation. The rigidity, or assumed rigidity, of Victorian sexual mores is a great help to a nineteenth-century plot, as it enables an author, not only to make a Wagnerian noise about a woman's extra-marital escapade, but to make the most frenzied activity on her part plausible as an effort to conceal the results of it. But the relation of melo-drama to the foreground action is far more important than this.

A realistic writer in the New Comedy tradition tends to work out his action on one plane: young and old, hero and humour, struggle for power within the same social group. The more romantic the writer, the more he tends to set over against his humorous world another kind of world, with which the romantic side of his story is associated. In a paper

written twenty years ago, I spoke of the action of romantic Shakespearean comedy as divided between a foreground world of humours and
a background 'green world', associated with magic, sleep and dreams,
and enchanted forests or houses, from which the comic resolution
comes. Dickens has no green world, except for a glint or two here and
there (e.g. the pastoral retreats in which Smike and Little Nell end
their days, Jenny Wren's paradisal dreams, the 'beanstalk' abode of
Tartar in *Edwin Drood*, and the like), but he does have his own way of
dividing his action. I have spoken of the nineteenth-century emphasis
on the presentable, on the world of public appearance to which the
nineteenth-century novelist is almost entirely confined. Behind this
world lies a vast secret world, the world of privacy, where there is little
or no communication. For Dickens this world is associated mainly with
dreams, memories, and death. He describes it very eloquently at the
opening of the third 'Quarter' of *The Chimes*, and again in the first
paragraph of the third chapter of *A Tale of Two Cities*, besides referring
frequently to it throughout his work.

Few can read Dickens without catching the infection of his intense
curiosity about the life that lies in the dark houses behind the lights of
his loved and hated London. We recognize it even at second hand:
when Dylan Thomas's *Under Milk Wood* opens on a night of private
dreams we can see an unmistakably Dickensian influence. For most of
the ironic fiction of the twentieth century, this secret world is essentially
the bedroom and bathroom world of ordinary privacy, as well as the
world of sexual drives, perversions, repressions, and infantile fixations
that not only complements the public world but conditions one's
behaviour in it at every point. Characters in twentieth-century fiction
have no privacy: there is no distinction between dressing-room and
stage. Dickens is by no means unaware of the importance of this aspect
of the hidden world, but it is of little use to him as a novelist, and he shows
no restiveness about being obliged to exclude it. This is because he is
not primarily an ironic writer, like Joyce or Flaubert. What he is really
curious about is a hidden world of *romantic* interest, not a world even
more squalid and commonplace than the visible one. His detective
interest in hidden life is comparable to other aspects of Victorian culture:
one thinks of the pre-Raphaelite paintings where we are challenged to
guess what kind of story is being told by the picture and its enigmatic

title, or of all the poems of Browning that appeal to us to deduce the reality hidden behind what is presented.

In following the main action of a Dickens novel we are frequently aware of a second form of experience being held up to it like a mirror. Sometimes this is explicitly the world of the stage. The kind of entertainment afforded by the Vincent Crummles troop in *Nicholas Nickleby* parallels the uninhibited melodrama of the main story: the dance of the savage and the Infant Phenomenon, in particular, mirrors the Dickensian theme of the girl-child in the monster-world. In *Hard Times*, where the relation is one of contrast, a circus company symbolizes an approach to experience that Gradgrind has missed out on. The Punch and Judy show in *The Old Curiosity Shop*, one of several popular dramatic entertainments in that book, has been mentioned, and in *Great Expectations* Pip, haunted by the ghost of a father, goes to see Mr Wopsle in *Hamlet*. Then again, Dickens makes considerable use of the curious convention in New Comedy of the doubled character, who is often literally a twin. In *The Comedy of Errors* the foreground Ephesus and the background Syracuse, in *Twelfth Night* the melancholy courts of Orsino and Olivia, are brought into alignment by twins. Similarly, the foreground action of *Little Dorrit* is related to the background action partly through the concealed twin brother of Flintwinch. In *A Tale of Two Cities*, where the twin theme is at its most complicated, the resemblance of Darnay and Carton brings the two cities themselves into alignment. In *Dombey and Son* the purse-proud world of Dombey and the other social world that it tries to ignore are aligned by the parallel, explicitly alluded to, between Edith Dombey and Alice Brown. There are many other forms of doubling, both of characters and of action, that I have no space here to examine. The role of Orlick in *Great Expectations*, as a kind of demonic double of Pip, is an example.

The basis for such a dividing of the action might be generalized as follows. There is a hidden and private world of dream and death, out of which all the energy of human life comes. The primary manifestation of this world, in experience, is in acts of destructive violence and passion. It is the source of war, cruelty, arrogance, lust, and grinding the faces of the poor. It produces the haughty lady with her guilty secret, like Lady Dedlock or Edith Dombey or Mrs Clennam, the lynching mobs that hunt Bill Sikes to death or proclaim the charity of the Protestant religion in *Barnaby Rudge*, the flogging schoolmasters and the hanging judges. It also produces the courage to fight against these things, and the instinctive virtue that repudiates them. In short, the hidden world expresses itself most directly in melodramatic action and rhetoric. It is not so much better or worse than the ordinary world of experience, as a world in which good and evil appear as much stronger and less disguised forces. We may protest that its moods are exaggerated, its actions unlikely, its rhetoric stilted and unconvincing. But if it were not there nothing else in Dickens would be there. We notice that the mainspring of melodramatic action is, like that of humorous action, mainly obsession. We notice, too, that Dickens's hair-raising descriptions, like that of Marseilles at the opening of *Little Dorrit* with its repetition of 'stare', are based on the same kind of associative rhetoric as the speech of the humours.

From this point of view we can look at the foreground action of the humours in a new light. Humours are, so to speak, petrified by-products of the kind of energy that melodrama expresses more directly. Even the most contemptible humours, the miserly Fledgeby or the hypocritical Heep, are exuberantly miserly and hypocritical: their vices express an energy that possesses them because they cannot possess it. The world they operate in, so far as it is a peaceable and law-abiding world, is a world of very imperfectly suppressed violence. They never escape from the shadow of a power which is at once Eros and Thanatos, and are bound to a passion that is never satisfied by its rationalized objects, but is ultimately self-destructive. In the earlier novels the emotional focus of this self-destroying passion is usually a miser, or a person in some way obsessed with money, like Ralph Nickleby, Dombey, Little Nell's grandfather, or Jonas Chuzzlewit. The folk-tale association of money and excrement, which points to the psychological origin of miserliness, appears in the 'Golden Dustman' theme of *Our Mutual Friend*, and is perhaps echoed in the names Murdstone and Merdle. In the later novels a more explicitly erotic drive gives us the victim-villain figures of Bradley Headstone and Jasper Drood. Food and animals are other images that Dickens often uses in sexual contexts, especially when a miser aspires to a heroine. Arthur Gride in *Nicholas Nickleby* speaks of Madeline Bray as a tasty morsel, and Uriah Heep is compared to a whole zoo of unpleasant animals: the effect is to give an

Andromeda pattern to the heroine's situation, and suggest a demonic ferocity behind the domestic foreground. The same principle of construction causes the stock-response humours like Podsnap or Gradgrind to take on a peculiar importance. They represent the fact that an entire society can become mechanized like a humour, or fossilized into its institutions. This could happen to Victorian England, according to *Hard Times*, if it takes the gospel of facts and statistics too literally, and did happen to pre-revolutionary France, as described in *A Tale of Two Cities*, dying of what Dickens calls 'the leprosy of unreality', and awaiting the melodramatic deluge of the Revolution.

The obstructing humours cannot escape from the ritual habits that they have set up to deal with this disconcerting energy that has turned them into mechanical puppets. The heroes and heroines, however, along with some of the more amiable humours, have the power to plunge into the hidden world of dreams and death, and, though narrowly escaping death in the process, gain from it a renewed life and energy. Sometimes this plunge into the hidden world is symbolized by a distant voyage. The incredible Australia that makes a magistrate out of Wilkins Micawber also enables the hunted convict Magwitch to become an ambiguous but ultimately genuine fairy godfather. Walter Gay in *Dombey and Son* returns from the West Indies, remarkably silent, long after he has been given up for dead, and the reader follows Martin Chuzzlewit into a place, ironically called Eden, where he is confidently expected to die and nearly does die, but where he goes through a metamorphosis of character that fits him for the comic conclusion. Other characters, including Dick Swiveller, Pip, and Esther Summerson, go into a delirious illness with the same result. *Our Mutual Friend* has a complex pattern of resurrection imagery connected with dredging the Thames, reviving from drowning, finding treasure buried in dust-heaps, and the like; a similar pattern of digging up the dead in *A Tale of Two Cities* extends from the stately Dr Manette to the grotesque Jerry Cruncher. We notice, too, that the sinister society is often introduced in a kind of wavering light between sleep and waking: the appearance of the faces of Fagin and Monks at Oliver Twist's window and the alleged dreams of Affery Flintwinch in *Little Dorrit* are examples. The most uninhibited treatment of this plunge into the world of death and dreams occurs, as we should expect, in the Christmas Books, where

Scrooge and Trotty Veck see in vision a tragic version of their own lives, and one which includes their own deaths, then wake up to renewed festivity. It seems clear that the hidden world, though most of its more direct expressions are destructive and terrible, contains within itself an irresistible power of renewing life.

The hidden world is thus, once again in literature, the world of an invincible Eros, the power strong enough to force a happy ending on the story in defiance of all probability, pushing all the obstructing humours out of the way, or killing them if they will not get out of the way, getting the attractive young people disentangled from their brothers and sisters and headed for the right beds. It dissolves all hardening social institutions and reconstitutes society on its sexual basis of the family, the shadowy old fathers and mothers being replaced by new and livelier successors. When a sympathetic character dies, a strongly religious projection of this power often appears: the 'Judgement' expected shortly by Miss Flite in *Bleak House*, for instance, stands in apocalyptic contrast to the Chancery Court. Dickens's Eros world is, above all, a designing and manipulating power. The obstructing humour can do only what his humour makes him do, and toward the end of the story he becomes the helpless pawn of a chess game in which black can never ultimately win.

The victorious hidden world is not the world of nature in the Rousseauistic context of that word. The people who talk about this kind of nature in Dickens are such people as Mrs Merdle in *Little Dorrit*, Mrs Chick in *Dombey and Son*, and Wackford Squeers – not an encouraging lot. Like most romancers, Dickens gives a prominent place to the fool or 'natural' – Smike, Mr Dick, Barnaby Rudge – whose instincts make up for retarded intelligence. But such people are privileged: elsewhere nature and *social* education, or human experience, are always associated. To say that Dora Copperfield is an unspoiled child of nature is also to say that she is a spoiled child. Dickens's nature is a human nature which is the same kind of thing as the power that creates art, a designing and shaping power. This is also true of Shakespeare's green world, but Dickens's Eros world is not the conserving force that the green world is, which revitalizes a society without altering its structure. At the end of a Shakespeare comedy there is usually a figure of authority, like Prospero or the various dukes, who represents this social conservation.

We have nothing in Dickens to correspond to such figures: the nearest to them are the empty Santa Claus masks of the Cheerybles, Boffin, and the reformed Scrooge. For all its domestic and sentimental Victorian setting, there is a revolutionary and subversive, almost a nihilistic, quality in Dickens's melodrama that is post-Romantic, has inherited the experience of the French Revolution, and looks forward to the world of Freud, Marx, and the existential thriller.

I used the word 'absurd' earlier about Dickens's melodramatic plots, suggesting that they were creatively and not incompetently absurd. In our day the word 'absurd' usually refers to the absence of purpose of meaning in life and experience, the so-called metaphysical absurd. But for literary criticism the formulating of the theory of the absurd should not be left entirely to disillusioned theologians. In literature it is design, the forming and shaping power, that is absurd. Real life does not start or stop; it never ties up loose ends; it never manifests meaning or purpose except by blind accident; it is never comic or tragic, ironic or romantic, or anything else that has a shape. Whatever gives form and pattern to fiction, whatever technical skill keeps us turning the pages to get to the end, is absurd, and contradicts our sense of reality. The great Victorian realists subordinate their storytelling skill to their representational skill. Theirs is a dignified, leisurely vehicle that gives us time to look at the scenery. They have formed our stock responses to fiction, so that even when travelling at the much higher speed of drama, romance, or epic we still keep trying to focus our eyes on the incidental and transient. Most of us feel that there is something else in Dickens, something elemental, yet un-connected with either realistic clarity or philosophical profundity. What it is connected with is a kind of story that fully gratifies the hope expressed, according to Lewis Carroll, by the original of Alice, that 'there will be nonsense in it'. The silliest character in *Nicholas Nickleby* is the hero's mother, a romancer who keeps dreaming of impossible happy endings for her children. But the story itself follows her specifications and not those of the sensible people. The obstructing humours in Dickens are absurd because they have overdesigned their lives. But the kind of design that they parody is produced by another kind of energy, and one which insists, absurdly and yet irresistibly, that what is must never take final precedence over what ought to be.

14 THE PROBLEM OF SPIRITUAL AUTHORITY IN THE NINETEENTH CENTURY

The aspect of Victorian literature represented by such names as Carlyle, Mill, Newman, and Arnold seems to me one of the seminal developments in English culture, ranking with Shakespeare and Milton, if not in literary merit, at least in many other kinds of importance. This is mainly because of the extraordinary fertility and suggestiveness of the educational theories it was so largely concerned with. I therefore speak of the problem of spiritual authority, because all educational theory seems to me to be essentially an application of that problem.

The source of actual or 'temporal' authority in society is seldom hard to locate. It is always in the near vicinity of whatever one pays one's taxes to. As long as it can be believed that might is right, and that the tax-collecting power is not to be questioned, there is no separate problem of spiritual authority. But the thesis that might is right, even when as carefully rationalized as it is in Hobbes, has seldom been regarded as much more than an irresponsible paradox. There has almost certainly never been a period in history when the taxpayer did not try to cheat the publican, and even the desire to cheat raises the question of what kinds of authority may be thought of as overriding the actual one. For self-interest also has a separate authority.

Spiritual authority is usually connected, of course, with religion, God being normally thought of as a sovereign spirit. Our cultural tradition has inherited from the Old Testament a conception of the will of God which may often be in the sharpest possible opposition to the will of man, especially an Egyptian or Babylonian or Philistine will. But if a religion can find an accredited human representative, the two kinds of authority again tend to merge. The medieval theory of the Pope's right to temporal power and the post-Renaissance conception of the divine right of kings are examples of an effort to make the spiritual order a guarantee of the stability of the temporal one. As far as the normal workings of the human mind can go, the will of God differs in degree but not in kind from the will of man, and the metaphors applied to it, such as the metaphor of divine 'sovereignty', are drawn from the more primitive forms of human society. When Greek philosophers began to frame ethical conceptions of justice and righteousness, they ran into similar problems. Their traditional gods, as they appear in Homer, still had all the arbitrary and whimsical quality of a human aristocracy, and submitting to a human conqueror would not be psychologically very different from praying to Poseidon the irascible earth-shaker. In Christianity the human product of spiritual authority is supposed to be charity, but Christian charity has usually been, down to quite recent times, supported by temporal power, and it may be significant that the word charity itself has come to mean chiefly a form of voluntary taxation.

Ordinary social consciousness usually begins in a sense of antithesis between what the ego wants and what society will allow it to have. Hence temporal authority comes to the individual first of all in the form of an external compulsion. In this stage freedom is identified with the ego's side of this antithesis. But education, and more particularly education of the reason, introduces us to a form of necessity or compulsion which is not opposed to freedom but seems to be rather another aspect of it. To assent to the truth of a geometrical demonstration is psychologically a contrast to assenting to the will of a social superior. Hence reason can do what faith, hope and even love by themselves cannot do: present us with the model or pattern of an authority which appeals to the mind rather than to the body, which compels but does not enforce. Such authority confers dignity on the person who accepts it, and such dignity has no context of hierarchy: there is nobody at whose expense the dignity is achieved.

The nineteenth-century social and political writers in Great Britain had inherited from Milton a conception of spiritual authority of this sort, and a singularly lucid and powerful one. For Milton the source of spiritual authority was a revelation from God, more particularly the revelation of the gospel which had spiritualized the law, and delivered those under the gospel from the sense of external constraint. St Paul tells us that where the spirit of the Lord is, there is liberty, and those under the gospel should do as they like, because what they like to do is the will of God, not the illusory pseudo-acts suggested by passion or selfishness. For Milton, again, the accredited human agent of spiritual authority is the church in the sense of the society of individuals who are under the gospel, among whom the one who has authority is the apostle or saint, which according to Milton is what the New Testament means by an *episcope* or overseer. Such authority clearly has no relevance to magistrates or penal codes. Revelation from God accommodates itself to man primarily in the form of reason. Reason manifests itself in the decisive acts of a free life ('Reason is but choosing', Milton says in *Areopagitica*, annexing Aristotle's conception of *proairesis* to the Christian *logos*), and as revelation is the opposite of mystery, there is no conflict between spiritual authority and reason. A revelation from an infinite mind may transcend the reason of a finite one, but does not contradict or humiliate it.

Human society, as Milton saw it, is conditioned by the inertia of original sin to seek the habitual and customary, to do things because they have been done before, to make an idol of tradition. The impact of revelation, coming through reason, is always subversive and revolutionary: it is bound to shake up the somnambulism of habit and confront it with the eternal opposition of God and fallen man. Such reason is also liberty, which man does not naturally want, but which God wants him to have. Purely social changes are, at best, gradual adjustments: genuine liberty is sudden and apocalyptic:

> In state many things at first are crude and hard to digest, which only time and deliberation can supple and concoct. But in religion, wherein is no immaturity, nothing out of season, it goes far otherwise. The door of grace turns upon smooth hinges, wide opening to send out, but soon shutting to recall the precious offers of mercy to a nation.

Temporal authority, however essential, is also provisional, the result of the permanent emergency in human affairs caused by the Fall. It can never be accepted as an end in itself: the reason why it is there is stated in scripture, and all non-scriptural ways of trying to justify it are suspect. There is no inherent authority, in other words, in tradition or custom or precedent, on which temporal authority may rest as a basis. Hence no church which bases its claim to authority on tradition can be a genuine embodiment of revelation. Milton's regicide pamphlet, *The Tenure of Kings and Magistrates*, is a work of extraordinary originality of thought, outlining an early theory of contract and being one of the earliest efforts to try to give some functional place to revolution in history. But even this involves an appeal to precedent, and Milton embarks on an appeal to precedent with the greatest unwillingness: 'But because it is the vulgar folly of men to desert their own reason, and shutting their eyes, to think they see best with other men's, I shall show, by such examples as ought to have most weight with us, what has been done in this case heretofore.'

We have, then, in Milton, a spiritual authority with its roots in revelation and manifesting itself largely in reason, and a temporal authority which is to be acknowledged and obeyed in its own sphere, but should not be rationalized by arguments drawn from precedent or custom. Temporal authority is primarily something that is there, whether we like it or not. If we don't like it, we turn to a conception of spiritual authority and subordinate the temporal power to it as far as possible, if only in our own minds. If we do like it or want to defend it, on the other hand, we tend to see in tradition, custom, habit, in short the process by which temporal authority came to be, some kind of inherent right. We may note in passing that if social revolution is not, for Milton, organically related to precedents, it is not organically related to the future either. The rebellions of the Jews against their overlords, as recorded in the Old Testament, had varying degrees of success, but none were permanently successful. Hence the significance of such a rebellion is typological, manifesting the power of the true God for and at the moment. The extent to which Milton was able to reconcile himself with the failure of the revolution of his own day is perhaps indicated in *Samson Agonistes*, where the temporary victory of Samson in destroying the Philistine temple has this kind of significance.

In the eighteenth century the conception of the natural society in Bolingbroke and Rousseau brought a new kind of revolutionary dialectic into social argument. Rousseau thought of man in his context as a child of nature, and not, as Milton did, in his context as a child of God whose original state was civilized. It was reason and nature that were associated in his thought, not reason and revelation, and the original free and equal society of man was not something intended for man by God which man irrevocably lost, but something man still has the power to recapture. Rousseau's thought resembles Milton's only in associating reason and revolution, and in thinking of reason as essentially the vision in the light of which the free act is performed. It is with the counter-revolutionary thought that developed in Britain in opposition to Rousseau, particularly in Burke, that the problem of spiritual authority in the nineteenth century begins.

For Burke, in almost direct contrast to Milton, the first justification for temporal authority consists in the fact that it is there: the right underlying its might, therefore, is the process of tradition and precedent that has brought it into being. The social contract of any society 'is collected from the form into which the particular society has been cast'. Any developed society is found to consist of various classes, and the tendency of each class is to promote its own interest by acting 'merely by their will'. This creates tyranny, whether exerted by the king (who is historically a class in himself), by the nobility, or, as in France, by the 'people', which means one class or group of people. The source of spiritual authority for Burke, therefore, is to be found, not so much in tradition as such, as in a kind of *telos*, a sense of belonging to a social organism whose health is preserved by maintaining a balance of power among the different organs. The health of the social structure is the end of all social action from any class, and the standard by which such action should be judged. Revolutionary action, which sets free an automatic and unconditioned will, is to society what the cancerous growth of tissue is in the individual. A social organism of this kind is the only genuine form of natural society, for nature is to be thought of as an order that preserves constancy in change by a process of continuous repair. 'Thus, by preserving the method of nature in the conduct of the state in what we improve, we are never wholly new; in what we retain, we are never wholly obsolete.'

Two factors in Burke's thought are particularly relevant here. In Milton, the current of liberty, so to speak, normally flows in a deductive direction, from revelation to reason, and from reason to social action. For Burke, liberty can only be preserved by the inductive, empirical, even *ad hoc* procedures of the political action that operates on the basis of what is there: prudence is the greatest of political virtues, and prejudice the only valuable form of deductive thinking. It is the revolutionary action leading to tyranny which is deductive, like the 'metaphysical' French Revolution which had begun with a set of major premises about the abstract rights of man, and had then attempted 'a decomposition of the whole civil and political mass, for the purpose of originating a new civil order out of the first elements of society'. Hence reason, given its full deductive and speculative head, is not an emancipating but a destructive and ultimately enslaving power in politics. Spiritual authority, at least, is something to which we owe loyalty, and loyalty is not primarily rational; hence society is held together by profounder forces than the reason can express or reach.

In the second place, most temporal authority is vested in the ascendant class: this class is faced with a strong revolutionary bid for power coming from further down in society: the maintenance of the health of the social organism, which means the maintenance of spiritual authority, is therefore bound up with preserving the existing rights and privileges of the ascendant class. 'We must suppose (society) to be in that state of habitual social discipline, in which the wiser, the more expert, and the more opulent conduct, and by conducting enlighten and protect the weaker, the less knowing, and the less provided with the goods of fortune.' Burke goes on to say that 'the state of civil society, which necessarily generates this aristocracy, is a state of nature' – i.e., once again, the genuine form of natural society. The ascendant class includes the church, as for Burke the church is a continuous social institution, and its spiritual authority is inconceivable without that continuity. Hence Burke says, in what from our present point of view is a key statement of his thought:

> Nothing is more certain, than that our manners, our civilization, and all the good things which are connected with manners and with civilization, have, in this European world of ours, depended for ages upon two principles; and were indeed the result of both combined; I mean the spirit of a gentleman, and the spirit of religion.

The ascendant class, therefore, and more particularly the aristocracy, comes to represent an ideal authority, expressed in the term 'gentleman', at the point in history at which its effective temporal authority had begun to decline (though, of course, its privileges and much of its prestige remained for another century). The social function of the aristocracy has always included the art of putting on a show, of dramatizing a way of life. It is natural that America, with no hereditary aristocracy as such, should have invented an *ad hoc* aristocracy out of its entertainers, who attract much the same kind of identification that royal figures do in British countries. In the thought of Carlyle, who has no interest in spiritual authority distinct from temporal authority, and wants only to identify the two, the reactivating of aristocracy naturally occupies a central place. For Carlyle the 'holiness' or radiance of the indwelling divinity in man, which is perceptible in the hero, is the source of an undifferentiated authority which is spiritual and temporal at once.

Yet even Carlyle distinguished the *de jure* authority of the aristocracy from the *de facto* authority of captains of industry and self-made heroes of the Napoleon and Cromwell category. The basis of the distinction seems to be that as *de facto* or temporal authority is essentially active, so *de jure* or spiritual authority has something about it associated with the contemplative. In his chapter on symbolism in *Sartor Resartus* Carlyle sees the heroic personality as an 'intrinsic' symbol (i.e. one that has value in itself, as distinct from the flag or the cross which are extrinsic and have value only as indicators). As a symbol, the hero is the focus of a community, and the *de jure* figure seems to be the most vivid one. Crowds gather to see the Queen in order to see their own unity as a society reflected in her. Here again there is a link between the recognition of spiritual authority and the dramatic function of an ascendant class.

Samuel Butler also associates spiritual authority with the aristocracy, in a more speculative and paradoxical way. He is, of course, particularly fascinated by the working of the evolutionary process in human society, and his conception of education, traditional as it is in itself, reflects this interest. He points out in *Life and Habit* that no skill is learned thoroughly until it passes through consciousness into the unconscious. It follows that the most profoundly educated people are those who have been born to wealth, leisure, and privilege, and have never been troubled by a conscious idea, which includes a good many of the aristocracy. Thus in *The Way of All Flesh* the hero, Ernest Pontifex, at that time engaged in social work in East London, meets an old classmate named Towneley who is large, handsome, simple-minded, well-to-do, and altogether admirable. Ernest asks Towneley effusively if he doesn't love the poor: Towneley says no, and gets away as quickly as possible. It could hardly be a briefer encounter, but it is an epiphany for Ernest: spiritual authority has spoken, as unmistakably as it spoke from the burning bush. Ernest considers this situation carefully, and finally decides:

> I see it all now. The people like Towneley are the only ones who know anything that is worth knowing, and like that of course I can never be. But to make Towneleys possible there must be hewers of wood and drawers of water – men, in fact, through whom conscious knowledge must pass before it can reach those who can apply it gracefully and instinctively as the Towneleys can.

We are reminded of the respect paid in Erewhon to those who are handsome, healthy, and rich, and how Erewhon considers it a crime to be ill or unfortunate. In Huxley's terms, society's sympathies are with nature, rather than with ethics, even though society itself is an ethical creation. Yet Ernest's solution is still a trifle immature, and *Erewhon* brings us a little closer to Butler's real view of spiritual authority. Most of the Erewhonians, according to Butler, are unthinking, instinctive conservatives, whose values are determined entirely by habit and prejudice: worshippers, as he says, of the goddess Ydgrun. But there is also in Erewhon a small group of 'high Ydgrunites', whom Butler describes as the best people he met in Erewhon. Of them he says: 'They were gentlemen in the full sense of the word; and what has one not said in saying this?' The high Ydgrunite would be somebody like Montaigne, presumably: able to live in and with society, able to see not only the power but the real significance of convention and prejudice, yet remaining intellectually detached from them. Such gentlemen are not only the natural aristocracy but the genuine apostles of society, correcting instinct by reason and reason by instinct, and never allowing the two to make that fatal alliance which is the mark of all bigots, whether reactionary or revolutionary.

The problem of spiritual authority, we see, has as its crucial point the problem of defining the community of such an authority. The writers we have been quoting, all of whom are deeply conservative, associate this community with the ideal aristocracy which the term 'gentleman' conveys. For a revolutionary thinker, such as William Morris, spiritual authority would be isolated from society, confined to the small conspiratorial group of those who repudiate its values and are shut out from its benefits. It is perhaps worth noting that Morris's revolutionary ideal, as outlined in the future Utopia depicted in *News from Nowhere*, is the assimilating of the conception of a natural aristocracy to the whole of society. In *News from Nowhere* everybody has the creative versatility and the *sprezzatura* that are the marks of the ideally educated courtier in Castiglione, except that, of course, there is no court and no prince, and no one to serve except one another. They are at once producers and consumers, and as consumers they have the sharply limited and defined quality of a privileged class. 'We know what we want,' says one of them, 'so we make no more than we want.' This applies even to the production of human beings: the population has become stabilized, apparently, because people are no longer rutting out of nervous instability, as they do in societies based on exploitation. The curiously childlike quality of Morris's ideal citizens is also significant, for, of course, the real natural aristocracy in all ages, the society of those who are genuinely entitled to leisure and privilege and consuming the goods produced for them by others, are the children.

11

We have just traced a parabola from the counter-revolutionary polemic of the later Burke to the revolutionary polemic of Morris. The former places spiritual authority in the middle of the ascendant class, or at least its centre of gravity is to be found there, and the *Appeal from the New to the Old Whigs* ends in contemptuous ridicule of John Ball, 'that reverend patriarch of sedition', who could not find the conception of 'gentleman' in the original producing society when Adam delved and Eve span. Morris, in contrast, places spiritual authority for his own time in the small alienated group who are possessed by the ambition of realizing the dream of John Ball. For Morris the Peasants' Revolt was the one brief moment when something like a proletariat appears in British history. In the thought of John Stuart Mill the problem of spiritual authority is located in a much less simplified view of society. For Mill, Burke's continuum of habit and prejudice is the way in which the majority of people live. Being a majority, they are not confined to a single class, and the progress of democracy involves making their will the source of *temporal* authority. As in Burke and Butler, their motivation is instinctive and empirical. Over against them are the smaller group of the liberal opposition, a much more highly individualized group, of whom Mill says that they initiate all wise and noble things.

Mill, somewhat unexpectedly, resembles Hegel in seeing the political opposition of Conservative and Liberal as the symbol of an ideal or intellectual opposition of conservative and liberal attitudes. As the liberal opposition is intellectually always a minority, it has the peculiar problem of getting enough mass support to be effective in a democratic election. Some of Mill's devices, such as a plurality of votes for the educated, are sufficiently desperate to indicate that this is a matter of some difficulty. To grasp the nature of the ideal opposition we have to grasp two principles. First, the majority is always right, for the majority is the source of temporal authority. Second, the majority is always wrong, for it is not the source of spiritual authority. The latter is to be found in the intellectual opposition, for 'almost all the greatest men who ever lived have formed part of such an Opposition'.

Authority in its two forms, therefore, rests on a paradoxical and illogical tension between majority rule and minority right. The minority are not a class but an élite, and no social epithet like 'gentleman' will apply to them. In practice most of them may be gentlemen, but that is not why they belong there. The gentleman behaves according to a social convention, and for Mill the toleration of unconventional or eccentric behaviour is the mark of a mature society. What holds this élite together is something intellectual, though it is certainly not intellectual agreement. To put the question in another way, what gives a minority a right? Criminals are a minority, but clearly have no right to be criminals. In the *Essay on Liberty* the right appears to be the ability to contribute something to the area of free thought and discussion, of what for Mill is the real parliament of man, the ideological debate that is close to being the source of spiritual authority because it supplies the vision for temporal power. To permit freedom of thought is to direct freedom of action, as unrestricted speculation is the best check so far discovered on premature, spasmodic, or panic-stricken action. Here again we run into a Hegelian element in Mill's thought: no idea contributed to this social debate has any real effectiveness unless it contains its own opposite: unless, therefore, the possibility of refuting it is also present. Mill draws our attention to the peculiar importance of Rousseau in challenging the validity of the structure of society itself.

Burke's counter-revolutionary argument was based on a completely inductive conception of political action; Mill's argument attempts to associate his liberal opposition with a more deductive point of view. He remarks, for example, that 'the non-existence of an acknowledged first principle has made ethics not so much a guide as a consecration of men's actual sentiments'. The Utilitarian philosophy held his loyalty because it provided a major premise for majority behaviour. That people will seek what they consider pleasure and avoid what they consider pain is individually probable and statistically certain. But this purely descriptive principle supplies no standard or value, no way even of distinguishing reality from illusion in the conception of pleasure. In Milton, who in *Areopagitica* presents a similar conception of truth as something arrived at dynamically through the conflict of opinion, the major premises come from scripture. Milton never conceived the possibility of a free society trying to find truth without the aid of scripture. In Mill there is no clear source of the premises of debate of this kind, no set of standards and assumptions that can be taken as given. The absence of such a source may be one reason for his curious attraction toward the most uncongenial types of political dogmatists, including Carlyle and Comte (it would take us too far afield to apply this principle to Harriet Taylor), as though he felt that they held some missing piece he was looking for.

In Newman, on the other hand, the source of spiritual authority is the church catholic: his great strength as a nineteenth-century thinker lay in his unvarying acceptance of that view. At no time in his adult life was Newman ever anything that a Protestant would call a Protestant: his problem was only to decide whether the Anglican or the Roman communion was the genuinely catholic one. He takes our present argument a step further by finding the road to spiritual authority through education. Education for him is partly social, and retains the social aim of producing the 'gentleman' which we met in Burke and

Butler. Even its intellectual characteristic, a disinterested or liberal quality in it which is 'its own end', has an analogy with the social ideal which is detachable from the necessity of earning a living. On its intellectual side, liberal education is essentially a discipline of reason, as in Milton, and, as in Mill, it seems to have something to do with a 'master view of things', a deductive or synoptic sense of intellectual form which gets one's head above the habit of living:

> The principle of real dignity in Knowledge, its worth, its desirableness, considered irrespectively of its results, is this germ within it of a scientific or a philosophical process. This is how it comes to be an end in itself; this is why it admits of being called Liberal.

But the university turns out to be a function of the church, and the education it gives confronts the student with a dilemma: he must either attach himself along with his education to the church or keep his education as a private possession. Recurrently we have come to this crucial point of having to define the community of spiritual authority. The individual can readily be seen to be capable of understanding more than society in general, and hence of possessing standards and values, with an authority superior in kind if not in power. But the conception 'gentleman', however interpreted, defines the superior individual rather than the superior group, even granted that one may recognize the individual as one of a group. For Newman only the church provides this community, and of the gentlemen who cannot commit themselves to it he says: 'When they do wrong, they feel, not contrition, of which God is the object, but remorse, and a sense of degradation. . . . They are victims of an intense self-contemplation.'

In Newman's view of the church there is no place, as there would have to be in Protestant thought, including Milton's, for a dialogue between scripture and church. The church for Newman is the definitive teacher of doctrine, hence it encloses scripture, and operates on ordinary society very much as the British constitution does in Burke. For Burke the conflict of classes and their interests, in a free society, is settled by a legal compromise which preserves the rights of both parties, and these compromises then form a series of precedents diffusing freedom through society, as the quarrels of king and barons produced Magna Carta and the quarrels of king and Parliament the

Bill of Rights. Newman sees church doctrine as developing in a somewhat similar way, being evolved out of the crises of history, defining a dogma here, marking off a heresy there, in an endless pilgrimage toward the City of God. Thus spiritual authority in Newman is, as in Milton, a revelation, but a revelation that has no place for metamorphosis, for the revolutionary and apocalyptic transformation of society.

In Arnold, the conception 'culture' is the basis from which we have to start. In using the phrase spiritual authority to describe a pervasive problem of nineteenth-century thought, I have been putting unfamiliar conceptions into the minds of some of my writers. For Mill, the problem is not exactly one of *spiritual* authority, and for Butler, it is not exactly a problem of authority. But Arnold is quite explicit about the authoritative nature of culture:

> If we look at the world outside us we find a disquieting absence of sure authority. We discover that only in right reason can we get a source of sure authority; and culture brings us towards right reason.

The traditional elements of gentleman and liberal education are both involved in Arnold's culture, but Arnold clears up a point about the social location of spiritual authority that has been confusing us thus far. We noticed that the more conservative a writer is, the more inclined he is to locate spiritual authority in the middle of actual society, in the place of greatest prestige and prominence. The more radical he is, the more inclined he is to locate it in an opposition, an alien or even excluded group. Something in Arnold – possibly the Romantic poet in him – realizes that the centre is the place of greatest isolation. The argument of *Culture and Anarchy* is to the effect that what is of greatest cultural value, such as a university or the established church, is central to society and demands to be placed at the centre, in the position of Carlyle's intrinsic symbol. Society itself presents a conflict of class interests, and culture for Arnold operates like law in Burke or doctrine in Newman, as a harmonizing principle creating a new kind of order out of this conflict. Those who support it have to begin by isolating themselves from class conflict, which means isolating themselves from the present structure of society: 'Within each of these classes there are a certain number of *aliens*, if we may so call them, – persons who are mainly led, not by their class spirit, but by a general *humane* spirit, by the love of human perfection.'

Culture represents an evaluation – the *best* that has been thought and said – and the conception of 'best' is bound up with permanence. Class conflict deals with temporary issues, and its arguments are rationalizations based on a temporary situation. Temporal power is based on the ascendancy of one class – here we come back to Milton's conception of temporal power as an interim power. The class *qua* class is always anti-cultural: the aristocracy, considered purely as a class, are only barbarians, the middle class only Philistines, the lower class only a populace. Hence it would be the wildest paradox to think of creating a new society through the dictatorship of one class. It is culture that is the genuinely revolutionary force in society, for culture 'seeks to do away with classes', and tends to create out of actual society an ideal order of liberty, equality, and fraternity. Culture for Arnold is a whole of which the church forms part, but as culture is not, like church, the name of a specific community, the problem of defining the community of spiritual authority is still with us.

The question of the origin of spiritual authority, and of whether that origin is purely human, partly human, or wholly superhuman has come up at various times in this inquiry. Anyone working out this question in Christian terms, whether Catholic or Protestant, would be likely to say that its origin is out of human reach, though the fact that Christ is at once God, Man, and Logos guarantees the validity of human reason as a means of receiving it, at least up to a point. For Burke and Butler, in different ways, spiritual authority, or whatever is homologous with it, comes to us as a process of nature, a datum or something given, which we may modify but must first of all accept. We have seen that spiritual authority begins in the recognition of truth, and truth usually has about it some quality of the objective, something presented to us. But for a liberal thinker, such as Mill, there can hardly be any real spiritual authority apart from what man himself creates. A revolutionary thinker would go a step farther and see in truth itself a human creation which, as man continues to create it, he may also re-create. Marx's second thesis on Feuerbach makes this quite clear:

> The question whether objective truth can be attributed to human thinking
> is not a question of theory, but is a practical question. In practice man must

prove the truth, that is, the reality and power, the this-sidedness of his thinking.

Arnold's 'culture' unites these qualities of the datum and the continuous creation, being a human construct which, so far as it is rooted in the past, possesses an objective authority. This authority, we should note, is not exclusively intellectual, for 'many things are not seen in their true nature and as they really are, unless they are seen as beautiful', and the imagination as well as the reason may recognize a monument of its own magnificence.

Wherever we turn in nineteenth-century thought we meet some version of a 'drunken boat' construct, where the values of humanity, intelligence, or cultural and social tradition keep tossing precariously in a sort of Noah's ark on top of a menacing and potentially destructive force. This is the relation of the world as idea to the world as will in Schopenhauer, of ethics to evolution in Darwin and Huxley, of the ascendant class to the proletariat in Marx, and, later, of ego to libido and id in Freud. There are also many variants of a 'saving remnant' theory, ranging from Coleridge's 'clerisy' to various pleas for a new kind of monastic movement (one thinks of the symbolic function of the idealized monastery in the argument of Carlyle's *Past and Present*). Of other metaphors of spiritual authority, two are conspicuous. One is the metaphor of the human body, whose seat of intelligence and authority ought to be somewhere on top, as it is in the individual body. The other is the thermostat or feedback metaphor which has organized so much social thinking in the last two centuries. In a sense the search for spiritual authority is really the search for a 'governor' in the mechanical sense, something that distributes the rhythm of a mechanism without being involved in the mechanism itself. This figure appears in Huxley's *Evolution and Ethics*: 'To this extent the general cosmic process begins to be checked by a rudimentary ethical process, which is, strictly speaking, part of the former, just as the "governor" in a steamengine is part of the mechanism of the engine.'

The problem dealt with in this paper could, of course, be extended over a far wider area of nineteenth-century thought than I am here able to cover. So far as I know, the twentieth century has not added much to the question, which may be one reason why the political axioms and assumptions of the twentieth century are still rooted in the nineteenth. It seems to me, however, appropriate to consider whether the university may not have a peculiarly close relationship to the question. In particular, the university seems to me to come closer than any other human institution to defining the community of spiritual authority. Newman's view that the university is a function of the church, with theology occupying a central role as the queen of sciences, does not seem to be borne out by the development of universities in the last century. I have no doubt that religion indicates where the ultimate source of spiritual authority is, nor that the churches have an essential function as custodians and interpreters of its tradition. But in the present-day shape of society, so dominated by science and technology, they clearly have only a partial and peripheral role in embodying the spiritual authority of that society.

Arnold comes nearest to seeing the universities in this light, but universities in his day, and more particularly as he conceived them, made it necessary for him to distinguish them from 'culture'. A century later we seem to be living our lives on two levels. One is the level of ordinary society, which is in so constant a state of revolution and metamorphosis that it cannot be accepted as the real form of human society at all, but only as the transient appearance of real society. Real society itself can only be the world revealed to us through the study of the arts and sciences, the total body of human achievement out of which the forces come that change ordinary society so rapidly. Of this world the universities are the social embodiment, and they represent what seems to me today the only visible direction in which our higher loyalties and obligations can go.

15 THE TOP OF THE TOWER: A Study of the Imagery of Yeats

All poets speak the same symbolic language, but they have to learn it either by instinct or unconsciously from other poets. In the poetry of the Western world from medieval times to our own, there has been a framework for poetic symbolism with four main levels. On the top level is what I should call the Logos vision, which includes the conventional heaven of religion, the place of the presence of God. The central symbol of the Logos vision is the city, the Biblical New Jerusalem, but it is also often described in metaphors taken from mathematics or from music, the two areas being connected by the conception of 'harmony'. Central to Logos imagery, in all poetry before Newton's time at least, is the image of the orderly stars moving in spheres which also give out a harmonious music, the archetype of the music we hear. The Logos vision is that of an order of existence designed by an intelligent Creator, and among its musical and mathematical images is that of the dance, which appears in Dante, in Sir John Davies's *Orchestra*, in the Eliot Quartets, and at the end of 'Among School Children'. In the last poem the image of the chestnut tree, immediately preceding, recalls the traditional image of the earthly paradise, just below the circling stars, in which man was originally placed.

The stars in their courses are all that is now left of the order of nature as God originally designed it: the earthly paradise for man was lost with the fall of Adam. But everything that inspires and ennobles man helps him to ascend from the world of his fallen nature to something nearer his original home, traditionally the Earthly Paradise or the Garden of Eden. This ascent of the soul is another area of poetic symbolism that I shall call the Eros vision, because some form of human love almost invariably prompts it. Eros symbolism usually begins with the figure of the alienated poet, who is forced into writing poetry by being frustrated as a lover. The creative life thus appears as what students of animal behaviour call a displaced activity, a substituted outlet of a mainly erotic energy. In medieval times this led to the convention begun by the Provençal love poets and expanded by Dante and Petrarch. According to the more typical forms of this, an erotic relation is established between a poet and a lady which does not aim either at marriage or at any sexual 'affair', but is intended from the beginning to pass through frustration to sublimation. The lady is too high in virtue or social rank to be sexually attainable: the poet is merely her servant and a servant of the God of Love, who has commanded him to love the lady. The lady then becomes the inspiration for everything good that the poet does, so that his dedication to her may also be an ascent of his soul toward virtue. In the chivalric romances this virtue is symbolized by the courage and strength of the knight-errant as he continues to rid the world of dragons and giants and tyrants. Such a convention is based on an erotic analogy to Christianity, and it was easy to fit it into the medieval Christian framework. In Christianity man has fallen from a higher state of being, and hence a love-inspired ascent of the soul may be thought of as a partial return to its original state, the state symbolized by Adam in Eden. I say a partial return, because for Christianity no one can complete the process in this life: for Catholic Christianity it is completed after death in purgatory.

There are two main varieties of Eros vision, the explicitly sexual and the sublimated. We may call them, following Milton, the allegro and the penseroso visions, though of course they are far older than Milton: Ovid, for example, writes an art of love which moves toward sexual intercourse, and then deals with the 'remedies' of love which take the opposite road. Milton's allegro vision is one of 'unreprovèd pleasures free' which take the narrator to an earthly Paradise, where Orpheus may hear an erotic (Lydian) music that might restore his Eurydice to him; the penseroso vision is a sublimated love for a nun (vestal virgin) which makes the narrator a philosopher studying Plato in a lonely tower, and leaves him a prophet and hermit. A similar duality in the Eros vision exists in medieval poetry. In *The Romaunt of the Rose* the poet is a lover whose quest ends with his physical possession of his mistress's body: in Dante's *Purgatorio* the poet is impelled by his love for Beatrice to climb the mountain of Purgatory to the Garden of Eden on top of it. There is no sexual culmination: Dante first meets a young girl, Matilda, but he is separated from her by a river; then he meets Beatrice, but Beatrice does not go farther than unveiling her mouth, the visible sex organ, so to speak.

The world that man entered with the fall of Adam and is now born into is a tragic world, and its central image is that of the dying god Adonis or Dionysus, a role which Christ adopts in his Incarnation. The tragic hero often recapitulates the dying god's typical life from mysterious birth to premature death; we also have an episodic form of this theme in the poems that deal with birth in this world as a loss of innocence or fall from a paradisal world to a lower one. Examples include poems by Vaughan and Traherne, Wordsworth's Intimations of Immortality Ode, Blake's *Book of Thel*, Dylan Thomas's 'Fern Hill', and a passage in Yeats's 'Among School Children'. Below this world of tragic or ironic experience is the Thanatos vision, including the hell of Christianity and the ironic visions of our day which present experience as an unending life in death.

All four of these worlds are clearly marked in Yeats's symbolism. The Logos vision, the 'Thirteenth Cone' where Chance and Choice are one, is not often referred to, but it is integral to his imagery none the less. It is most explicitly described, perhaps, in the fourth of the 'Supernatural Songs':

> There all the barrel-hoops are knit,
> There all the serpent-tails are bit,
> There all the gyres converge in one,
> There all the planets drop in the Sun.

This world is regularly associated with the sun in Yeats, and it stands above the cycle of life and death represented by the ouroboros or tail-biting serpent of the second line. Yeats tells us that this world in Plato is a world of pure Idea or Form, but that Plotinus transformed it into a 'timeless individuality or daimon', preferring Socrates to his thought, and seeing the Logos world existentially as a total person rather than a total idea, containing 'archetypes of all possible existences whether of man or brute'. Plotinus was, Yeats says, the first to establish this individuality as the sole source of being, though Yeats's Christian and

Jewish readers, at least, might feel that a few other people had got to the conception a little earlier than Plotinus. The traditional associations of harmony appear in a remarkable early evocation of this Logos world in the poem 'Paudeen':

> on the lonely height where all are in God's eye,
> There cannot be, confusion of our sound forgot,
> A single soul that lacks a sweet crystalline cry.

It is, however, the imagery of Eros that I want to consider more particularly in this essay. The theme of the sexually inspired ascent of the soul underlies the 'tower' and 'winding stair' images in Yeats. The most obvious source for the image is, again, the spiral *escalina* or staircase going up and around the mountain of Purgatory in Dante. It is interesting that the only contemporary poet producing work of comparable value to that of Yeats, T. S. Eliot, was also fascinated by staircases, and his *Ash Wednesday*, with its winding stair and its explicit debt to the *Purgatorio*, belongs to the same period as the appearance of the same imagery in Yeats. The spiral shape of Dante's mountain links the winding stair with Yeats's gyre image. The gyre for Yeats is one of the central images of the cycle of life because it can be an emblem either of fertility and life or of death. The former produces the cornucopia or horn of plenty, an image appearing in 'A Prayer for My Daughter', and the latter the Charybdis or maelstrom. The activity of the poet, moving from a broad receptivity to the concentrated effort of creation, may be thought of as a spiral or vortex of energy moving from base to apex. This activity recapitulates, in its turn, the whole movement of life, of plants from receptive root to climactic fruit or blossom, and of animals who pass through the vortex of birth from one world to another. Once entered into the world of birth, another vortex pulls them back through its apex into death, which is symbolically a return to the mother. The death-gyre appears in Dante's hell, which, like his purgatory, is a cone narrowing from base to apex.

The gyre is, of course, also a sexual symbol, male on the outside and female on the inside, and sex is closely connected with rising flames and the spiralling of smoke, fire being a traditional purgatorial image also. We may compare the rites of kindling the 'need-fire' described in *The Golden Bough*, where a naked boy and girl go into a room together and make fire by twirling a pointed stick in a hole, or what Yeats calls perning in a gyre. Sexual intercourse and the birth resulting from it form a double gyre or reversing movement into and out of the mother's body. The seashell, which appears in the first poem in Yeats's *Collected Poems*, is another helical emblem of life arising out of the sea, and the ear, described by Blake, in a more sinister context, as 'a whirlpool fierce to draw creations in', is the vortex through which the Word is born in the Virgin's body in Yeats's 'Mother of God'. Dante's greatest predecessor as an Eros poet was Plato, whose ascent of the soul is usually associated with the ladder. But, if we can believe Aristophanes' *The Clouds*, where Socrates is represented as dethroning the gods and replacing them with a new deity called *dinos* or 'whirl', perhaps the gyre underlies the Socratic tradition too.

In the Bible the ascent from earth to heaven is also first represented by a ladder, the image of Jacob's, that is, Israel's, dream. From the point of view of later Christian typology, this ladder would be identical spiritually with the later journey of Israel as a people through the labyrinth of the desert toward their original home or Promised Land. The gyre is a conventionalized labyrinth, the crooked path of the serpent as distinct from the straight path of the arrow. The Promised Land is symbolically identical with the original Garden of Eden, and is represented in the New Testament by the vision of the Virgin Mother and her divine Child, the epiphany of divine innocence. The connecting link between the Promised Land and the Virgin is the *hortus conclusus* or enclosed garden of the Song of Songs, identified with the body of the Virgin in Christian symbolism. All these Biblical archetypes are incorporated in Dante. Dante begins with the standard medieval Eros theme, the alienated lover who is inspired by his love in the form of a vision. He goes up the Mountain of Purgatory, shedding one of the seven deadly sins at each stage, the last sin to be purged being, appropriately enough, lechery or excessive physical love, where again the image of fire appears. After this Dante finds himself in Eden, so that he has really regained his own childhood, not his individual childhood but his generic childhood as a son of Adam.

Thus Dante's quest up the mountain has in a sense gone backward in time, removing the sins which accumulated in his ordinary experience like, to use a Yeatsian image, the wrappings of a mummy cloth around a mummy, and thus proceeding from his situation as a poet in mid-career back to the ultimate source of his life. Similarly, Yeats says of the spirits in his equivalent of purgatory: 'They examine their past if undisturbed by our importunity, tracing events to their source, and as they take the form their thought suggests, seem to live backward through time.' After Virgil has left Dante with a grave benediction, in possession of his free will, his own pope and emperor, Beatrice appears, scolding like an Italian mamma, and Dante is immediately reduced to a whimpering and tearful child. An erotic impulse drives Dante from the sexual into the pre-sexual, and from there to his own original state of innocence. It looks as though, psychologically, one of the goals of the Eros ascent is connected with the mother and the mother's encircling body (one thinks of another modern treatment of the theme in Auden's and Isherwood's *Ascent of F6*).

As the lover or visionary proceeds on his quest toward his own eternal youth, the shadow of ordinary life appears beside him in the form of an old man, who guides and instructs him on the journey but cannot enter the final paradise. This figure is represented by Moses in the Exodus story and by Virgil in Dante. In the New Testament we have Joseph, who also cannot enter the *hortus conclusus*, as well as the Magi of Matthew and the Simeon of Luke. I have mentioned Milton's allegro and penseroso visions, where there is a modulation of this theme. The figure of the philosopher in the tower, studying the stars of the Logos vision, is linked by Yeats both with Il Penseroso and with Shelley's Prince Athanase. In Milton's *Comus* the usual associations of hero or heroine and guardian are reversed: the Lady's chastity puts her in tune with the Logos harmonies of the heavenly world, but her attendant spirit goes back to an earthly Paradise, identified with Spenser's Gardens of Adonis, of which more later. Most comedy is written in the Eros mode, and we notice in Shakespeare the penseroso figures of Jaques and Prospero, who withdraw from the festivity and multiple marriages at the end into a meditative solitude.

In Yeats the theme of a journey backward in time is reinforced by the 'ancestral stair' in which the poet travels in the track of his great predecessors, and by the personal and cultural memories in 'The Tower'. Long before Yeats had made what he calls 'the connection, still vague in my imagination, between pilgrimage and vision, scenery and the pilgrim's salvation', he had picked up the conception of two levels of existence, one that of ordinary life and the other a land of eternal youth, from the Irish legends of the Tir na nOg and the Sidhe dancing in the gyres of the whirling wind. In many stories of fairyland, the mortals who enter it find that time is arrested there, and that when they return to ordinary life they have become incredibly aged, in the role of the old man excluded from the earthly paradise.

There has been, as already indicated, an old feud between the sexual and the sublimated or religious versions of the Eros quest, and even in the sublimated versions some ambiguity recurs. The Israelites were able to enter the Promised Land only through the help of the harlot Rahab, and Rahab in Dante marks the boundary of what is in effect the total area of the lower Paradise, which stretches from the Garden of Eden, at the top of Mount Purgatory, just below the moon, to the sphere of Venus, the limit of the earth's shadow in Dante's astronomy. Rahab, the last soul seen in Venus, balances the virginal figure of Matilda, the first soul seen in Eden. Similarly, the story of the Virgin Birth in the Bible comes very close to being a story of a forgiven harlot, and the forgiven harlot appears in the Gospels and later legends in the form of another Mary. In most paintings of the Crucifixion, Christ is flanked by both Marys, the forgiven harlot in red and the Virgin in blue. There is a similar duality in Yeats's portrayals of two aspects of the personality, one seeking the sexual cycle and the other trying to escape from it: an early example[1] presents it in its true colours:

> She opened her door and her window,
> And the heart and the soul came through,
> To her right hand came the red one,
> To her left hand came the blue.

For a complete Eros vision, therefore, we need a virgin, a child, and a harlot. When we add to them the eagle which flies upward into the Logos unity of the sun, and the lion which wanders alone in the wilderness, we have the five elements 'That make the Muses sing'[2].

In Dante, the Mountain of Purgatory stands on an island on the other side of the earth, and the souls of the dead reach it by crossing water on the ship of death. As Dante emerges from hell, an angel arrives with a boatload of souls, dumps them down at the foot of the mountain, and hurries back for more. Similarly the wandering of Israel in the desert begins with the crossing of the Red Sea (identical with the escape from Egypt, which is symbolically under the Red Sea with Pharaoh's army). The ancient ship of death image enters Yeats's poem 'His Dream', in *The Green Helmet* volume, but in 'Byzantium' and in 'News for the Delphic Oracle' the vehicular form, as Blake would call it, is not a ship but a dolphin, an equally traditional image of salvation out of the sea. The ascent up the desert mountain culminates in the vision of unfallen nature, symbolized as a rule by an unspoiled or redeemed female. Sometimes this female figure is identified with the moon, the traditional boundary between temporal and eternal worlds, which stands directly above the mountain in Dante and elsewhere. Thus the quest for ideal beauty of Keats's hero Endymion is represented by Endymion's love for Phoebe the moon goddess. In Spenser's Muta-bilitie Cantos a great debate, anticipating some of the similar debates in Yeats, is held in the sphere of the moon, which is also just above the top of an Irish mountain, 'Arlo Hill'. The debate is between Mutability, the ruler of everything below the moon, who claims that everything above the moon is also hers, and Jove, the representative of the higher order of nature. The judge is Nature herself, who decides in favour of Jove, though she admits that there are cycles, and therefore some principle of change, on both levels. In other words, it is essential for a Renaissance Christian poet to keep a higher Logos vision above an Eros one.

The sublimated version of the Eros quest has been more popular in the past, not only for religious reasons, but because of the underlying paradox in the sexual relation expressed by Sir Thomas Browne: 'United souls are not satisfied with embraces, but desire to be truly each other.' Poets insist on the imagery of mutual identity anyway, though, as we see in Donne's 'The Extasie' and Shakespeare's 'The Phoenix and the Turtle', usually with some underlying humour and sense of the paradox involved. This tone of paradoxical humour recurs in Yeats's 'Solomon and the Witch', where it is suggested that perfect sexual intercourse would restore the fallen world to its paradisal form. But perfect intercourse would be, as Blake says, a complete union of bodies rather than 'a pompous high priest entering by a secret place'. The capacity for such complete union is ascribed to the angels by Swedenborg, in a passage frequently referred to by Yeats, and one which connects this theme with that of a world adjacent to but different from ours where time runs backward from age towards youth.

In the course of history there are certain gigantic cycles which are started off by a supernatural sex act of this kind, of the type preserved in mythology by the legends of the intercourse of a male bird and a woman, Leda and the swan, the Dove and the Virgin, Attracta and the Irish heron. Such cycles are marked by certain 'conjunctions' – an astrological term with an obvious sexual overtone – of planets. The word 'consummation' also has a sexual meaning, though in Christian theology it refers primarily to the eventual burning up of the world by fire. But fire, we saw, is a sexual image too, appearing in Dante's ring of fire and Shakespeare's phoenix, and Blake says in *The Marriage of Heaven and Hell* that the apocalypse by fire will take place through 'an improvement of sensual enjoyment'. This image of the flame of the apocalypse being lit by sex comes into the image at the end of the 'The Winding Stair' where the poet strikes a match to set fire to 'the great gazebo', which is now a structure of guilt.

Yeats carries his preference for the sexual to the sublimated quest to the point of making several parodies of the latter. The early volume *Responsibilities* is polarized in its symbolism between the figures of the sleeper and the wanderer, the figure who, like the traditional Enoch and Elijah, remains quietly awaiting the final end of things, and the figure who, like Cain or the Wandering Jew, is condemned to wander in the cycle of time. The latter figure is closely connected with the old man who is prevented from entering the earthly paradise, and appears in *Last Poems* as the 'pilgrim' and the 'wild old wicked man', who gets randier as he gets older. Then again, we said that in traditional Christian symbolism the higher Logos vision is described in mathematical imagery, which indicates the Christian sense of the superiority of the sublimated and conceptual vision over the sexual one. Yeats makes the point that the element of mathematical formality in Greek art does not transcend the sexual, but is itself a powerful expression of the sexual. The art that 'Pythagoras planned' turns out to be an apotheosis of physical and sexual beauty, and the same is true of Renaissance art:

> Michael Angelo left a proof
> On the Sistine Chapel roof,

> Where but half-awakened Adam
> Can disturb globe-trotting Madam
> Till her bowels are in heat.

On the other hand, Ribh denounces Patrick for being obsessed by a mathematical notion of a divine Trinity and replacing the old sexual trinity of father, mother, and child with it. Plotinus, whose vision culminates in a flight of the solitary to the solitary, and who was said by his biographer to have been ashamed of being in the body, makes some surprising discoveries about his spiritual goal when he finally reaches it.

In *The Shadowy Waters* the hero and heroine are led on by Aengus, the Irish Eros, towards a world of total love in which the frustrations of ordinary experience have ceased to exist. Consequently they are leaving the world for a paradise:

> ... in some island where the life of the world
> Leaps upward, as if all the streams o' the world
> Had run into one fountain.

We recall that in the Song of Songs the image of the enclosed garden is paired with that of a 'fountain sealed', and the Eros image of journeying upstream to the source or spring of a river appears later in 'The Tower' and elsewhere. *The Shadowy Waters* quest reaches a point at the limit of the cyclical world of time, where it impinges on the eternal world. The cycle of time is often symbolized in literature by a dragon or serpent, particularly the ouroboros serpent with its tail in its mouth, referred to in the 'Supernatural Song' quoted above. Whether or not the ouroboros is the precise image in Yeats's mind in *The Shadowy Waters*, at any rate Dectora says:

> O ancient worm,
> Dragon that loved the world and held us to it,
> You are broken, you are broken.

The sailors, on the other hand, follow the cycle and return to the world of time, laden with the treasure that is the more conventional reward of killing the dragon. In *The Herne's Egg*, although there is the apocalyptic embrace of the heron with his priestess, the priestess also requires a sexual act with a human lover in the cycle of time, in order to provide a womb for the body of the dead Conchubar seeking reincarnation, a theme which Yeats adapts from a sardonic Tibetan folk-tale.

These examples suggest that there are, in fact, three possible conclusions for the Eros ascent: the sublimated, the sexual, and the return back down the mountain to ordinary existence. In Dante it is impossible to go back down: the sacramental cable car runs in only one direction. But that is because ordinary life, running from birth to death, has already taken place: purgatory is the reversing movement after death, and for the same reason only the sublimated goal is possible for Dante. Obviously the sexual goal and the return are closely connected, for the natural result of intercourse with the bride is birth, and birth begins the descending movement. One reason why Virgil in Dante cannot get past the top of purgatory is that his imagination reached its limit, from Dante's point of view, in his vision of a world renewed by the birth of a divine child in the Fourth Eclogue. Renewal in time merely turns the cycle of time.

Yet even in Dante there is a faint suggestion that from Eden on top of the mountain all forms of life except human ones fall back into the lower world, and in Spenser's description of the Gardens of Adonis, or sexual paradise, there is a 'Time', who is continually forcing seeds and embryos out of this world into the lower one. We saw that the typical figure of the descending movement from birth to death is Adonis, who forsakes the love of Venus for war and hunting, and who is killed when still young. Adonis symbolism thus complements Eros symbolism. In Christianity the downward journey is pre-eminently the journey of Christ from Incarnation to Crucifixion, the Agape or descent of love from creator to creature, in which Christ takes on an Adonis or dying-god role, clothed in Luvah's robes of blood, as Blake says, Luvah or Orc being Blake's Eros-Adonis figure. This journey is made by Christ in his capacity as the second Adam, a conscious and voluntary descent repeating and redeeming the first Adam's passionate fall. Thus Spenser, after writing two Hymns on Love and Beauty in the regular Eros convention, follows them with a 'Hymn of Heavenly Love' describing the incarnation of Christ. The response of Christian faith to Christ's act forms one of the sublimated versions of the Eros ascent, the version symbolized by Eliot in 'Little Gidding' as the ascending movement of fire. The conception of the Eros journey as a reversal of or response to a previous fall is Platonic also, though it is the Neoplatonists rather than Plato who lay stress on the original fall of the soul. Neoplatonic imagery merges with Christianity in the poems about the fall from innocence in childhood already mentioned.

Yeats was, as his *Autobiographies* tell us, fascinated by the notion of a double movement in life, and in the early play *The Hour-Glass* the conception of an antithetical world, whose summer is our winter, is presented in the symbol of the hour-glass itself, the image of time as a double gyre, narrowing and broadening simultaneously. Thus the goal of the Eros ascent, the 'land of heart's desire', was from the beginning linked to the tragedy and irony of the world of experience. The goal of the journey of love is usually beauty in some form or other, often an ideal beauty which combines the allegro figure of the imprisoned or sleeping maiden with the penseroso sense of harmony and order. A medieval symbol for such a goal of vision is the Holy Grail, which has female associations in its chalice shape and in its functions as a provider of food and as the container of the body or blood of Christ. The corresponding symbol in Yeats's early poetry is the rose, the symbol of sexual passion as the lily is of virginity, a symbol, as Yeats says, corresponding also to Shelley's intellectual beauty, except that he sees it 'as suffering with man and not as something pursued and seen from afar'. The phrase implies, among other things, the interconnection of Eros and Adonis symbols. The rose is on the rood of time, just as, in 'The Two Trees', the tree of life is reflected in the tree of death. The colours of Eros are the red and white of St Valentine, the patron of coupling birds like Shakespeare's red phoenix and white turtle; the colours of Adonis are the white and red of the dead body and spilled blood. These colours recur in an episode of the Parzival legend referred to by Yeats, where Parzival sees some blood drops on snow reminding him of his mistress so vividly that he falls into a trance. The poet-lover, inspired by Eros, moves upward toward a female figure who may be virgin mother or mistress; the hero, the incarnation of Adonis, is frequently born of a calumniated mother who may also be a virgin or mistress of a divine bird. Eros shoots arrows, and Adonis figures like St Sebastian are stuck full of them; Eros seeks his mother Venus, and Adonis escapes Venus to go to his death. In some versions of the dying-god story, including the one Yeats prefers, Adonis is killed by Venus, or rather by the figure whom Robert Graves calls the white goddess, Blake Tirzah or the sinister mother, and Yeats the 'staring virgin'. The complementary nature of Eros and Adonis imagery comes out vividly in 'Parnell's Funeral':

> A beautiful seated boy; a sacred bow;
> A woman, and an arrow on a string;
> A pierced boy, image of a star laid low.
> That woman, the Great Mother imaging,
> Cut out his heart.

The torn-out heart and the severed head are the two most frequent images of the martyrdom of the hero: they have also some connection with the four suits of cards featured in the Hanrahan stories. Lance and chalice (the two red suits) are the emblems of the Passion of Christ; sword and dish symbolize the death of John the Baptist, who was born at the summer solstice, as Christ was at the winter solstice, decreasing as Christ increases in a double gyre relation to him. Except for one very significant passage in *A Vision* (p. 212), there is not much about John the Baptist in Yeats, but there is a fair amount about Salome, one of the manifestations of the 'staring virgin'.

Yeats had grasped, even before Frazer's *Golden Bough* appeared, the identity in symbolism between the dying Christ and the Classical dying gods. The association he made all his life between Christ and Dionysus appears as early as 'The Secret Rose', where the rose may be sought either in the Holy Sepulchre or in the wine vat. The Adonis symbols in Yeats cluster around two central and traditional images. One is the image of hunting. The Celtic hounds of the other world, white with red ears, appear in the earlier poems with sexual associations, representing, according to Yeats, the frustrated and elusive pursuits of the sex war. Similar animals reappear in the 'Hound Voice' of *Last Poems* and the silenced dogs of 'To Dorothy Wellesley', and the theme of 'violence of horses' incorporates the archetype of the Wild Hunt into the anarchy of Yeats's own time. The other is the image of the tangled and bloody wood, associated with the setting sun, where the hero lies dead or hung on a tree like Absalom, gored by a beast like Adonis, or torn to pieces by drunken Bacchantes like Orpheus. This wood forms the setting of 'Her Vision in the Wood', a poem in *A Woman Young and Old*.

We said that *The Shadowy Waters* portrays two lovers escaping to a paradisal Eros world, while the sailors return to the ordinary one. There had previously been threats of mutiny and conspiracy from the sailors, hence this poem is the earliest example in Yeats of the theme of debate at or near the limit of the Eros journey, which recurs in 'A Dialogue of Self and Soul' and 'Vacillation'. The point on the boundary of the cycle of this world and an immortal world above it, usually associated with the earthly paradise or the moon, or both, the symbolic top of the tower or mountain, is what I have elsewhere called the point of epiphany. In 'A Dialogue of Self and Soul' the soul is a disciple of Plotinus, and wants to go upward from the point of epiphany into the pure mystical identity of solitude of which Plotinus speaks. The self looks downward, fascinated by the Adonis symbols of the ceremonial sword and its silk covering embroidered with flowers of 'heart's purple'. These things are 'Emblematical of love and war', and the soul wants no part of them. The self speaks for the poet, who, unlike the mystic, is committed to images, to sense experience, and to the recurring wheel of life. It is clear that the Eros dialogue between the wise old guide and the impetuous lover is not always a matter of the guide's informing his charge. Perhaps, however, we should think of both speakers as aspects of the old man in the tower, as a development of the two figures of *Responsibilities* previously mentioned, the sleeper and the wanderer: those who await a final consummation either in repose or in restlessness.

We are left with a strong impression that, as in Eliot, the way up and the way down are the same (except that Eliot's directions are reversed, the 'dark night' vision being the upward one in Yeats), and that if one succeeds in either, one gets both. It should be noticed, however, that the soul associates *guilt* with the double gyre of descent and return, speaking of 'the *crime* of death and birth', and that the self does not finally accept guilt. In his resolve to 'cast out remorse' the self's proposed descent is more like that of the bodhisattva in Eastern religions, and what he reaches by descent is the genuine Earthly Paradise, the total vision of innocence in which, going even beyond Blake's 'Everything that lives is holy', he can say 'Everything we look upon is blest.'

In 'Among School Children' there is again a contrast between the nun, whose image retains 'a marble or a bronze repose', and the mother, who is bound to the cycle of recurrence. Here the two ideals are seen more ironically as equally half-achievements, perfection being symbolized by the tree and the dancer, in whom spontaneity and discipline, vitality and harmony, have become the same thing, and where the body has not been broken by the soul, like the nuns', or by birth, like the mother's. 'Vacillation' begins with one of the standard point-of-epiphany symbols, the tree of life or 'labyrinth of the birds', also represented by the chestnut tree in 'Among School Children' and the living tree with its demonic reflection in 'The Two Trees'. In 'Vacillation', as in 'The Two Trees', the tree has two aspects, one of which is the 'Attis' tree on which the dying god, or his image, is hung. This tree thus again illustrates the interconnection of innocence and experience, Eros and Adonis. Here again the poet considers the sublimated goal of the perfection of life, whose symbol, a subtler one than the 'marble and bronze' of 'Among School Children', is the incorruptible body of the dead saint. The poet again, however, chooses the cycle of death and rebirth out of corruption, the lion and honeycomb of Samson's riddle, though without challenging the traditional moral contrast between corruptible and incorruptible body.

Yeats, then, consistently rejects for himself, though not necessarily for anyone else, the sublimated goals of the Eros vision that lead on to the Logos vision, and prefers the sexual goal which leads inevitably to going back down into the cycle again. Because he is a poet, Yeats tells us, he must choose the path of the hero and the 'swordsman' rather than the saint. This is not simply a temperamental choice: there is a major complication in Yeats's winding-stair imagery that did not exist for, say, Dante. In Christianity, and in Neoplatonism more speculatively, the sublimation of the sexual instinct is the preferred programme, because the man inspired by love is ultimately not seeking a sexual partner, but is a creature returning to his creator. But for Yeats there is no creator in the picture except man himself. The sources of creation are not in a divine mind beyond the stars: they are in the 'foul rag-and-bone shop of the heart' at the *bottom* of the ladder. The alienation symbolized by the disdainful mistress of Eros poetry and by the 'staring virgin' of Adonis poetry, who tear out the poet's or hero's heart, is the point to which all creation regularly recurs. To return to his creator, man has to come back down again, return on himself, seek the source of the creative powers which are close to the sexual instincts, and are therefore in 'the place of excrement', as Crazy Jane says, partaking of the corruption out of which all life comes.

What is the consequence of such a choice? One consequence certainly is the incorporation into Yeats's imagery of a purely ironic view of human life and history, in which all things are ordered by a relentlessly turning cycle. The cycle is the form that the double gyre assumes when it becomes the controlling image of all life. It is a central doctrine of *A Vision* that reality can manifest itself only in a series of opposites, a doctrine Yeats associates with Nicholas Cusanus, as Joyce associates it with Bruno, and seeing a double gyre as a single cycle is the same principle in reverse. This cyclical and fatalistic view of history is the one that is set out in *A Vision*. The fatalism of *A Vision* is in part a reflection of the passivity of mind in which Yeats received it, but even so it is important to realize that *A Vision* is Yeats's *Inferno*, his demonic or Thanatos vision. We said that the Eros theme, which enters into the Petrarchan or Courtly Love convention, normally begins with frustration, in which the lover complains of and bewails the inflexible cruelty of his lady. Yeats's love for Maud Gonne provides the corresponding theme in his poetry, and Maud Gonne is repeatedly associated with Helen of Troy. Helen of Troy in turn, hatched from the egg of Leda, is the symbol of the eternal recurrence of history, the misery she caused inevitably repeating itself in future ages. We are not surprised to find *A Vision* astrological in symbolism: all hells contain parodies of heavens, and visions of harmony and fatality alike tend to be astrological in reference.

We are not surprised either to find the imagery of *A Vision* completely dominated by

> the circle of the moon
> That pitches common things about,

for, in the traditional cosmology we have been dealing with, the world of the closed cycle of time is a sublunary world. Solar imagery never gets really integrated into *A Vision*, and references to solar symbolism elsewhere in Yeats suggest a pattern of far greater comprehensiveness than *A Vision* ever achieved. The same ironic sublunary perspective comes into 'Blood and the Moon', which turns on the melancholy adage *si la jeunesse savait, si la vieillesse pouvait*. The Eros vision of youth is inseparable from the Adonis vision with its premature death and its 'odour of blood', and the vision of wisdom pursued by age is an attempt to grasp the static order of something that must be dead before it can be understood. In this perspective every civilization leaves its structure unfinished, dying at the top, like Swift and his tree, and the rare individual who gets near the top finds only an empty lumber room full of dead butterflies. In this ironic perspective the 'tower' built by human creative power is a structure of pride and arrogance, identical with the Tower of Babel which stretched upwards towards the moon, only to be abandoned to ruin by dissensions in the mob. It is also the great 'clock tower' which marks but never escapes from the wheel of time. In the end it becomes the 'black tower' of death, where 'the dead upright' are watched by an immovable guard. At the end of 'Blood and the Moon' the moon appears, symbol, as it so often is, of a teasing and elusive perfection which is out of reach of both the red blood of power and the white bones of wisdom. The moon stared at by the cat Minnaloushe is the image of a cycle that is always changing and yet never changing, as Oedipus kills his father and Cuchulain his son, age after age, through earth and purgatory alike. Behind it are the greater cycles symbolized by the 'Full Moon in March', associated with the two great events of what may have been the one period of decisive change in history, the period between the death of Julius Caesar and the resurrection of Jesus Christ.

In *A Vision*, human life struggles upward to the complete subjectivity of Phase Fifteen and downward to the complete objectivity of Phase One without ever attaining either. The struggle upward is said to be toward nature and the struggle downward toward God, but the completely natural Phase Fifteen is supernatural, and at Phase One 'God' occupies the place of death. What is really at Phase One is the mob, the undifferentiated mass of a late civilization, the mob to which 'Church and State' have been reduced in Yeats's time, according to the poem of that name, and which every great man, or at least every great Irishman, has despised. The 'primary' mob is Yeats's Satan, the accuser of mankind. It accuses by making the standard appeals of slave morality, the appeals to conscience, equality, and altruism. In short, it inspired the guilt-ridden political activism of Maud Gonne and the Gore-Booth sisters. The dragon that kills the hero is, ultimately, the mob that drags him down, as the Irish mob slandered Parnell, attacked Synge, and murdered O'Higgins. One thinks of Spenser's Blatant

Beast, the emblem of slander and envy. The opinionated female, according to one of Yeats's more tedious themes, expressed in 'Michael Robartes and the Dancer' and elsewhere, fights for the dragon instead of the knight trying to rescue her, and thereby impersonates the 'staring virgin' tearing out the hero's heart. A more serious aspect of this theme is the connection between Christianity and slave morality which made the sacrifice of Christ, according to *Calvary*, an outrage to Judas and Lazarus and meaningless to the heron and the swan, emblems of an 'antithetical' cycle which complements and completes the 'primary' half-achievement of Christ.

It is important to notice that the great wheel of *A Vision* turns in the opposite direction from the Eros-Adonis cycle. In the latter the comic rises and the tragic falls. All our language about comedy and tragedy, such as the metaphor in 'catastrophe', and the word 'fall' itself, shows how inevitable these associations are. But in *A Vision* Yeats is interested in the heroic rather than the tragic, and associates comedy with the kind of realism that he regarded as decadent. Hence in *A Vision* the tragic and heroic are the 'antithetical' themes that rise out of the mass, and the comic is the 'primary' mass that pulls everything down to itself. This introduces into the poetry certain tragic aspects of the Eros ascent, with the proud Furies climbing the stair of the bloody tower in 'To Dorothy Wellesley', and with the 'odour of blood on the ancestral stair' in 'Blood and the Moon'. Similarly, there is an innocent aspect of tragedy, which is the inward exuberance or gaiety of the heroic spirit, a gaiety much insisted on in the later poems, notably 'Lapis Lazuli'. Such gaiety is unaffected by the tragic or ironic aspects of the world it is in, and which are seen only from the outside. It enables heroes like 'the great lord of Chou' in 'Vacillation' to say 'Let all things pass away' in triumph or in disaster alike, the moment of experience having the reality that anything which dissolves in time misses. It is also this gay science, as it has been called, that encourages the poet to identify himself with the process of death and corruption and rebirth instead of attempting to escape from it like the saint or mystic.

We began by saying that traditionally there is a Logos vision in poetry, a vision of an intelligently ordered nature, and that this vision can also be found in Yeats. But the Logos vision is, again, traditionally attained only after an arduous upward striving of the soul, and Yeats, once he has attained this point, deliberately turns his back on the Logos vision and goes downward again. This in turn brings him into an infernal or ironic vision of an unending cyclical alternation of forces all through history. But, we said, the real reason for Yeats's turning away from the Logos vision was that for him the sources of creation were within man, in the corruption of the human heart. The language of symbolism usually begins with a creation myth, the story of how things came to be. In the history of mythology, it is the sexual creation myths that come first, stories of how the world was born, or revived like spring from winter. Such myths are centred on an earth-mother, and the more sophisticated myths of a sky-father who *makes* the world and imposes an intelligible pattern on it come later. Yeats speaks of

> the red-rose-bordered hem
> Of her, whose history began
> Before God made the angelic clan.[3]

It is the mother-centred sexual myth that Yeats appears to follow back to its source in the return to the mother who is at once birth and death, womb and tomb.

But having made this descent, Yeats finds that he has once again been sliding down half of a double gyre, this time the one given us by Heraclitus. Once he has made his journey to the heart of the corruptible, he finds that he can now go back again, up from the 'fury and mire' of human veins toward a dry light, or genuine Logos vision (Heraclitus also uses the term *Logos*), in which the gleaming city of light is seen once more, but seen this time as a city whose maker and builder is man. The contrast between Yeats and Shelley on this point is instructive. Yeats speaks of Shelley as 'constantly' using towers as poetic images, and it is true that the word occurs very frequently in Shelley. But when it means a building, Shelley's tower tends to be a rather sinister image, like the 'Tower of Famine' or the madhouse in *Julian and Maddalo*. Towers used apocalyptically, along with 'domes' and 'pyramids', are often not buildings, but mountains or clouds or other images of a regenerate nature. This is true even of the *Prometheus Unbound* passage misquoted by Yeats in 'Blood and the Moon', and even Prince Athanase only sits apart from men '*as* in a lonely tower'. Shelley is certainly a poet in the Eros tradition of Plato and Dante, but his contemplative counterpart of the Earthly Paradise (as presented in 'The Sensitive Plant' and elsewhere) is rather the oracular cave, a much more obviously maternal symbol. The point is small but significant: Shelley, who died at thirty, revolves around an identification of man and a feminine nature; and Yeats's tower, building, and city imagery indicates a symbolism appropriate to an art that looks beyond nature into 'the artifice of eternity'. Like Blake, Yeats finds his real hero not in the Orc of the sexual and historical cycle, much less in the old man Urizen with his premature Logos vision, but in Los the blacksmith, the creative power that builds the eternal golden city out of time.

In 'Sailing to Byzantium' the city is seen from afar, and the tower has expanded into an entire chain of being, ranging from the divine ('drowsy Emperor') through the spiritual (traditionally the angels and the stars, here the sages in the fire) and the human ('lords and ladies of Byzantium') down through the rest of creation with the bird and the tree transformed into gold. 'Sailing to Byzantium' is very like a conventional Christian poem about the New Jerusalem awaiting the soul after death, except for the paradox in 'the artifice of eternity'. The builder of Byzantium is not a God conceived as independent of man, and when man is thought of as the only visible creator, nature is no longer a creation but a ruin, and man builds his palaces out of and in defiance of nature. In such a world the tree no longer has the 'blind lush leaf' of the dying Attis, but is golden only; yet its gold is not the 'staring fury' of 'Vacillation' either. Just as the imagery both of the traditional Logos vision and of Yeats's ironic *Vision* is astrological, so the image of Byzantium arising out of the sea of death is alchemical, alchemy being the symbol of a creative *process* in which humanity and nature alike are burned up in the 'consummation' of an immortal world of gold, the Golden Age come again.

This reversal of perspective from descent to the corrupt source of creation back up again through the process of creation is a reversal which affects the whole personality, not merely the technical skill of the poet. In *The Shadowy Waters* we are told that those who live ordinary passion-driven lives are helpless puppets of a dream dreamed by the gods. Their passions seem to operate on them as external forces, because, of course, the gods who are dreaming them are their own projected selves. In their view of things, this passive puppet-life is reality, and genuine desire, as expressed in dreams and in love, seems utterly impotent against it. The dreamer, the lover, and the poet are all engaged in reversing the current of reality: they are identifying themselves with the true gods, who are the powers of dream and love and creation themselves. These powers have become reality for them, and what the world calls reality has subsided into dream, the world of 'living' that ought to be left to servants. The true gods are the 'fire-born moods' of an early poem, the 'Presences' of 'Among School Children', and the 'Daimons' of the later, profounder, and yet less well understood parts of *A Vision*.

In 'Byzantium' the imagery is again Heraclitean and alchemical, the vision of 'Sailing to Byzantium' seen from within as a process. We start out in the sea, the beginning and the end of life, and move from the 'fury and mire' of human passion upward to the 'changeless metal'. This is the movement of discarnation, opposite to the birth-to-death movement of incarnation, in which the spiral wrappings of the dead mummy are unwound, a movement taking us beyond the world that is 'by the moon embittered', and where the gong never ceases to strike. Perhaps, then, the intuition of so many poets, including Dante, that this journey of the soul is also connected with another life after ordinary death has something to be said for it. If man has invented death, as Yeats says, he can recover what he has projected, and find his home in the 'translunar Paradise' which he himself can make, and has made.

The poet of the Byzantium poems has gone far beyond the mystery of the Fifteenth Phase of *A Vision*, presented there as something for ever beyond human capacities. The Fifteenth Phase is guarded, we are told, by Christ and Buddha. Christ descended into the bottom of the cyclical world – made himself of no account, as Paul says – and then rose out of it, with a great company following. Buddha meditated on the deliverance of man from his own Narcissus image, 'mirror on mirror mirrored', the genuine Hercules in heaven liberated from his shadow in Hades. Just as in Eliot's 'Burnt Norton' the summit of vision and the depth of annihilation are the same point, the still point of the turning world, so in Yeats the top of the tower is both the rag-and-bone shop of the heart and the translunar Paradise that the heart alone has created.

16 CONCLUSION TO *A LITERARY HISTORY OF CANADA*

Some years ago a group of editors met to draw up the first tentative plans for a history of English Canadian literature. What we then dreamed of is substantially what we have got, changed very little in essentials. I expressed at the time the hope that such a book would help to broaden the inductive basis on which some writers on Canadian literature were making generalizations that bordered on guesswork. By 'some writers' I meant primarily myself: I find, however, that more evidence has in fact tended to confirm most of my intuitions on the subject.

To study Canadian literature properly, one must outgrow the view that evaluation is the end of criticism, instead of its incidental by-product. If evaluation is one's guiding principle, criticism of Canadian literature would become only a debunking project, leaving it a poor naked *alouette* plucked of every feather of decency and dignity. True, what is really remarkable is not how little but how much good writing has been produced in Canada. But this would not affect the rigorous evaluator. The evaluative view is based on the conception of criticism as concerned mainly to define and canonize the genuine classics of literature. And Canada has produced no author who is a classic in the sense of possessing a vision greater in kind than that of his best readers (Canadians themselves might argue about one or two, but in the perspective of the world at large the statement is true). There is no Canadian writer of whom we can say what we can say of the world's major writers, that their readers can grow up inside their work without ever being aware of a circumference. Thus the metaphor of the critic as 'judge' is more appropriate for the student of a literature which seldom raises the larger issues of criticism.

This fact about Canadian literature, so widely deplored by Canadians, has one advantage. It is much easier to see what literature is trying to do when we are studying a literature that has not quite done it. If no Canadian author pulls us away from the Canadian context toward the centre of literary experience itself, then at every point we remain aware of his social and historical setting. The conception of what is literary has to be greatly broadened for such a literature. The literary, in Canada, is often only an incidental quality of writings which, like those of many of the early explorers, are as innocent of literary intention as a mating loon. Even when it is literature in its orthodox genres of poetry and fiction, it is more significantly studied as a part of Canadian life than as a part of an autonomous world of literature.

So far from merely admitting or conceding this, the editors have gone out of their way to emphasize it. We have asked for chapters on political, historical, religious, scholarly, philosophical, scientific, and other non-literary writing, to show how the verbal imagination operates as a ferment in all cultural life. We have included the writings of foreigners, of travellers, of immigrants, of emigrants – even of emigrants whose most articulate literary emotion was their thankfulness at getting the hell out of Canada. The reader of this book, even if he is not Canadian or much interested in Canadian literature as such, may still learn a good deal about the literary imagination as a force and function of life generally. For here another often deplored fact also becomes an advantage: that many Canadian cultural phenomena are not peculiarly Canadian at all, but are typical of their wider North American and Western contexts.

This book is a collection of essays in cultural history, and of the general principles of cultural history we still know relatively little. It is, of course, closely related to political and to economic history, but it is a separate and definable subject in itself. Like other kinds of history, it has its own themes of exploration, settlement, and development, but these themes relate to a social *imagination* that explores and settles and develops, and the imagination has its own rhythms of growth as well as its own modes of expression. It is obvious that Canadian literature, whatever its inherent merits, is an indispensable aid to the knowledge of Canada. It records what the Canadian imagination has reacted to, and it tells us things about this environment that nothing else will tell us. By examining this imagination as the authors of this book have tried to do, as an ingredient in Canadian verbal culture generally, a relatively small and low-lying cultural development is studied in all its dimensions. There is far too much Canadian writing for this book not to become, in places, something of a catalogue; but the outlines of the structure are clear. Fortunately, the bulk of Canadian non-literary writing, even today, has not yet declined into the state of sodden specialization in which the readable has become the impure.

I stress our ignorance of the laws and conditions of cultural history for an obvious reason. The question: why has there been no Canadian writer of classic proportions? may naturally be asked. At any rate it often has been. Our authors realize that it is better to deal with what is there than to raise speculations about why something else is not there. But it is clear that the question haunts their minds. And we know so little about cultural history that we not only cannot answer such a question, but we do not even know whether or not it is a real question. The notion, doubtless of romantic origin, that 'genius' is a certain quantum that an individual is born with, as he might be born with red hair, is still around, but mainly as a folk-tale motif in fiction, like the story of Finch in the Jalna books. 'Genius' is as much, and as essentially, a matter of social context as it is of individual character. We do not know what the social conditions are that produce great literature, or even whether there is any causal relation at all. If there is, there is no reason to suppose that they are good conditions, or conditions that we should try to reproduce. The notion that the literature one admires must have been nourished by something admirable in the social environment is persistent, but has never been justified by evidence. One can still find books on Shakespeare that profess to make his achievement more plausible by talking about a 'background' of social euphoria produced by the defeat of the Armada, the discovery of America a century before, and the conviction that Queen Elizabeth was a wonderful woman. There is a general sense of filler about such speculations, and when similar arguments are given in a negative form to explain the absence of a Shakespeare in Canada they are no more convincing. Puritan inhibitions, pioneer life, 'an age too late, cold climate, or years' – these may be important as factors or conditions of Canadian culture, helping us to characterize its qualities. To suggest that any of them is a negative cause of its merit is to say much more than anyone knows.

One theme which runs all through this book is the obvious and unquenchable desire of the Canadian cultural public to identify itself through its literature. Canada is not a bad environment for the author, as far as recognition goes: in fact, the recognition may even hamper his development by making him prematurely self-conscious. Scholarships, prizes, university posts, await the dedicated writer: there are so many medals offered for literary achievement that a modern Canadian Dryden might well be moved to write a satire on medals, except that if he did he would promptly be awarded the medal for satire and humour. Publishers take an active responsibility for native literature, even poetry; a fair proportion of the books bought by Canadian readers are by Canadian writers; the C.B.C. and other media help to employ some writers and publicize others. The efforts made at intervals to boost or hard-sell Canadian literature, by asserting that it is much better than it actually is, may look silly enough in retrospect, but they were also, in part, efforts to create a cultural community, and the aim deserves more sympathy than the means. Canada has two languages and two literatures, and every statement made in a book like this about 'Canadian literature' employs the figure of speech known as synecdoche, putting a part for the whole. Every such statement implies a parallel or contrasting statement about French-Canadian literature. The advantages of having a national culture based on two languages are in some respects very great, but of course they are for the most part potential. The difficulties, if more superficial, are also more actual and more obvious.

Canada began as an obstacle, blocking the way to the treasures of the East, to be explored only in the hope of finding a passage through it. English Canada continued to be that long after what is now the United States had become a defined part of the Western world. One reason for this is obvious from the map. American culture was, down to about 1900, mainly a culture of the Atlantic seaboard, with a western frontier that moved irregularly but steadily back until it reached the other coast. The Revolution did not essentially change the cultural unity of the English-speaking community of the North Atlantic that

had London and Edinburgh on one side of it and Boston and Phila-
delphia on the other. But Canada has, for all practical purposes, no
Atlantic seaboard. The traveller from Europe edges into it like a tiny
Jonah entering an inconceivably large whale, slipping past the Straits
of Belle Isle into the Gulf of St Lawrence, where five Canadian
provinces surround him, for the most part invisible. Then he goes up
the St Lawrence and the inhabited country comes into view, mainly a
French-speaking country, with its own cultural traditions. To enter the
United States is a matter of crossing an ocean; to enter Canada is a
matter of being silently swallowed by an alien continent.

It is an unforgettable and intimidating experience to enter Canada
in this way. But the experience initiates one into that gigantic east-to-
west thrust which historians regard as the axis of Canadian development, the 'Laurentian' movement that makes the growth of Canada
geographically credible. This drive to the west has attracted to itself
nearly everything that is heroic and romantic in the Canadian tradition.
The original impetus begins in Europe, for English Canada in the
British Isles, hence though adventurous it is also a conservative force,
and naturally tends to preserve its colonial link with its starting-point.
Once the Canadian has settled down in the country, however, he then
becomes aware of the longitudinal dimension, the southward pull
toward the richer and more glamorous American cities, some of which,
such as Boston for the Maritimes and Minneapolis for the eastern
prairies, are almost Canadian capitals. This is the axis of another kind
of Canadian mentality, more critical and analytic, more inclined to see
Canada as an unnatural and politically quixotic aggregate of disparate
northern extensions of American culture – 'seven fishing-rods tied
together by the ends', as Goldwin Smith put it.

The simultaneous influence of two larger nations speaking the same
language has been practically beneficial to English Canada, but
theoretically confusing. It is often suggested that Canada's identity is
to be found in some *via media*, or *via mediocris*, between the other two.
This has the disadvantage that the British and American cultures have
to be defined as extremes. Haliburton seems to have believed that the
ideal for Nova Scotia would be a combination of American energy and
British social structure, but such a chimera, or synthetic monster, is hard
to achieve in practice. It is simpler merely to notice the alternating

current in the Canadian mind, as reflected in its writing, between two moods, one romantic, traditional, and idealistic, the other shrewd, observant, and humorous. Canada in its attitude to Britain tends to be more royalist than the Queen, in the sense that it is more attracted to it as a symbol of tradition than as a fellow nation. The Canadian attitude to the United States is typically that of a smaller country to a much bigger neighbour, sharing in its material civilization but anxious to keep clear of the huge mass movements that drive a great imperial power. The United States, being founded on a revolution and a written constitution, has introduced a deductive or *a priori* pattern into its cultural life that tends to define an American way of life and mark it off from anti-American heresies. Canada, having a seat on the sidelines of the American Revolution, adheres more to the inductive and the expedient. The Canadian genius for compromise is reflected in the existence of Canada itself.

The most obvious tension in the Canadian literary situation is in the use of language. Here, first of all, a traditional standard English collides with the need for a North American vocabulary and phrasing. As long as the North American speaker feels that he belongs in a minority, the European speech will impose a standard of correctness. This is to a considerable extent still true of French in Canada, with its campaigns against 'joual' and the like. But as Americans began to out-number the British, Canada tended in practice to fall in with the American developments, though a good deal of Canadian theory is still Anglophile. A much more complicated cultural tension arises from the impact of the sophisticated on the primitive, and vice versa. The most dramatic example, and one I have given elsewhere, is that of Duncan Campbell Scott, working in the Department of Indian Affairs in Ottawa. He writes of a starving squaw baiting a fish-hook with her own flesh, and he writes of the music of Debussy and the poetry of Henry Vaughan. In English literature we have to go back to Anglo-Saxon times to encounter so incongruous a collision of cultures.

Cultural history, we said, has its own rhythms. It is possible that one of these rhythms is very like an organic rhythm: that there must be a period, of a certain magnitude, as Aristotle would say, in which a social imagination can take root and establish a tradition. American literature had this period, in the northeastern part of the country, between the Revolution and the Civil War. Canada has never had it. English Canada was first a part of the wilderness, then a part of North America and the British Empire, then a part of the world. But it has gone through these revolutions too quickly for a tradition of writing to be founded on any one of them. Canadian writers are, even now, still trying to assimilate a Canadian environment at a time when new techniques of communication, many of which, like television, constitute a verbal market, are annihilating the boundaries of that environment. This foreshortening of Canadian history, if it really does have any relevance to Canadian culture, would account for many features of it: its fixation on its own past, its penchant for old-fashioned literary techniques, its preoccupation with the theme of strangled articulateness. It seems to me that Canadian sensibility has been profoundly disturbed, not so much by our famous problem of identity, important as that is, as by a series of paradoxes in what confronts that identity. It is less perplexed by the question 'Who am I?' than by some such riddle as 'Where is here?'

We are obviously not to read the mystique of Canadianism back into the pre-Confederation period. Haliburton, for instance, was a Nova Scotian, a Bluenose: the word 'Canadian' to him would have summoned up the figure of someone who spoke mainly French and whose enthusiasm for Haliburton's own political ideals would have been extremely tepid. The mystique of Canadianism was specifically the cultural accompaniment of Confederation and the imperialistic mood that followed it. But it came so suddenly after the pioneer period that it was still full of wilderness. To feel 'Canadian' was to feel part of a no-man's-land with huge rivers, lakes, and islands that very few Canadians had ever seen. 'From sea to sea, and from the river unto the ends of the earth' – if Canada is not an island, the phrasing is still in the etymological sense isolating[1]. One wonders if any other national consciousness has had so large an amount of the unknown, the unrealized, the humanly undigested, so built into it. Rupert Brooke speaks of the 'unseizable virginity' of the Canadian landscape. What is important here, for our purposes, is the position of the frontier in the Canadian imagination. In the United States one could choose to move out to the frontier or to retreat from it back to the seaboard. The tensions built up by such migrations have fascinated many American novelists and historians. In the Canadas, even in the Maritimes, the frontier was all around one, a part and a condition of one's whole imaginative being. The frontier was primarily what separated the Canadian, physically or mentally, from Great Britain, from the United States, and even more important, from other Canadian communities. Such a frontier was the immediate datum of his imagination, the thing that had to be dealt with first.

After the Northwest passage failed to materialize, Canada became a colony in the mercantilist sense, treated by others less like a society than as a place to look for things. French, English, Americans plunged into it to carry off its supplies of furs, minerals, and pulpwood, aware only of their immediate objectives. From time to time recruiting officers searched the farms and villages to carry young men off to death in a European dynastic quarrel. Travellers visit Canada much as they would visit a zoo: even when their eyes momentarily focus on the natives they are still thinking primarily of how their own sensibility is going to react to what it sees. A feature of Canadian life that has been noted by writers from Susanna Moodie onward is the paradox of empty spaces and lack of privacy, with no defences against the prying or avaricious eye. The resentment expressed against this in Canada seems to have taken political rather than literary forms: this may be partly because Canadians have learned from their imaginative experience to look at each other in much the same way: 'as objects, even as obstacles', as one writer says.

It is not much wonder if Canada developed with the bewilderment of a neglected child, preoccupied with trying to define its own identity, alternately bumptious and diffident about its own achievements. Adolescent dreams of glory haunt the Canadian consciousness (and unconsciousness), some naïve and some sophisticated. In the naïve area are the predictions that the twentieth century belongs to Canada, that our cities will become much bigger than they ought to be, or, like Edmonton and Vancouver, 'gateways' to somewhere else, reconstructed Northwest passages. The more sophisticated usually take the form of a Messianic complex about Canadian culture, for Canadian culture, no less than Alberta, has always been 'next year country'[2]. The myth of the hero brought up in the forest retreat, awaiting the moment when his giant strength will be fully grown and he can emerge into the world, informs a good deal of Canadian criticism down to our own time.

Certain features of life in a new country that are bound to handicap its writers are obvious enough. In drama, which depends on a theatre and consequently on a highly organized urban life, the foreshortening of historical development has been particularly cruel, as drama was strangled by the movie just as it was getting started as a popular medium. Other literary genres have similar difficulties. Culture is born in leisure and an awareness of standards, and pioneer conditions tend to make energetic and uncritical work an end in itself, to instil a gospel of social unconsciousness, which lingers long after the pioneer conditions have disappeared. The impressive achievements of such a society are likely to be technological. It is in the inarticulate part of communication, railways and bridges and canals and highways, that Canada, one of whose symbols is the taciturn beaver, has shown its real strength. Again, Canadian culture, and literature in particular, has felt the force of what may be called Emerson's law. Emerson remarks in his journals that in a provincial society it is extremely easy to reach the highest level of cultivation, extremely difficult to take one step beyond that. In surveying Canadian poetry and fiction, we feel constantly that all the energy has been absorbed in meeting a standard, a self-defeating enterprise because real standards can only be established, not met. Such writing is academic in the pejorative sense of that term, an imitation of a prescribed model, second-rate in conception, not merely in execution. It is natural that academic writing of this kind should develop where literature is a social prestige symbol. However, it is not the handicaps of Canadian writers but the distinctive features that appear in spite of them which are our main concern at present.

II

The sense of probing into the distance, of fixing the eyes on the skyline, is something that Canadian sensibility has inherited from the *voyageurs*. It comes into Canadian painting a good deal, in Thomson whose focus is so often farthest back in the picture, where a river or a gorge in the hills twists elusively out of sight, in Emily Carr whose vision is always, in the title of a compatriot's book of poems[3], 'deeper into the forest'.

Even in the Maritimes, where the feeling of linear distance is less urgent, Roberts contemplates the Tantramar marshes in the same way, the refrain of 'miles and miles' having clearly some incantatory power for him. It would be interesting to know how many Canadian novels associate nobility of character with a far-away look, or base their perorations on a long-range perspective[4]. This might be only a cliché, except that it is often found in sharply observed and distinctively written books. Here, as a random example, is the last sentence of W. O. Mitchell's *Who Has Seen the Wind*: 'The wind turns in silent frenzy upon itself, whirling into a smoking funnel, breaking up top soil and tumbleweed skeletons to carry them on its spinning way over the prairie, out and out to the far line of the sky.'

A vast country sparsely inhabited naturally depends on its modes of transportation, whether canoe, railway, or the driving and riding 'circuits' of the judge, the Methodist preacher, or the Yankee peddler. The feeling of nomadic movement over great distances persists even into the age of the aeroplane, in a country where writers can hardly meet one other without a social organization that provides travel grants. Pratt's poetry is full of his fascination with means of communication, not simply the physical means of great ships and locomotives, though he is one of the best of all poets on such subjects, but with communication as message, with radar and asdic and wireless signals, and, in his war poems, with the power of rhetoric over fighting men. What is perhaps the most comprehensive structure of ideas yet made by a Canadian thinker, the structure embodied in Innis's *Bias of Communication*, is concerned with the same theme, and a disciple of Innis, Marshall McLuhan, continues to emphasize the unity of communication, as a complex containing both verbal and non-verbal factors, and warns us against making unreal divisions within it. Perhaps it is not too fanciful to see this need for continuity in the Canadian attitude to time as well as space, in its preoccupation with its own history (the motto of the Province of Quebec is *je me souviens*) and its relentless cultural stock-takings and self-inventories. The Burke sense of society as a continuum – consistent with the pragmatic and conservative outlook of Canadians – is strong and begins early. As I write, the centennial of Confederation in 1967 looms up before the country with the moral urgency of a Day of Atonement: I use a Jewish metaphor because there is something Hebraic about the Canadian tendency to read its conquest of a promised land, its Maccabean victories of 1812, its struggles for the central fortress on the hill at Quebec, as oracles of a future. It is doubtless only an accident that the theme of one of the most passionate and intense of all Canadian novels, A. M. Klein's *The Second Scroll*, is Zionism.

Civilization in Canada, as elsewhere, has advanced geometrically across the country, throwing down the long parallel lines of the railways, dividing up the farm lands into chessboards of square-mile sections and concession-line roads. There is little adaptation to nature: in both architecture and arrangement, Canadian cities and villages express rather an arrogant abstraction, the conquest of nature by an intelligence that does not love it. The word conquest suggests something military, as it should – one thinks of General Braddock, preferring to have his army annihilated rather than fight the natural man on his own asymmetrical ground. There are some features of this generally North American phenomenon that have a particular emphasis in Canada. It has often been remarked that Canadian expansion westward had a tight grip of authority over it that American expansion, with its outlaws and sheriffs and vigilantes and the like, did not have in the same measure. America moved from the back country to the wild west; Canada moved from a New France held down by British military occupation to a northwest patrolled by mounted police. Canada has not had, strictly speaking, an Indian war: there has been much less of the 'another redskin bit the dust' feeling in our historical imagination, and only Riel remains to haunt the later period of it, though he is a formidable figure enough, rather like what a combination of John Brown and Vanzetti would be in the American conscience. Otherwise, the conquest, for the last two centuries, has been mainly of the unconscious forces of nature, personified by the dragon of the Lake Superior rocks in Pratt's *Towards the Last Spike*:

> On the North Shore a reptile lay asleep –
> A hybrid that the myths might have conceived,
> But not delivered.

Yet the conquest of nature has its own perils for the imagination, in a country where the winters are so cold and where conditions of life have so often been bleak and comfortless, where even the mosquitoes have been described as 'mementoes of the fall'. I have long been impressed in Canadian poetry by a tone of deep terror in regard to nature, a theme to which we shall return. It is not a terror of the dangers or discomforts or even the mysteries of nature, but a terror of the soul at something that these things manifest. The human mind has nothing but human and moral values to cling to if it is to preserve its integrity or even its sanity, yet the vast unconsciousness of nature in front of it seems an unanswerable denial of those values. A sharp-witted Methodist circuit rider speaks of the 'shutting out of the whole moral creation' in the loneliness of the forests.

If we put together a few of these impressions, we may get some approach to characterizing the way in which the Canadian imagination has developed in its literature. Small and isolated communities surrounded with a physical or psychological 'frontier', separated from one another and from their American and British cultural sources: communities that provide all that their members have in the way of distinctively human values, and that are compelled to feel a great respect for the law and order that holds them together, yet confronted with a huge, unthinking, menacing, and formidable physical setting – such communities are bound to develop what we may provisionally call a garrison mentality. In the earliest maps of the country the only inhabited centres are forts, and that remains true of the cultural maps for a much later time. Frances Brooke, in her eighteenth-century *Emily Montague*, wrote of what was literally a garrison; novelists of our day studying the impact of Montreal on Westmount write of a psychological one.

A garrison is a closely knit and beleaguered society, and its moral and social values are unquestionable. In a perilous enterprise one does not discuss causes or motives: one is either a fighter or a deserter. Here again we may turn to Pratt, with his infallible instinct for what is central in the Canadian imagination. The societies in Pratt's poems are always tense and tight groups engaged in war, rescue, martyrdom, or crisis, and the moral values expressed are simply those of that group. In such a society the terror is not for the common enemy, even when the enemy is or seems victorious, as in the extermination of the Jesuit missionaries or the crew of Franklin (a great Canadian theme that

Pratt pondered but never completed). The real terror comes when the individual feels himself becoming an individual, pulling away from the group, losing the sense of driving power that the group gives him, aware of a conflict within himself far subtler than the struggle of morality against evil. It is much easier to multiply garrisons, and when that happens, something anti-cultural comes into Canadian life, a dominating herd-mind in which nothing original can grow. The intensity of the sectarian divisiveness in Canadian towns, both religious and political, is an example: what such groups represent, of course, *vis-à-vis* one another, is 'two solitudes'[5], the death of communication and dialogue. Separatism, whether English or French, is culturally the most sterile of all creeds. But at present I am concerned rather with a more creative side of the garrison mentality, one that has had positive effects on our intellectual life.

Earlier Canadian writers were certain of their moral values: right was white, wrong black, and nothing else counted or even existed. Such certainty invariably produced a sub-literary rhetoric. Or, as Yeats would say, we make rhetoric out of quarrels with one another, poetry out of the quarrel with ourselves. To use words, for any other purpose than straight description or command, is a form of play, a manifestation of *homo ludens*. But there are two forms of play, the contest and the construct. The editorial writer attacking the Family Compact, the preacher demolishing imaginary atheists with the argument of design, are using words aggressively, in theses that imply antitheses. Ideas are weapons; one seeks the verbal *coup de grace*, the irrefutable refutation. Such a use of words is congenial enough to the earlier Canadian community: all the evidence, including the evidence of this book, points to a highly articulate and argumentative society in nineteenth-century Canada. We notice that scholarship in Canada has so often been written with more conviction and authority, and has attracted wider recognition, than the literature itself. There are historical reasons for this, apart from the fact, which will become clearer as we go on, that scholarly writing is more easily attached to its central tradition.

Leacock has a story which I often turn to because the particular aspect of Canadian culture it reflects has never been more accurately caught. He tells us of the rivalry in an Ontario town between two preachers, one Anglican and the other Presbyterian. The latter taught ethics in the local college on weekdays – without salary – and preached on Sundays. He gave his students, says Leacock, three parts Hegel and two parts St Paul, and on Sunday he reversed the dose and gave his parishioners three parts St Paul and two parts Hegel. Religion has been a major – perhaps the major – cultural force in Canada, at least down to the last generation or two. The churches not only influenced the cultural climate but took an active part in the production of poetry and fiction, as the popularity of Ralph Connor reminds us. But the effective religious factors in Canada were doctrinal and evangelical, those that stressed the arguments of religion at the expense of its imagery.

Such a reliance on the arguing intellect was encouraged by the philosophers, who in the nineteenth century were invariably idealists with a strong religious bias. One writer quotes the Canadian philosopher George as saying that civilization consists 'in the conscience and intellect' of a cultivated people, and Watson as asserting that 'we are capable of knowing Reality as it actually is. . . . Reality when so known is absolutely rational.' An even higher point may have been reached by that triumphant nineteenth-century theologian[6] whose book I have not read but whose title I greatly admire: *The Riddle of the Universe Solved.* Naturally sophisticated intelligence of this kind was the normal means of contact with literature. We are told that James Cappon judged poetry according to whether it had a 'rationalized concept' or not – this would have been a very common critical assumption. Sara Jeannette Duncan shows us a clergyman borrowing a copy of Browning's *Sordello,* no easy reading, and returning it with original suggestions for interpretation. Such an interest in ideas is not merely cultivated but exuberant.

But using language as one would use an axe, formulating arguments with sharp cutting edges that will help to clarify one's view of the landscape, remains a rhetorical and not a poetic achievement. To quote Yeats again, one can refute Hegel (perhaps even St Paul) but not the *Song of Sixpence.* To create a disinterested structure of words, in poetry or in fiction, is a very different achievement, and it is clear that an intelligent and able rhetorician finds it particularly hard to understand how different it is. A rhetorician practising poetry is apt to express himself in spectral arguments, generalizations that escape the feeling of possible refutation only by being vast enough to contain it, or vaporous enough to elude it. The mystique of Canadianism was accompanied by an intellectual tendency of this kind. World-views that avoided dialectic, of a theosophical or transcendentalist cast, became popular among the Canadian poets of that time, Roberts and Carman particularly, and later among painters, as the reminiscences of the Group of Seven make clear. Bucke's *Cosmic Consciousness*, though not mentioned by any of our authors so far as I remember, is an influential Canadian book in this area. When minor rhetorically-minded poets sought what Samuel Johnson calls, though in a very different context, the 'grandeur of generality', the result is what has been well described as 'jejune chatter about infinity'.

The literature of protest illustrates another rhetorical tradition. In the nineteenth century the common assumption that nature had revealed the truth of progress, and that it was the duty of reason to accommodate that truth to mankind, could be either a conservative or a radical view. But in either case it was a revolutionary doctrine, introducing the conception of change as the key to the social process. In the proletarian social Darwinists, who represented a fusion of secularism, science and social discontent, there was a strong tendency to regard literature as a product and a symbol of a ruling-class mentality, with, as we have tried to indicate, some justification. Hence radicals tended either to hope that 'the literature of the future will be the powerful ally of Democracy and Labour Reform', or to assume that serious thought and action would by-pass the creative writer entirely, building a scientific socialism and leaving him to his Utopian dreams.

The radicalism of the period up to the Russian Revolution was, from a later point of view, largely undifferentiated. A labour magazine could regard Ignatius Donnelly, with his anti-Semitic and other crank views, as an advanced thinker equally with William Morris and Edward Bellamy. Similarly, even today, in Western Canadian elections, a protest vote may go Social Credit or NDP without much regard to the difference in political philosophy between these parties. The depression introduced a dialectic into Canadian social thought which profoundly affected its literature. In one writer's striking phrase, 'the Depression was like an intense magnetic field that deflected the courses of all the poets who went through it'. In this period there were, of course, the inevitable Marxist manifestoes, assuring the writer that only social significance, as understood by Marxism, would bring vitality to his work. The *New Frontier*, a far-left journal of that period, shows an uneasy sense on the part of its contributors that this literary elixir of youth might have to be mixed with various other potions, not all favourable to the creative process: attending endless meetings, organizing, agitating, marching, demonstrating, or joining the Spanish Loyalists. It is easy for the critic to point out the fallacy of judging the merits of literature by its subject-matter, but these arguments over the role of 'propaganda' were genuine and serious moral conflicts. Besides helping to shape the argument of such novels as Grove's *The Master of the Mill* and Callaghan's *They Shall Inherit the Earth*, they raised the fundamental issue of the role of the creative mind in society, and by doing so helped to give a maturity and depth to Canadian writing which is a permanent part of its heritage.

It is not surprising, given this background, that the belief in the inspiration of literature by social significance continued to be an active force long after it had ceased to be attached to any specifically Marxist or other political programmes. It is still strong in the *Preview* group in the forties, and in their immediate successors, though the best of them have developed in different directions. The theme of social realism is at its most attractive, and least theoretical, in the poetry of Raymond Souster. The existentialist movement, with its emphasis on the self-determination of social attitudes, seems to have had very little direct influence in Canada: the absence of the existential in Pratt suggests that this lack of influence may be significant.

During the last decade or so a kind of social Freudianism has been taking shape, mainly in the United States, as a democratic counterpart of Marxism. Here society is seen as controlled by certain anxieties, real or imaginary, which are designed to repress or sublimate human impulses toward a greater freedom. These impulses include the creative and the sexual, which are closely linked. The enemy of the poet is not the capitalist but the 'square', or representative of repressive morality. The advantage of this attitude is that it preserves the position of rebellion against society for the poet, without imposing on him any specific social obligations. This movement has had a rather limited development in Canada, somewhat surprisingly considering how easy a target the square is in Canada: it has affected Layton and many younger Montreal poets, but it has not affected fiction to any great degree, though there may be something of it in Richler. It ignores the old political alignments: the Communists are usually regarded as Puritanic and repressive equally with the bourgeoisie, and a recent poem of Layton's contrasts the social hypocrisy in Canada with contemporary Spain. Thus it represents to some extent a return to the undifferentiated radicalism of a century before, though no longer in a political context.

As the centre of Canadian life moves from the fortress to the metropolis, the garrison mentality changes correspondingly. It begins as an expression of the moral values generally accepted in the group as a whole, and then, as society gets more complicated and more in control of its environment, it becomes more of a revolutionary garrison within a metropolitan society. But though it changes from a defence of to an attack on what society accepts as conventional standards, the literature it produces, at every stage, tends to be rhetorical, an illustration or allegory of certain social attitudes. These attitudes help to unify the mind of the writer by externalizing his enemy, the enemy being the anti-creative elements in life as he sees life. To approach these elements in a less rhetorical way would introduce the theme of self-conflict, a more perilous but ultimately more rewarding theme. The conflict involved is between the poetic impulse to construct and the rhetorical impulse to assert, and the victory of the former is the sign of the maturing of the writer.

III

There is, of course, nothing in all this that differentiates Canadian from other related cultural developments. The nineteenth-century Canadian reliance on the conceptual was not different in kind from that of the Victorian readers described by Douglas Bush, who thought they were reading poetry when they were really only looking for Great Thoughts. But if the tendency was not different in kind, it was more intense in degree. Here we need another seminal fact, one that we have stumbled over already: the fact that the Canadian literary mind, beginning as it did so late in the cultural history of the West, was established on a basis, not of myth, but of history. The conceptual emphasis in Canadian culture we have been speaking of is a consequence, and an essential part, of this historical bias.

Canada, of course, or the place where Canada is, can supply distinctive settings and props to a writer who is looking for local colour. Tourist-writing has its own importance (e.g. *Maria Chapdelaine*), as has the use of Canadian history for purposes of romance, of which more later. But it would be an obvious fallacy to claim that the setting provided anything more than novelty. When Canadian writers are urged to use distinctively Canadian themes, the fallacy is less obvious, but still there. The forms of literature are autonomous: they exist within literature itself, and cannot be derived from any experience outside literature. What the Canadian writer finds in his experience and environment may be new, but it will be new only as content: the form of his expression of it can take shape only from what he has read, not from what he has experienced. The great technical experiments of Joyce and Proust in fiction, of Eliot and Hopkins in poetry, have resulted partly from profound literary scholarship, from seeing the formal possibilities inherent in the literature they have studied. A writer who is or who feels removed from his literary tradition tends rather to take over forms already in existence. We notice how often critics of Canadian fiction have occasion to remark that a novel contains a good deal of sincere feeling and accurate observation, but that it is spoiled by an unconvincing plot, usually one too violent or dependent on coincidence for such material. What has happened is that the author felt he could make a novel out of his knowledge and observation, but had no story in particular to tell. His material did not come to him in the form of a story, but as a consolidated chunk of experience, reflection, and sensibility. He had to invent a plot to put this material in causal shape (for writing, as Kafka says, is an art of causality), to pour the new wine of content into the old bottles of form. Even Grove works in this way, though Grove, by sheer dogged persistence, does get his action powerfully if ponderously moving.

Literature is conscious mythology: as society develops, its mythical stories become structural principles of storytelling, its mythical concepts, sun-gods and the like, become habits of metaphorical thought. In a fully mature literary tradition the writer enters into a structure of traditional stories and images. He often has the feeling, and says so, that he is not actively shaping his material at all, but is rather a place where a verbal structure is taking its own shape. If a novelist, he starts with a storytelling impetus; if a poet, with a metaphor-crystallizing impetus. Down to the beginning of the twentieth century at least, the Canadian who wanted to write started with a feeling of detachment from his literary tradition, which existed for him mainly in his school books. He had probably, as said above, been educated in a way that heavily stressed the conceptual and argumentative use of language. We have been shown how the Indians had a mythology which included all the main elements of our own, but it was, of course, impossible for Canadians to establish any real continuity with it: Indians, like the rest of the country, were seen as nineteenth-century literary conventions. Certain elements in Canadian culture, too, such as the Protestant revolutionary view of history, may have minimized the importance of the oral tradition in ballad and folk song, which seems to have survived best in Catholic communities. In Canada the mythical was simply the 'prehistoric' (this word, we are told, is a Canadian coinage), and the writer had to attach himself to his literary tradition deliberately and voluntarily. And though this may be no longer true or necessary, attitudes surviving from an earlier period of isolation still have their influence.

The separation of subject and object is the primary fact of consciousness, for anyone so situated and so educated. Writing for him does not start with a rhythmical movement, or an impetus caught from or encouraged by a group of contemporaries: it starts with reportage, a single mind reacting to what is set over against it. Such a writer does not naturally think metaphorically but descriptively; it seems obvious to him that writing is a form of self-expression dependent on the gathering of a certain amount of experience, granted some inborn sensitivity toward that experience. We note how many Canadian novelists have written only one novel, or only one good novel, how many Canadian poets have written only one good book of poems, generally their first. Even the dream of 'the great Canadian novel', the feeling that somebody some day will write a Canadian fictional classic, assumes that whoever does it will do it only once. This is a characteristic of writers dominated by the conception of writing up experiences or observations: nobody has enough experience to keep on writing about it, unless his writing is an incidental commentary on a non-literary career.

The Canadian writers who have overcome these difficulties and have found their way back to the real headwaters of inspiration are heroic explorers. There are a good many of them, and enough of them to say that the Canadian imagination has passed the stage of exploration and has embarked on that of settlement. But it is, of course, full of the failures as well as the successes of exploration, imaginative voyages to Golconda that froze in the ice, and we can learn something from them too. Why do Canadians write so many historical romances, of what has been called the rut and thrust variety? One can understand it in the earlier period: the tendency to melodrama in romance makes it part of a central convention of that time. But romances are still going strong in the early twentieth century, and if anything even stronger in our own day. They get a little sexier and more violent as they go on, but the formula remains much the same: so much love-making, so much 'research' about antiquities and costume copied off filing-cards, more love-making, more filing cards. There is clearly a steady market for this, but the number of writers engaged in it suggests other answers. There is also a related fact, the unusually large number of Canadian popular best-selling fiction-writers, from Agnes Fleming through Gilbert Parker to Mazo de la Roche.

In nineteenth-century Canadian literature not all the fiction is romance, but nearly all of it is formula-writing. In the books of this type that I have read I remember much honest and competent work. Some of them did a good deal to form my own infantile imagination, and I could well have fared worse. What there is not, of course, is a re-created view of life, or anything to detach the mind from its customary attitudes. In the early twentieth century we begin to notice a more consistent distinction between the romancer, who stays with established values and usually chooses a subject remote in time from himself, and the realist, who deals with contemporary life, and therefore – it appears to be a therefore – is more serious in intention, more concerned to unsettle a stock response. One tendency culminates in Mazo de la Roche, the other in Morley Callaghan, both professional writers and born storytellers, though of very different kinds. By our own time the two tendencies have more widely diverged. One is mainly romance dealing with Canada's past, the other is contemporary realism dealing with what is common to Canada and the rest of the world, like antique and modern furniture stores. One can see something similar in the poetry, a contrast between a romantic tradition closely associated with patriotic and idealistic themes, and a more intellectualized one with a more cosmopolitan bias. This contrast is prominently featured in the first edition of A. J. M. Smith's anthology, *A Book of Canadian Poetry* (1943).

This contrast of the romantic and the realistic, the latter having a moral dignity that the former lacks, reflects the social and conceptual approach to literature already mentioned. Here we are looking at the same question from a different point of view. Literature, we said, is conscious mythology: it creates an autonomous world that gives us an imaginative perspective on the actual one. But there is another kind of mythology, one produced by society itself, the object of which is to persuade us to accept existing social values. 'Popular' literature, the kind that is read for relaxation and the quieting of the mind, expresses this social mythology. We all feel a general difference between serious and soothing literature, though I know of no critical rule for distinguishing them, nor is there likely to be one. The same work may belong to both mythologies at once, and in fact the separation between them is largely a perspective of our own revolutionary age.

In many popular novels, especially in the nineteenth century, we feel how strong the desire is on the part of the author to work out his situation within a framework of established social values. In the success-story formula frequent in such fiction the success is usually emotional, i.e. the individual fulfils himself within his community. There is nothing hypocritical or cynical about this: the author usually believes very deeply in his values. Moral earnestness and the posing of serious problems are by no means excluded from popular literature, any more than serious literature is excused from the necessity of being entertaining. The difference is in the position of the reader's mind at the end, in whether he is being encouraged to remain within his habitual social responses or whether he is being prodded into making the steep and lonely climb into the imaginative world. This distinction in itself is familiar enough, and all I am suggesting here is that what I have called the garrison mentality is highly favourable to the growth of popular literature in this sense. The role of romance and melodrama in consolidating a social mythology is also not hard to see. In romance the characters tend to be psychological projections, heroes, heroines, villains, father-figures, comic-relief caricatures. The popular romance operates on Freudian principles, releasing sexual and power fantasies without disturbing the anxieties of the superego. The language of melodrama, at once violent and morally conventional, is the appropriate language for this. A subliminal sense of the erotic release in romance may have inspired some of the distrust of novels in nineteenth-century pietistic homes. But even those who preferred stories of real life did not want 'realism': that, we learn, was denounced on all sides during the nineteenth century as nasty, prurient, morbid, and foreign. The garrison mentality is that of its officers: it can tolerate only the conservative idealism of its ruling class, which for Canada means the moral and propertied middle class.

The total effect of Canadian popular fiction, whatever incidental merits in it there may be, is that of a murmuring and echoing literary collective unconscious, the rippling of a watery Narcissus world reflecting the imaginative patterns above it. Robertson Davies's *Tempest Tost* is a sardonic study of the triumph of a social mythology over the imaginative one symbolized by Shakespeare's play. Maturity and individualization, in such a body of writing, are almost the same process. Occasionally a writer is individualized by accident. Thus Susanna Moodie in the Peterborough bush, surrounded by a half-comic, half-sinister rabble that she thinks of indifferently as Yankee, Irish, native, republican, and lower class, is a British army of occupation in herself, a one-woman garrison. We often find, too, as in Leacock, a spirit of criticism, even of satire, that is the complementary half of a strong attachment to the mores that provoke satire. That is, a good deal of what goes on in Mariposa may look ridiculous, but the norms or standards against which it looks ridiculous are provided by Mariposa itself. In Sara Jeannette Duncan there is something else again, as she watches the garrison parade to church in a small Ontario town: 'The repressed magnetic excitement in gatherings of familiar faces, fellow-beings bound by the same convention to the same kind of behaviour, is precious in communities where the human interest is still thin and sparse.' Here is a voice of genuine detachment, sympathetic but not defensive either of the group or of herself, concerned primarily to understand and to make the reader see. The social group is becoming external to the writer, but not in a way that isolates her from it.

This razor's edge of detachment is naturally rare in Canadian writing, even in this author, but as the twentieth century advances and Canadian society takes a firmer grip of its environment, it becomes easier to assume the role of an individual separated in standards and attitudes from the community. When this happens, an ironic or realistic literature becomes fully possible. This new kind of detachment of course often means only that the split between subject and object has become identified with a split between the individual and society. This is particularly likely to happen when the separated individual's point of view is also that of the author, as in the stories of misunderstood genius with which many minor authors are fascinated. This convention was frequent in the plays of the twenties, and even more so in the fiction. But some of the most powerful of Canadian novels have been those in which this conflict has been portrayed objectively. Buckler's *The Mountain and the Valley* is a Maritime example, and Sinclair Ross's *As for Me and My House* one from the prairies.

The essayist B. K. Sandwell remarks: 'I follow it (society) at a respectful distance . . . far enough away to make it clear that I do not belong to it.' It is clear that this is not necessarily any advance on the expression of conventional social values in popular romance. The feeling of detachment from society means only that society has become more complex, and tensions have developed within it. We have traced this process already. The question that arises is: once society, along with physical nature, becomes external to the writer, what does he then feel a part of? For rhetorical or assertive writers it is generally a smaller society, the group that agrees with them. But the imaginative writer, though he often begins as a member of a school or group, normally pulls away from it as he develops.

If our general line of thought is sound, the imaginative writer is finding his identity within the world of literature itself. He is withdrawing from what Douglas LePan calls a country without a mythology into the country of mythology, ending where the Indians began. The dramatist John Coulter says of his play, or libretto, *Deirdre of the Sorrows*: 'The art of a Canadian remains . . . the art of the country of his forebears and the old world heritage of myth and legend remains his heritage . . . though the desk on which he writes be Canadian.' But the progress may not be a simple matter of forsaking the Canadian for the international, the province for the capital. It may be that when the Canadian writer attaches himself to the world of literature, he discovers, or rediscovers, by doing so, something in his Canadian environment which is more vital and articulate than a desk.

IV

At the heart of all social mythology lies what may be called, because it usually is called, a pastoral myth, the vision of a social ideal. The pastoral myth in its most common form is associated with childhood, or with some earlier social condition – pioneer life, the small town, the *habitant* rooted to his land – that can be identified with childhood. The nostalgia for a world of peace and protection, with a spontaneous response to the nature around it, with a leisure and composure not to be found today, is particularly strong in Canada. It is overpowering in our popular literature, from *Anne of Green Gables* to Leacock's Mariposa, and from *Maria Chapdelaine* to *Jake and the Kid*. It is present in all the fiction that deals with small towns as collections of characters in search of an author. Its influence is strong in the most serious writers: one thinks of Gabrielle Roy, following her *Bonheur d'occasion* with *La poule d'eau*. It is the theme of all the essayists who write of fishing and other forms of the simpler life, especially as lived in the past. We may quote MacMechan: 'golden days in memory for the enrichment of less happier times to come'. It even comes into our official documents – the Massey Report begins, almost as a matter of course, with an idyllic picture of the Canada of fifty years ago, as a point of departure for its investigations. One writer speaks of the eighteenth-century Loyalists as looking 'to a past that had never existed for comfort and illumination', which suggests that the pastoral myth has been around for some time.

The Indians have not figured so largely in the myth as one might expect, though in some early fiction and drama the noble savage takes the role, as he does to some extent even in the Gothic hero Wacousta. The popularity of Pauline Johnson and Grey Owl, however, shows that the kind of rapport with nature which the Indian symbolizes is central to it. Another form of pastoral myth is the evocation of an earlier period of history which is made romantic by having a more uninhibited expression of passion or virtue or courage attached to it.

This, of course, links the pastoral myth with the vision of vanished grandeur that comes into the novels about the *ancien régime*. In *The Golden Dog* and *The Seats of the Mighty* the forlorn little fortress of seventeenth-century Quebec, sitting in the middle of what Madame de Pompadour called 'a few arpents of snow', acquires a theatrical glamour that would do credit to Renaissance Florence. The two forms of the myth collide on the Plains of Abraham, on the one side a marquis, on the other a Hanoverian commoner tearing himself reluctantly from the pages of Gray's *Elegy*.

Close to the centre of the pastoral myth is the sense of kinship with the animal and vegetable world, which is so prominent a part of the Canadian frontier. I think of an image in Mazo de la Roche's *Delight*. Delight Mainprize – I leave it to the connoisseurs of ambiguity to explore the overtones of that name – is said by her creator to be 'not much more developed intellectually than the soft-eyed Jersey in the byre'. It must be very rarely that a novelist – a wide-awake and astute novelist – can call her heroine a cow with such affection, even admiration. But it is consistent with her belief in the superiority of the primitive and the instinctive over the civilized and conventional. The prevalence in Canada of animal stories, in which animals are closely assimilated to human behaviour and emotions, illustrates the same point. Conversely, the killing of an animal, as a tragic or ironic symbol, has a peculiar resonance in Canadian poetry, from the moose in Lampman's Long Sault poem to the Christmas slaughter of geese which is the informing theme of James Reaney's *A Suit of Nettles*. More complicated pastoral motifs are conspicuous in Morley Callaghan, who turns continually to the theme of betrayed or victorious innocence – the former in *The Loved and the Lost*, the latter in *Such is My Beloved*. The Peggy of *The Loved and the Lost*, whose spontaneous affection for Negroes is inspired by a childhood experience and symbolized by a child's toy, is particularly close to our theme.

The theme of Grove's *A Search for America* is the narrator's search for a North American pastoral myth in its genuinely imaginative form, as distinct from its sentimental or socially stereotyped form. The narrator, adrift in the New World without means of support, has a few grotesque collisions with the hustling mercantilism of American life – selling encyclopedias and the like – and gets badly bruised in spirit. He becomes convinced that this America is a false social development which has grown over and concealed the real American social ideal, and tries to grasp the form of this buried society. In our terms, he is trying to grasp something of the myth of America, the essential imaginative idea it embodies. He meets, but irritably brushes away, the tawdry and sentimentalized versions of this myth – the cottage away from it all, happy days on the farm, the great open spaces of the west. He goes straight to the really powerful and effective versions: Thoreau's *Walden*, the personality of Lincoln, Huckleberry Finn drifting down the great river. The America that he searches for, he feels, has something to do with these things, though it is not defined much more closely than this.

Grove drops a hint in a footnote near the end that what his narrator is looking for has been abandoned in the United States but perhaps not yet in Canada. This is not our present moral: pastoral myths, even in their genuine forms, do not exist as places. They exist rather in such things as the loving delicacy of perception in Grove's own *Over Prairie Trails* and *The Turn of the Year*. Still, the remark has some importance because it indicates that the conception 'Canada' can also become a pastoral myth in certain circumstances. One writer, speaking of the nineteenth-century mystique of Canadianism, says: 'A world is created, its centre in the Canadian home, its middle distance the loved landscape of Canada, its protecting wall the circle of British institutions . . . a world as centripetal as that of Sherlock Holmes and as little liable to be shaken by irruptions of evil.' The myth suggested here is somewhat Virgilian in shape, pastoral serenity serving as a prologue to the swelling act of the imperial theme. Nobody who saw it in that way was a Virgil, however, and it has been of minor literary significance.

We have said that literature creates a detached and autonomous mythology, and that society itself produces a corresponding mythology, to which a good deal of literature belongs. We have found the pastoral myth, in its popular and sentimental social form, to be an idealization of memory, especially childhood memory. But we have also suggested that the same myth exists in a genuinely imaginative form, and have found its influence in some of the best Canadian writers. Our present problem is to see if we can take a step beyond Grove and attempt some characterization of the myth he was looking for, a myth which would naturally have an American context but a particular reference to Canada. The sentimental or nostalgic pastoral myth increases the feeling of separation between subject and object by withdrawing the subject into a fantasy world. The genuine myth, then, would result from reversing this process. Myth starts with the identifying of subject and object, the primary imaginative act of literary creation. It is therefore the most explicitly mythopoeic aspect of Canadian literature that we have to turn to, and we shall find this centred in the poetry rather than the fiction. There are many reasons for this: one is that in poetry there is no mass market to encourage the writer to seek refuge in conventional social formulas.

A striking fact about Canadian poetry is the number of poets who have turned to narrative forms (including closet drama) rather than lyrical ones. The anthologist who confines himself wholly to the lyric will give the impression that Canadian poetry really began with Roberts' *Orion* in 1880. Actually there was a tradition of narrative poetry well established before that (Sangster, Heavysege, Howe, and several others), which continues into the post-Confederation period (Mair, Isabella Crawford, Duvar, besides important narrative works by Lampman and D. C. Scott). It is clear that Pratt's devotion to the narrative represents a deep affinity with the Canadian tradition, although so far as I know (and I think I do know) the affinity was entirely unconscious on his part. I have written about the importance of narrative poetry in Canada elsewhere, and have little new to add here. It has two characteristics that account for its being especially important in Canadian literature. In the first place, it is impersonal. The bald and dry statement is the most effective medium for its treatment of action, and the author, as in the folk-song and ballad, is able to keep out of sight or speak as one of a group. In the second place, the natural affinities of poetic narrative are with tragic and ironic themes, not with the more manipulated comic and romantic formulas of prose fiction. Consistently with its impersonal form, tragedy and irony are expressed in the action of the poem rather than in its moods or in the poet's own comment.

We hardly expect the earlier narratives to be successful all through, but if we read them with sympathy and historical imagination, we can see how the Canadian environment has exerted its influence on the poet. The environment, in nineteenth-century Canada, is terrifyingly cold, empty and vast, where the obvious and immediate sense of nature is the late Romantic one, increasingly affected by Darwinism, of nature red in tooth and claw. We notice the recurrence of such episodes as shipwreck, Indian massacres, human sacrifices, lumbermen mangled in log-jams, mountain climbers crippled on glaciers, animals screaming in traps, the agonies of starvation and solitude – in short, the 'shutting out of the whole moral creation'. Human suffering, in such an environment, is a by-product of a massive indifference which, whatever else it may be, is not morally explicable. What confronts the poet is a moral silence deeper than any physical silence, though the latter frequently symbolizes the former, as in the poem of Pratt that is explicitly called 'Silences'.

The nineteenth-century Canadian poet can hardly help being preoccupied with physical nature; the nature confronting him presents him with the riddle of unconsciousness, and the riddle of unconsciousness in nature is the riddle of death in man. Hence his central emotional reaction is bound to be elegiac and sombre, full of loneliness and fear, or at least wistful and nostalgic, hugging, like Roberts, a 'darling illusion'. In Carman, Roberts, and D. C. Scott there is a rhetorical strain that speaks in a confident, radio-announcer's voice about the destiny of Canada, the call of the open road, or the onward and upward march of progress. As none of their memorable poetry was written in this voice, we may suspect that they turned to it partly for reassurance. The riddle of unconsciousness in nature is one that no moralizing or intellectualizing can answer. More important, it is one that irony cannot answer:

> The gray shape with the paleolithic face
> Was still the master of the longitudes.

The conclusion of Pratt's *Titanic* is almost documentary: it is as stripped of irony as it is of moralizing. The elimination of irony from the poet's view of nature makes that view pastoral – a cold pastoral, but still a pastoral. We have only physical nature and a rudimentary human society, not strong enough yet to impose the human forms of tragedy and irony on experience.

The same elegiac and lonely tone continues to haunt the later poetry.

Those who in the twenties showed the influence of the death-and-resurrection myth of Eliot, notably Leo Kennedy and A. J. M. Smith, were also keeping to the centre of a native tradition. The use of the Eliot myth was sometimes regarded as a discovery of myth, but, of course, the earlier poets had not only used the same myth, but were equally aware of its origins in classical poetry, as Carman's *Sappho* indicates. The riddle of the unconscious may be expressed by a symbol such as the agonies of a dying animal, or it may be treated simply as an irreducible fact of existence. But it meets us everywhere: I pick up Margaret Avison and there it is, in a poem called 'Identity':

> But on this sheet of beryl, this high sea,
> Scalded by the white unremembering glaze,
> No wisps disperse. This is the icy pole.
> The presence here is single, worse than soul,
> Pried loose forever out of nights and days
> And birth and death
> And all the covering wings.

In such an environment, we may well wonder how the sentimental pastoral myth ever developed at all. But of course there are the summer months, and a growing settlement of the country that eventually began to absorb at least eastern Canada into the north temperate zone. Pratt's Newfoundland background helped to keep his centre of gravity in the elegiac, but when he began to write the feeling of the mindless hostility of nature had largely retreated to the prairies, where a fictional realism developed, closely related to this feeling in mood and imagery. The Wordsworthian sense of nature as a teacher is apparent as early as Mrs Traill, in whom we note a somewhat selective approach to the subject reminiscent of Miss Muffet. As the sentimental pastoral myth takes shape, its imaginative counterpart takes shape too, the other, gentler, more idyllic half of the myth that has made the pastoral itself a central literary convention. In this version nature, though still full of awfulness and mystery, is the visible representative of an order that man has violated, a spiritual unity that the intellect murders to dissect. This form of the myth is more characteristic of the second phase of Canadian social development, when the conflict of man and nature is expanding into a triangular conflict of nature, society, and individual. Here the individual tends to ally himself with nature against society. A very direct and haunting statement of this attitude occurs in John Robins's *Incomplete Anglers*: 'I can approach a solitary tree with pleasure, a cluster of trees with joy, and a forest with rapture; I must approach a solitary man with caution, a group of men with trepidation, and a nation of men with terror.' The same theme also forms part of the final cadences of Hugh MacLennan's *The Watch That Ends the Night*: 'In the early October of that year, in the cathedral hush of a Quebec Indian summer with the lake drawing into its mirror the fire of the maples, it came to me that to be able to love the mystery surrounding us is the final and only sanction of human existence.'

It is the appearance of this theme in D. C. Scott which makes him one of the 'ancestral voices' of the Canadian imagination. It is much stronger and more continuous in Lampman, who talks less than his contemporaries and strives harder for the uniting of subject and object in the imaginative experience. This union takes place in the contact of individual poet and a landscape uninhabited except for Wordsworth's 'huge and mighty forms' that are manifested by the union:

> Nay more, I think some blessèd power
> Hath brought me wandering idly here.

Again as in Wordsworth, this uniting of individual mind and nature is an experience from which human society, as such, is excluded. Thus when the poet finds a 'blessèd power' in nature it is the society he leaves behind that tends to become the God-forsaken wilderness. Usually this society is merely trivial or boring; once, in the unforgettable 'City of the End of Things', it becomes demonic.

The two aspects of the pastoral tradition we have been tracing are not inconsistent with each other; they are rather complementary. At one pole of experience there is a fusion of human life and the life in nature; at the opposite pole is the identity of the sinister and terrible elements in nature with the death wish in man. In Pratt's 'The Truant' the 'genus *homo*' confronts the 'great Panjandrum' of nature who is also his own death wish: the great Panjandrum is the destructive force in the Nazis and in the Indians who martyred Brébeuf, the capacity in man that enables him to be deliberately cruel. Irving Layton shows us not only the cruelty but the vulgarity of the death-wish consciousness:

as it has no innocence, it cannot suffer with dignity, as animals can; it loses its own imaginary soul by despising the body:

> Listen: for all his careful fuss,
> Will this cold one ever deceive us?
>   Self-hating, he rivets a glittering wall;
> Impairs it by a single pebble
> And loves himself for that concession.

We spoke earlier of a civilization conquering the landscape and imposing an alien and abstract pattern on it. As this process goes on, the writers, the poets especially, tend increasingly to see much of this process as something that is human but still dehumanized, leaving man's real humanity a part of the nature that he continually violates but is still inviolate.

Reading through any good collection of modern Canadian poems or stories, we find every variety of tone, mood, attitude, technique, and setting. But there is a certain unity of impression one gets from it, an impression of gentleness and reasonableness, seldom difficult or greatly daring in its imaginative flights, the passion, whether of love or anger, held in check by something meditative. It is not easy to put the feeling in words, but if we turn to the issue of the *Tamarack Review* that was devoted to West Indian literature, or to the Hungarian poems translated by Canadians in the collection *The Plough and the Pen*, we can see by contrast something of both the strength and the limitations of the Canadian writers. They too have lived, if not in Arcadia, at any rate in a land where empty space and the pervasiveness of physical nature have impressed a pastoral quality on their minds. From the deer and fish in Isabella Crawford's 'The Canoe' to the frogs and toads in Layton, from the white narcissus of Knister to the night-blooming cereus of Reaney, everything that is central in Canadian writing seems to be marked by the imminence of the natural world. The sense of this imminence organizes the mythology of Jay Macpherson; it is the sign in which Canadian soldiers conquer Italy in Douglas LePan's *The Net and the Sword*; it may be in the foreground, as in Alden Nowlan, or in the background, as in Birney; but it is always there.

To go on with this absorbing subject would take us into another book: *A Literary Criticism of Canada*, let us say. Here we can only sum up the present argument emblematically, with two famous primitive American paintings. One is 'Historical Monument of the American Republic', by Erastus Salisbury Field. Painted in 1876 for the centennial of the Revolution, it is an encyclopedic portrayal of events in American history, against a background of soaring towers, with clouds around their spires, and connected by railway bridges. It is a prophetic vision of the skyscraper cities of the future, of the tremendous technological will to power of our time and the civilization it has built, a civilization now gradually imposing a uniformity of culture and habits of life all over the globe. Because the United States is the most powerful centre of this civilization, we often say, when referring to its uniformity, that the world is becoming Americanized. But of course America itself is being Americanized in this sense, and the uniformity imposed on New Delhi and Singapore, or on Toronto and Vancouver, is no greater than that imposed on New Orleans or Baltimore. A nation so huge and so productive, however, is deeply committed to this growing technological uniformity, even though many tendencies may pull in other directions. Canada has participated to the full in the wars, economic expansions, technological achievements, and internal stresses of the modern world. Canadians seem well adjusted to the new world of technology and very efficient at handling it. Yet in the Canadian imagination there are deep reservations to this world as an end of life in itself, and the political separation of Canada has helped to emphasize these reservations in its literature.

English Canada began with the influx of defeated Tories after the American Revolution, and so, in its literature, with a strong anti-revolutionary bias. The Canadian radicalism that developed in opposition to Loyalism was not a revival of the American revolutionary spirit, but a quite different movement, which had something in common with the Toryism it opposed: one thinks of the Tory and radical elements in the social vision of William Cobbett, who also finds a place in the Canadian record. A revolutionary tradition is liable to two defects: to an undervaluing of history and an impatience with law, and we have seen how unusually strong the Canadian attachment to law and history has been. The attitude to things American represented by Haliburton is not, on the whole, hostile: it would be better described as non-committal, as when Sam Slick speaks of a Fourth of July as 'a splendid spectacle; fifteen millions of freemen and three millions of slaves a-celebratin' the birthday of liberty'. The strong romantic tradition in Canadian literature has much to do with its original convervatism. When more radical expressions begin to creep into Canadian writing, as in the poetry of Alexander McLachlan, there is still much less of the assumption that freedom and national independence are the same thing, or that the mercantilist Whiggery which won the American Revolution is necessarily the only emancipating force in the world. In some Canadian writers of our own time – I think particularly of Earle Birney's *Trial of a City* and the poetry of F. R. Scott – there is an opposition, not to the democratic but to the oligarchic tendencies in North American civilization, not to liberal but to *laissez-faire* political doctrine. Perhaps it is a little easier to see these distinctions from the vantage-point of a smaller country, even one which has, in its material culture, made the 'American way of life' its own.

The other painting is the much earlier 'The Peaceable Kingdom', by Edward Hicks, painted around 1830. Here, in the background, is a treaty between the Indians and the Quaker settlers under Penn. In the foreground is a group of animals, lions, tigers, bears, oxen, illustrating the prophecy of Isaiah about the recovery of innocence in nature. Like the animals of the Douanier Rousseau, they stare past us with a serenity that transcends consciousness. It is a pictorial emblem of what Grove's narrator was trying to find under the surface of America: the reconciliation of man with man and of man with nature: the mood of Thoreau's Walden retreat, of Emily Dickinson's garden, of Huckleberry Finn's raft, of the elegies of Whitman. This mood is closer to the haunting vision of a serenity that is both human and natural which we have been struggling to identify in the Canadian tradition. If we had to characterize a distinctive emphasis in that tradition, we might call it a quest for the peaceable kingdom.

The writers of the last decade, at least, have begun to write in a world which is post-Canadian, as it is post-American, post-British, and post everything except the world itself. There are no provinces in the empire of aeroplane and television, and no physical separation from the centres of culture, such as they are. Sensibility is no longer dependent on a specific environment or even on sense experience itself. A remark of one critic about Robert Finch illustrates a tendency which is affecting literature as well as painting: 'The interplay of sense impressions is so complicated, and so exhilarating, that the reader receives no sense impression at all.' Marshall McLuhan speaks of the world as reduced to a single gigantic primitive village, where everything has the same kind of immediacy. He speaks of the fears that so many intellectuals have of such a world, and remarks amiably: 'Terror is the normal state of any oral society, for in it everything affects everyone all the time.' The Canadian spirit, to personify it as a single being dwelling in the country from the early voyages to the present, might well, reading this sentence, feel that this was where he came in. In other words, new conditions give the old ones a new importance, as what vanishes in one form reappears in another. The moment that the peaceable kingdom has been completely obliterated by its rival is the moment when it comes into the foreground again, as the eternal frontier, the first thing that the writer's imagination must deal with. Pratt's 'The Truant', already referred to, foreshadows the poetry of the future, when physical nature has retreated to outer space and only individual and society are left as effective factors in the imagination. But the central conflict, and the moods in which it is fought out, are still unchanged.

One gets very tired, in old-fashioned biographies, of the dubious embryology that examines a poet's ancestry and wonders if a tendency to fantasy in him could be the result of an Irish great-grandmother. A reader may feel the same unreality in efforts to attach Canadian writers to a tradition made up of earlier writers whom they may not have read or greatly admired. I have felt this myself whenever I have written about Canadian literature. Yet I keep coming back to the feeling that there does seem to be such a thing as an imaginative continuum, and that writers are conditioned in their attitudes by their predecessors, or by the cultural climate of their predecessors, whether there is conscious influence or not. Again, nothing can give a writer's experience and sensitivity any form except the study of literature itself. In this study the great classics, 'monuments of its own magnificence', and the best contemporaries have an obvious priority. The more such monuments or such contemporaries there are in a writer's particular cultural traditions, the more fortunate he is; but he needs those traditions in any case. He needs them most of all when what faces him seems so new as to threaten his identity. For present and future writers in Canada and their readers, what is important in Canadian literature, beyond the merits of the individual works in it, is the inheritance of the entire enterprise. The writers of Canada have identified the habits and attitudes of the country, as Fraser and Mackenzie have identified its rivers. They have also left an imaginative legacy of dignity and of high courage.

NOTES

PREFACE

1 I deeply regret having to say now the late Philip Wheelwright.

CHAPTER I

1 Sonnet 124:11.

2 *The Human Condition* (1959).

CHAPTER 3

1 'So-and-so Reclining on a Couch,' *Collected Poems*.

2 This refers to what is usually called spiritualism, not to controlled experiments in extra-sensory perception and the like, where there is no question of fraud.

3 *Feeling and Form*, by Susanne Langer (1953).

CHAPTER 4

1 I am not speaking specifically of the *Biblia Pauperum*, but of a generalization about religious art based on the phrase.

2 I have developed this argument further in *The Modern Century* (1967): see particularly the second lecture, 'Improved Binoculars'.

CHAPTER 7

1 The book is *Four Ages of Man: The Classical Myths*, by Jay Macpherson

(1962). I should add that many teachers I have talked to since writing this article prefer to put the beginning of the study of mythology earlier than grade nine, and certainly this book could be used earlier.

2 This is one of the 'Adagia' in *Opus Posthumous*, 157.

3 These include both the fundamentalists of the Bible belt and the fundamentalists of the anti-Bible belt. There are many who seem to think that the early study of the Bible in school would lead to obscurantism, racialism, imperialism, and the reactivating of the Inquisition: their mental processes are identical with those of the people who believe that detaching the science of geology from the Book of Genesis will inevitably destroy all moral values.

4 True in its context, but the real reason for stressing resemblances rather than differences is that discrimination and analysis are not functional in poetic thinking, which is almost entirely constructive. It is different with criticism, as the next paragraph shows, but even criticism must follow the shape of its subject.

5 *Centuries of Meditation*, I, 85.

CHAPTER 9

1 These conceptions of Eros and Agape have been drawn ultimately from *Agape and Eros*, by Bishop Nygren, tr. Hebert and Watson, 1932–39, but are very differently applied.

2 Proverbs viii, 30; *P. L.* vii, 10.

CHAPTER 11

1 See also the pyramids in the design at the top of *The Marriage of Heaven and Hell*, Plate 21 (not in all copies).

CHAPTER 12

1 See the article 'On the Discrimination of Romanticisms,' *Essays in the History of Ideas* (1948).

2 See *Sarah Binks*, by Paul G. Hiebert (1947). The joke, however, like so many jokes, is anticipated in *Finnegans Wake*, 203.

3 *Newton Demands the Muse*, by Marjorie H. Nicolson (1946).

4 *The Heavenly City of the Eighteenth-Century Philosophers*, by Carl Becker (1951).

5 I am not assuming that man was not regarded as responsible for his civilization in pre-Romantic times, but it makes a good deal of psychological difference whether man is regarded as the continuous creator of his civilization or merely as the trustee of an original form given him by God.

6 See 'The Correspondent Breeze', reprinted in *English Romantic Poets: Modern Essays in Criticism*, ed. M. H. Abrams (1960).

7 *The Romantic Ventriloquists* (1963).

8 The allusions to Blake are to the 'Introduction' to the *Songs of Experience*, the 'And did those feet' lyric from *Milton*, and the poem from the Rossetti MS beginning 'The Caverns of the Grave I've seen'.

9 Of particular interest is the Yeatsian identification of chance and choice in the passage quoted (cf. p. 259, below).

10 A topical allusion to a new book when the paper was written.

CHAPTER 13

1 Cf. *Anatomy of Criticism*, 166.

2 *Aspects of the Novel* (1927).

CHAPTER 15

1 'The Cap and Bells', from *The Wind Among the Reeds* (1899).

2 'Those Images', *Last Poems* (1939).

3 'To Ireland in the Coming Times', from *The Rose* (1893).

CHAPTER 16

1 Non-Canadian readers may not be aware of the traditional application to Canada of Psalm 72:8: 'And he shall have dominion from sea to sea, and from the river unto the ends of the earth'. Canada was called the 'Dominion' of Canada for many years; the motto on the Canadian coat of arms is *a mari usque ad mare*, and the vertical red stripes on the Canadian flag were originally blue to represent the two oceans. Canadian politicians

seem to be endeavoring to obliterate this symbolism for reasons which elude me.

2 The allusion is to *Next Year Country*, by Jean Burnet (1951), a sociological study of Alberta.

3 *Deeper into the Forest*, by Roy Daniells (1948), who, like Emily Carr, is from British Columbia.

4 One may also compare the last sentences of the two volumes of Professor Donald Creighton's biography of John A. Macdonald (1952, 1955).

5 The title (a phrase from Rilke) of Hugh MacLennan's novel (1946) about the English and French communities in Montreal.

6 This is the subtitle of a book significantly called *Hegel not Haeckel*: the allusion is to Ernst Haeckel's *The Riddle of the Universe*, tr. McCabe, 1900, a book much refuted in clerical circles.